GW00975929

Anthony Babb BEM

U-BOAT ENIGMAS

Royal Navy Salvage & Secrecy in WW1

A novel and a reference book

First published in 2019 by Anthony Babb BEM
Copyright © Anthony Babb BEM

Anthony Babb BEM asserts his right under the Copyright, Design
and Act 1988 to be identified as the author of this work.

All rights reserved. No part of this publication may be reproduced,
stored, or transmitted in any form, or by any means, electronic,
mechanical or photocopying, recording or otherwise, without the
express permission of the publisher.

ISBN: 9781070501239 (Paperback Edition)

The author made every effort to ensure the accuracy of the
information in this book at the time of going to press.
However, he cannot accept any responsibility for any loss, injury
or inconvenience resulting from the use of the information
contained in this book.

This book is sold subject to the condition that it shall not, by way
of trade or otherwise, be lent, resold, hired out or otherwise
circulated without the publisher's prior consent in any form of
binding or cover than that in which it is published and without a
similar condition, including this condition, being imposed on the
subsequent purchaser.

iii

Contents

Introduction

The unique pictures that you will find at the back of this book initially came to my attention in 1972, when I first visited my future wife's home. Knowing that I was in the Royal Navy and that her father's collection of pictures came from his time in the Royal Navy during World War One, it was not long before they were presented to me for viewing. Of course, it was her daughter I was more interested in and my knowledge of naval matters from that period was extremely small. All I could do was agree that they were naval and that they involved mostly damaged ships. They were then returned to their resting place in a Paxo stuffing box.

My wife sadly passed away before her mother did, and so my son took on the mantle of next of kin, which meant that when Nellie needed to go into a care home and her house rented out, Andrew took care of matters. That was how the pictures came to me in 2007 and being retired I had the time to do them justice.

Luckily, the collector of the pictures, John Foulkes had written notes on the back of most of them and very quickly I was able to establish that he had been involved in ship salvage in that war. There are even a few books on the subject and I started to realise how important this work was in the Great War. A visit to the BBC's Antique Roadshow was a little disappointing because the pictures themselves were worthless and the advice was to write a book.

Instead, I created a lecture from the information gathered and in 2012 on board P & O's cruise ship Oriana I started my lecturing career. Having developed a small portfolio of Naval Lectures including my Falklands experiences I decided to add some WW1 talks to go with the Salvage lecture. During my visits to The National Archives, I continued to collect salvage reports.

Now a book started to make sense because the salvage report for UC-44 provided lots of information; however it also left me with the feeling that I was missing something. The strangest part was the instruction to hide the U-boat out of sight especially when it had been in public view for over 2 weeks.

I found UC-44 items in the Imperial War Museum and thus joined their Facebook page. Regularly I would search the internet using keywords and one day found a plea for help, from a man in Dunmore East, looking for an expert on the salvage of UC-44.

Answering that call put me in touch with a local historical society, the Barony of Gaultier Historical Society who planned an event called Friend or Foe to celebrate the 100th Anniversary of the saving of the Captain of the U-boat, and the laying of a memorial to commemorate those lost. Intrigued, I became their UC-44 expert and began researching again.

Finally, in Kew, I discovered the codebook that was recovered and then a spy book that mentioned this very submarine, now I had both Salvage and a Secrecy story. Luck had enabled me to link these strange bedfellows and then view many of the activities in a really new light.

The book, Strange Intelligence memoirs of Naval Secret Service, mentions the very submarine (UC-44). This could easily be dismissed as fiction, but not with such an obvious and telling link, now I think it is fact. Too much fits in with the salvage facts.

It also describes the tracking of U-boats using direction finding of their radio signals and includes liaison with convoys. Add to this the ability to read every U-boat transmission, using the documents recovered from UC-44 for a considerable time, and Room 40 had all they needed to route the convoys away from danger and to upset any German U-boat plans.

Without a doubt, the greatest threat to Britain in World War One was actually the German U-boat offensive. This followed the

Battle of Jutland, where they failed to strike a decisive blow against the British Grand Fleet.

We were eventually victorious because the Royal Navy blockade starved Germany of food. The German's final land attack of WW1, the spring offensive of 1918 was a result of the Russian Revolution, the ceasefire on that front released a large number of troops. This was their last great effort which was to be in vain. The German troops were very hungry and sometimes stopped to enjoy the bounty they discovered in our trenches.

The work of the Royal Navy Salvage Section ensured that we had enough ships to keep our troops well fed and supplied. American troops and supplies were also able to cross the Atlantic fairly easily, and eventually, we were able to launch a successful counter-offensive which led directly to the end of the war.

The German U-boat blockade included unrestricted submarine warfare in their attempts to starve Britain but failed.

The history books mention many factors that are relevant to their defeat, including, Q ships, Depth Charges, airplane patrols, non-rigid airship patrols, attacks on submarine bases, ramming by warships and Motor Launch patrols equipped with hydrophones in all our local harbours, all of which contributed a little.

Convoys, of course, are almost always quoted as being the most effective factor; however, there has always been some debate, about the introduction of this ultimately successful strategy. The Royal Navy wanted to protect those vulnerable ships but we had limited tools. Room 40 was to provide the essential information so that convoys would work.

It was the availability of enough merchant ships which was critical. Shipbuilding contributed but was working flat out.

It was the salvage of the many damaged ships around our coasts which gave us the breathing space, putting many ships back to work very quickly. Additionally, the salvage teams recovered much cargo and so adding to the value of their work.

Salvage was carried out by many people, including civilian salvage companies and dockyard workers, but there is one group that did more than most.

The Royal Navy's Salvage Section was set up early in WW1, with a view to salvaging our damaged warships after battle with the German High Seas Fleet. Operating as Royal Fleet Auxiliaries, it was soon realised that they had to be used to salvage merchant ships as well.

This section was ably led by the ex-Royal Navy diver, Captain Frederick Young of the Liverpool Salvage Association. Salvage Officers were appointed to oversee each job but it was the experienced Able Seaman that was the key to the salvage teams. He is the foundation stone that the Royal Navy is built on and John Foulkes was such a man, serving on the salvage ship RFA Racer.

That most secret of organisations Room 40, Naval Intelligence in WW1 is Bletchley Park's heritage and much has been written about the Zimmerman telegram decoding, but this other work, described here is almost unknown and as important.

It is quite worthy of note that the head of Room 40 in World War 1, A G Denniston became the head of Bletchley Park.

Scattered throughout this book are WW1 incidents that mirror many of the highly acclaimed activities carried out by Bletchley Park in World War 2; that cannot be a coincidence.

The majority of Salvage Riggers were Royal Fleet Reserve ratings, generally slightly older and very experienced, just the type of people necessary for this work.

John's early life and Royal Navy career were instrumental in him being in the right place at the right time, thus I use the early chapters to set the scene and describe life below the decks.

The events, people, locations and ships are as factual as possible. Unfortunately, Room 40 documentation, available in the archives is very sparse, a great deal was destroyed.

Whilst there were some shortages at home these were minimal, more importantly, the troops and animals, on our front line were always very well supplied until eventually, the German leaders realised that they could not carry on.

The story starts just before the start of World War 2, simply because HMS Thetis was recalled by my mother in Law.

From HMS Theseus to HMS Thetis

Thursday 1st June 1939

Nellie, John's 25-year-old daughter arrives home from work in the late afternoon, to find her dad sitting at the kitchen table. Her mother Jessie is busy at the range, cooking the evening meal and asks if she would like a cup of tea. Saying yes please, the kettle is dropped on the top with a quite a bang, there is some tension in the air.

Her dad has that day's Liverpool Echo spread out in front of him, along with his prized collection of photographs. They are from his time in the Royal Navy when he was salvaging ships and submarines during WW1, and it is obvious that something is afoot.

The headlines are about the sinking of HMS Thetis, a brand new Royal Navy submarine, which has been built just down the road at Cammell Lairds, and the fate of the men on board whose lives are in great jeopardy.

Just off Llandudno in Liverpool Bay, they had been carrying out their first diving trial but had not surfaced afterward. There are 103 men trapped, 54 crew, 27 shipyard workers and 22 others, John is describing how difficult the task is to save them. Nellie loves to hear about his WW1 experiences, and he goes on to explain that it should be possible to save them, of course, her mother wants to lay the table but she senses there is more to her attitude.

Tomorrow he plans to go to Llandudno and up the Great Orme so that he can see what is happening, and Nellie agrees to go with him. As they tidy up the paper and photographs, John talks about his very first involvement in salvage. It was on the cruiser HMS Theseus stationed in the Mediterranean in 1899 and how strikingly similar, are the names HMS Theseus and HMS Thetis which just happen to span his salvage experiences. Jessie his wife listens to the two of them, thinking of the four hard years of war, but saying nothing.

The next day there is a huge crowd on the Great Orme, and in the distance they can just see the many ships gathering round, trying to rescue the trapped men.

John says to his daughter 'those are the warships and those are the salvage ships, probably belonging to the Liverpool Salvage Association.'

A man with binoculars standing nearby; realises that John has an understanding of the events unfolding before them, 'take these so you can see more, and perhaps you can explain what is happening'.

John gratefully and eagerly accepts the binoculars and studies the scene. 'Yes that is the salvage ship Ranger out there; I worked with her a few times in WW1. I can see the stern of the submarine sticking out of the water. The salvage ship has lifting cables attached to the submarine stern, holding it up and there is a man actually sitting on the hull by the propeller.'

'What are they trying to do?' asks the stranger.

'Hopefully, they will have a line connected to supply air to those inside whilst they open up a way for them to get out.'[1]

---

[1] *It was the Royal Fleet Auxiliary Salvage Section in World War 1, following the raising of C16 that actually advised the Admiralty to fit these valves. In this way air and food can be supplied in emergency. All future submarines were fitted with these valves, which gives the rescuers much more time to save them. The air-lines could also be used help to push out any water in the hull. Telephone connections for communications were also provided.*

Those standing close by hearing what he is saying gather round, keen to hear more, as the news is very sparse from the authorities. They also want to know why he knows so much, and he is happy to tell them all he knows, describing some of his salvage work in World War 1, but especially his involvement in the salvage of the British Submarine C16 and the German Coastal Submarine UC-44.

He tells them that in those early days of submarines, it was really difficult to rescue trapped sailors. However this submarine will be fitted with valves so that an air hose can be connected, this should keep the trapped men alive until they can be rescued.

Then John lets out a gasp which startles them all, 'Some men have just appeared at the surface and they are being hauled on board, 4 of them.'

Everyone turns to look out to sea, and John hands the binoculars back, they are all more hopeful now, but time just drags on and there are no more escapes.

The stranger turns to John 'Do you know how long their air will last?'

'With 100 people on board they will be using it up very quickly' he replies.

The hours pass slowly until it gets dark, at this the crowd reluctantly disperses and they all go home.

What they did not know, was that the submarine's bow was held firmly on the seabed, and there are very swift local sea currents, making life very difficult for the divers. They had been unable to connect a hose to this valve, so the men on board were running out of air. Four men did escape, but unknown to the watchers the escape system then jammed. Eventually, all the rest of the men on board died when the oxygen ran out, which may even have been whilst they were all watching.

Nellie was really proud of her dad's knowledge and the way he spoke to the crowd. She knew he had a great love of the sea, which had been strengthened when he had listened to his Norwegian father in law, Bernt Anderson telling him his seagoing adventures.

Bernt had worked for Cunard as a seaman on their transatlantic voyages, taking immigrants to America. His sea stories were apparently things of legend for John, these tales made being a sailor exciting, and even romantic. Her Grandfather had died before she was born, but her dad had often told her the story, of how he had met her Grandmother Ellen and came to be in England.

The family story is that he was at school in Southern Norway, and the school teacher had been verbally abusing his sister. Getting annoyed, he threw an inkwell at the teacher, then regretting his actions, ran out of school and stowed away on a ship in Oslo. On-board this ship, he was discovered by a young lady, who was engaged to the Captain. Amazingly they fell in love and were put ashore together when the ship docked in Liverpool.

After marrying Ellen, he worked as an Able Seaman, on those many Immigration ships which travelled from Liverpool to New York. One of these was the Cunard Line SS Gallia. She firmly believed this had been one of the reasons why her dad had stayed in the Royal Naval Reserve to continue his love of the sea.

Her dad was now a successful businessman, still involved in the running of the family hotel. Her wonderful mother loved her dad but she never said much about him being in the Navy, it was almost as if she did not really approve and perhaps the war had taken its toll although their marriage appeared to be very strong.

HMS Caledonia Training 1897

Finishing school at the age of 13, John's first job is as a barman in the Crown Hotel Birkenhead, where the family lives, which is managed by his dad Vaughan. The truth is he is only filling in time because he already knows that he has to wait until he is at least 15 years and 3 months before he can fulfil his dream, which is to join the Royal Navy.

His ambition is to be a seaman, and one of his friends William has recently joined the Royal Navy. This appears very attractive to this young boy because they have uniforms, guns and an opportunity to see something of the world. His mother and father have insisted that he attend school despite his dislike of learning, but at least this means he can read and write, which is an essential skill for anyone planning to join up.

There would be many other young boys trying to enlist, but his friend William had given him lots of useful information when he was home on leave. This gave him great confidence that he would be successful. The only problem is that he needs a letter from his father, allowing him to sign up if selected and this is proving very difficult to get.

It is the 2nd December 1897 when John reaches that special date, but despite telling his parents many times; that he wants to join the Royal Navy, his mother is not at all happy. She keeps telling him to wait, and see how he feels when he is old enough, but he has never been very patient.

Eventually a couple of weeks later, he finally gets what he wants, his father calls him into the kitchen and hands him the letter, although his mother does not look too happy he does not really care. Thus on the 15th Dec 1897, he sets off by train, using the ticket given to him by the recruiting office, on the long and very exciting journey into the unknown to a strange place called Queensferry. This is where the old wooden training ship HMS Caledonia is moored, waiting for him and many other boys like him wanting to join the senior service.

It is his first long train journey, taking him from Liverpool via Carlisle to Edinburgh. The short last leg of this long journey being completed using a smaller local train. It takes him over the recently completed and amazing Forth Bridge, to the station at the far end of it. By now he is used to the general noise of the train, the wheels clacking over the joints, the engine puffing away. However, when they reach the bridge, the noise is then magnified by the many huge steel tubes, which flash past the windows alternating patterns of light and shadow into his carriage. It sounds almost like weird bells heralding his arrival into a new and very different world.

There are many Royal Navy ships stretched out below them in the Firth of Forth and he doesn't know which way to look, as they trundle between the great steel girders. The train eventually squeals to a halt at the platform just past the end of the great bridge where quite a few sailors appear to be looking in his direction and waiting for them.

Being collected at the station, by the smart-looking Petty Officers, inspires him and makes him even more determined to do well and so it transpires.

The train journey has taken most of the day, so after a short boat journey, out to the old wooden hulk lying almost sleeping in the calm waters, they are fed, and then given a hammock to sleep in, which is a very strange experience. The surprisingly comfortable contraption hangs from the ceiling on short ropes, but he soon sleeps after the tiring journey, the excitement of the travel and all the new sights. Every new sight had not allowed him to rest on his journey into the unknown, nothing William had told him could have prepared him for all the wonders to be seen having travelled almost half of the country.

Next morning after breakfast, they are taken ashore by boat, to complete the formalities of examinations, medicals, and interviews, in order to establish their suitability, for service in the Royal Navy.

Many boys, for that, is what John still is, do not make the required grade; education is essential and so is good health, John is blessed with both. Eventually, in the afternoon he is taken into an office and is quite surprised when he is asked if he has been in trouble with the police at all. Despite having been clipped about the ears a couple of times by the local bobby he answers 'No' in a confident manner, and it is only then that he realises that Royal Navy really want him, plus he has his father's written permission, so he is able to join the very next day.

On the 17th December 1897 after being read the Naval Discipline Act, he and his 17 other classmates, sign on for 12 years from the age of 18. He has a slight moment of hesitation before signing because he is actually committing to almost fifteen years which seems like forever, but he knows it is what he wants and then they start the new joiner's routine. Each class is assigned to a Petty Officer, and this fearsome looking bearded man quickly gets to work. His job is to turn these scruffy civilians, into the smart, clean, disciplined seamen, that the navy needs to man its many warships.

They all get haircuts, new uniforms; all of their new kit has to be marked with his name, and then many periods of drill. This involves hours out on the upper deck, learning to march in step and to salute the naval way. They are not allowed out (or ashore in naval language), for at least 6 weeks, and even then only for a very few hours at a time on certain days. This process instils discipline and fitness, as they start the long road to being a seaman on a warship.

The Royal Navy has the greatest fleet in the world and is continually modernising, there are many changes in technology going on at this time and many more to come. The old wooden sailing warship HMS Caledonia is nothing like the steam driven, steel-hulled ships with large guns that are being built, she is simply being used to accommodate and train these young recruits.

The training ship is divided up by decks, with the upper deck used exclusively for sail drill, gunnery and recreation; it is here that he spends most of the first 6 weeks. Accommodation is in the lower and Orlop decks where the 800 boys sling their hammocks. He is quickly learning how to keep himself and his kit clean, followed by even more cleaning, of his living space or more correctly his mess deck. Having everything inspected very thoroughly by his seniors, is vastly different to the life he is used to at home, but he soon settles in, the routine just sweeps you along leaving little time to question things.

Collecting his pay of 2 ½ p per day involves lining up with his classmates in alphabetic order. When his name is called out, he steps forward smartly, salutes the paymaster, says his name and official number, '196912' out loud, then holds his cap out, upside down, whilst staying at attention. The paymaster then repeats his name and number but adds the amount of money he is due. The coins are then dropped into his upturned cap, physical contact between a rating and an officer is not allowed. He then turns smartly to the side and marches off, counting the coppers as soon as he can and realising this money is his to do as he wishes with.

Eventually, after the 6 weeks, they are considered smart enough to venture out in uniform, but even this is not straight forward. Leave is only granted for a few hours at weekends and involves catching the liberty boat, that only departs every hour. To further complicate the process, there is a meticulous inspection carried out by the Officer of the Day, before being allowed to proceed ashore.

Being ashore is even weirder, as he walks with his shipmates down the road. He is very self-conscious of his smart square rig and his cap with HMS Caledonia proudly written in shining gleaming gold letters across the front. There is little to do ashore, but it is good to have a walkabout for a couple of hours and feel freedom from orders being barked at them.

Sometimes they enjoy a cup of tea and a cake, in the local teashop. The serving girls occasionally give them the eye; however, there are far too many sailors. There are only a few girls, and their fathers are well aware of the attraction of a naval uniform; but they still give them the eye, despite the warnings they have been given at home.

Back on board, the training takes place on the main and middle decks, starting with lessons in subjects such as parts of the ship, seamanship, and rope work including many knots. The school rooms on these decks hold 200 boys at a time. Most days they also spend some time in a whaler learning to pull the oars in unison, even doing this when they are taken ashore, for sporting activities such as football.

Regular examinations take place, and it is essential to pass each of these, before progressing to the next stage. Time passes very quickly, and soon it is the end of the preliminary course. In these 12 weeks, he has also learned to swim, thus only half of his time is spent in instruction. At the end of this period, there is another examination; this is the time when the cream of the recruits is selected. These boys are to train as an advanced class, probably becoming signalmen or maybe a few wireless-men because radio is now in its infancy.

John does not qualify for this class, and spends a further 5 months as an "ordinary boy", receiving instruction in gunnery, mechanical training, and practical seamanship.

Before all this, it is time to go home for a couple of weeks by train, so that now his family and friends will see him in his splendidly smart uniform. To accommodate all the boys going home, a special train is arranged to Edinburgh; here they split up onto the various railway lines, to continue their journey home. All boys are required to write home regularly, so he knows that his family will be expecting him for his leave period.

The journey takes most of the day, but he is soon home in familiar surroundings, sitting in the large kitchen of the Crown Hotel in Birkenhead that his family runs. They are so pleased to see him and comment on how much he has grown in the 3 months he has been away.

His mother fusses over him, so pleased to see her growing son whilst his father looks on proudly. His elder brother Henry is now the Barman, as he had been, and his younger brother Vaughan and sister Ellen are at school. Also in the house is his other brother George, who is due to start school soon and the youngest, 3-year-old Alice who is fascinated by his uniform and especially his naval collar.

His mother tells him to go to Morris's and get a photograph taken in uniform the next day, his friend William is also home on leave from HMS Dolphin and they could have one taken together. That night around the dinner table, the whole family buzzes with news and questions, but of course, at 6 pm it is necessary to open the bar.

John takes up his old place serving behind the bar, meeting all the regulars, and it turns into a really good night. Eventually much later, after helping to clean up the bar, he falls into his old bed; it is most strange to sleep on a flat wide soft mattress after 3 months in a hammock, but he is soon in a deep sleep.

Late the next morning he suddenly wakes up, wonders where he is, it feels like he has slept for an absolute eternity. Whilst he had no problem sleeping on the ship, it is really nice to be in his old bed, which seems to swallow him up, surround him and welcome him home, not wanting to let him go.

The whole of his leave passes all too quickly, with visits to family and friends, who are all keen to hear about his experiences. He is the centre of attention which is really understandable, but of course, he has to go back and continue his training.

The pattern is now set as he returns to HMS Caledonia, with new subjects being introduced on a regular basis, which is broken down into, 12 weeks seamanship and school, 2 weeks mechanical training, 10 weeks gunnery, 4 weeks practical seamanship, and finally kitting up for sea.

There are many new experiences, and every day he and his friends will look out over the ship's side to the Firth of Forth, to see what new ships are in view. In the anchorage, there are a few ships like the old wooden hulk Caledonia, but many which have both sails and funnels for steam, and some which have no sails at all. Each new modern arrival is inspected by the boys. They all hope that one of these marvels would end up being their new home. However, they also know that first, they have to go to the harbour and sea training ships, which are based in Portland at the other end of the country.

At the end of his 3rd term, he travels home to Birkenhead on leave, with instructions to report to the harbour training ship HMS Minotaur, on 16th September 1898. This ship provides a four months practical course, which includes seamanship, gunnery, and school with special attention being paid to boat work.

During this time on the harbour training ship, it is clear that John is finding the exams tough, and although he is just managing to get a pass each time, the words of encouragement from his Petty Officer are having little real effect and he is struggling to keep up with his classmates, he is one of the youngest.

Eventually, just before his 16th birthday, he is ordered to see his Divisional Officer and John fears for his naval future, will his dream be shattered? At the meeting with his divisional officer, Lt Swan tells him that he is due to be rated Boy 1st Class on his upcoming birthday, but he will be recommending to the Captain, that he should go back to "Caledonia" to take the course again. It is clear he is struggling with his exams, and it would be better for John and the Navy if he starts again.

At the age of sixteen, John is promoted to Boy 1st Class, but 2 weeks later on 31st October, he is sent back to HMS Caledonia, as a "backward boy" because the Captain has agreed with Lt Swan, that this is the best course of action both for John and the navy.

On his way back he visits home, and as far as they are concerned it is just a normal visit, but of course, his friend William, will know what has happened. Fortunately, William is also home, and is sworn to secrecy which is not a problem; naval ratings will always support each other, especially when dealing with civilians, even when they are family.

Back at HMS Caledonia, John is put in a class that is full of "sprogs" (a naval inspired term for youngsters. This comes from notes made on old sailing ship's logs. When a child was born to some of the "ladies" who lived on these old wooden ships, they would record the event in the log. If the father was unknown, which was quite often the case; they would write "SPROG" which stands for "Son Produced Recoil Of Gun", the birth taking place on the table slung over the gun).

John, who is now the "old hand" despite only being 16 is made class leader, even though some of his class are much older than he is. Having done the course before, he is able to relax and take on the responsibility without undue effect. It is only now that he realises, just how many different accents there are on board and that even his own "scouse" has been rounded off slightly, although his roots will always show when he speaks.

26 weeks later he is again on route to a training ship at Portland, but this time he is sent to HMS Agincourt, which is the same class of ship as "HMS Minotaur". He successfully completes his training and then awaits his first sea draft as a real sailor, and he will no longer be a MUT; that is a "Man Under Training".

The Mediterranean & HMS Theseus

1899 to 1902

On 31st May 1899 our junior seaman, finally sails through the narrow breakwater, into a sunny and very warm Malta, to join HMS Hood. She is sitting tethered between two buoys, in the middle of a very impressive Harbour. The towering sandstone walls embrace the anchorage, with cannons peeping between the breaks in the fortifications; there is the town of Valetta to the right and St Julian to the left, cradling the aptly named Grand Harbour.

The Royal Navy's most impressive Mediterranean fleet lies within, including the great Battleship, which he is about to join and become a crew member of. The harbour is busy with steam pinnaces, taking their important passengers on business, and there are also one or two whalers, being pulled by naval crews.

Most of the other small boats in the harbour consist of colourful strange looking ones, with a high curved stem and stern pieces; a single man stands at the front using 2 oars to pull it along sweeping his arms backward and forwards in a strange but effective motion. He later learns that each warship has its own water taxi called a dgħajsa (pronounced dysa), which is manned by a local and can be used instead of the ship's liberty boat.

Transferring to HMS Hood in her steam pinnace; provides him with an excellent view of this 8-year-old battleship, fitted with 2 huge turrets, and he finally feels that all his wishes have come true at once. Climbing aboard and standing to attention at the top of the gangway, it is normal to salute the quarterdeck. However he is laden with a kitbag and hammock so doesn't need to salute, just stand to attention briefly. Seeing the 2 large barrels of the 13.5" main armament on the rear turret halts his advance. The man climbing up behind him; mutters something not very complimentary, about daydreaming Junior sailors. At which he wakes up, and marches over to the quartermaster, to report.

'Put your kit over to the side, and go with Mick here, the Bosuns mate to the Master at Arms office' he says.

Led by Mick who is also a gunner they head below.

The Master at Arms sits in his office, resplendent in his all-white tropical uniform, he eyes this new young member of the crew, through a large white beard or full set as it is known and takes his paperwork from him. 'We have been expecting you Foulkes; you will be messing in the forward seamen's mess, with all the other junior seamen. Here is your joining routine which you need to complete today.'

'Thank you Master' says John who takes the proffered card.

'Get back up to the quarterdeck and wait by your kit, I will get the Killick of your mess, Jock, to collect you and show you where you will be billeted. In the morning, you will muster on the quarterdeck sharply at 0800, with the rest of the seaman. Don't be late' are his final sharp words, but lurking under that magnificent beard, John thinks he can detect the makings of a smile, as he replies smartly.

'Yes, Master' and heads off back to the quarterdeck.

On leaving the office, Mick says 'come on Scouse let's get back up top'.

'My name is John'. He quickly replies.

To which Mick says 'I'm afraid you will be Scouse from now on, with that accent.'

John is very proud of his Liverpool roots, and it will take a while to get used to this nickname. He is however actually proud to have one, and it shows that the people on board are friendly.

Jock arrives on deck shortly afterward, looking for the new member of his mess, grabs John's hammock, and leads him down into the main deck, and forward to the mess deck.

The steel hull is starting to warm up, this is despite the small open portholes which are fitted with wind catchers, but there is no breeze. It is warm and humid in the mess, where a number of ratings are busy scrubbing out. Jock tells him all the Junior Seamen live in this corner, as he slings his hammock into the correct stowage and then finds the allocated place for his kitbag, which will serve as his wardrobe.

The rest of the day is taken up with visits to, the seaman's office, where he finds out that he is Port watch, and will be working Focsle part of ship. Then to the pay office, to ensure he gets his pay, and the stores office, for new cap tallies, bearing the proud words HMS Hood, one of which is soon in place.

That evening sitting on the upper deck, as the heat diminishes; alongside him are a couple of his new messmates, Jim and Peter. They are watching a Japanese Cruiser enter harbour, as he learns a little about Malta, from these new friends. A little later, when it is dark, the ship exercises its searchlights, to practice anti-torpedo drill, and it is almost like bonfire night. Candle lights are flickering from the many openings in the walls; the portholes on the many ships also twinkle.

The bright white searchlight beams sweep the harbour searching for torpedo boats that might be sneaking up on the ship. The shafts of light bounce off the water surface onto the vertical walls of the harbour, creating patterns which reflect on the almost still water. In the port, the lights reveal the many dysa's, taking sailors ashore for a break from ship's routine.

Jim and Peter have promised to take him ashore, they are all Port watch, and will have the opportunity for some leave on Saturday. He is enticed with tales of a strange place called The Gut. Its proper name is Straight Street and is full of bars and other delights, all ready to part him from his hard earned dosh.

Early next morning, the duty Petty Officer strides into the mess, rousing those asleep with calls of 'Show a Leg' and banging the pillars, making a great deal of noise, to ensure all are awake. After breakfast, it is time to muster on the quarterdeck, with the rest of the sailors who make up his part of ship.

There he meets the Petty Officer in charge of the Focsle, who will allocate his work for the day. Prayers are followed by an inspection, and then it is time to muster on the Focsle and start cleaning the wooden decks, mostly by hand with a scrubbing brush. Shortly after HMS Theseus sails past, to the shrill calls of pipes, bringing them all smartly to attention, as she steams quickly out of the harbour, her wake causing the Hood to sway slightly from side to side.

Peter whispers to him that Theseus is a first-class cruiser, and is always rushing about, unlike these battleships, which don't go to sea quite as much. John likes the sleek look of Theseus but keeps his opinion to himself, as his mind wanders, to the delights of The Gut, which is only a couple of days away. Today it is even warmer than yesterday, but at least they are out in the fresh air and with the canvas awnings up covering the whole deck, they are at least shaded from direct sunlight.

Saturday afternoon soon arrives, as the three of them muster on the Quarterdeck, ready to catch the liberty boat, for his first run ashore in Malta with his two new friends. The dysa lands them at the nearby Custom House steps, this is a large square building, sited under the towering walls, and they wonder which way to head off into the town of Valetta; right takes them the back way and is shorter, left is longer but there is more to see.

Lined up on the roads, are very smart open sided Carriages pulled by a single horse, these are called Karozzins, and nicknamed Karis by sailors. They are driven by locals, who call to them in a friendly way, but that costs money, so they ignore the pleas of the drivers.

It is a steep walk, up to the main town, whichever way you go, and Jim decides that it's a bit early to head to the Gut, so they will take the long route, and turn left, to take the winding road up to the Baraka Gardens.

Once at the top, they look over the walls, above the harbour, and laid out before them are all of the ships, lying in the sparkling waters under the glorious sun. Now he can also see the many creeks where other ships are berthed. John is quite used to ports and has spent many hours looking at ships, in both Birkenhead and Liverpool, but the magnificence of the harbour, almost takes his breath away, as he takes in the wondrous view.

On his way to Malta, the transport ship stopped at the impressive Gibraltar, which is supposed to be one of the 7 wonders of the world, and he cannot understand how Malta was missed off the list.

His two friends almost have to drag him away, but of course, in the end, the wish to see the famous Gut, gets the better of him and he quickly follows.

The town of Valetta is almost as magnificent, as they pass the large square sandstone fortress-like buildings, which hint at its great past. Then the passageways start to narrow, and his friends tell him to be quiet, as they pass the police station, which is where the naval patrols sit and wait for the evening revelries to start.

At the top of The Gut, where the passageway narrows, even more, he can glimpse down the slope the Mediterranean visible in the distance. He can see some men and sailors, standing outside small arched doorways, with just the heads of ladies peering out, and smiling to invite the sailors inside.

There are small signs hanging over each doorway, and John is led well down the street, past most of these doorways to the Red Barrel, which is apparently the Hood's favourite haunt.

Outside the doorman, recognises his companions, and smiles a welcome, as the 2 ladies who had been peering out scurry inside getting ready to serve the 3 young sailors, who are the first to arrive that night. Junior Seaman must be back by 11 pm, and so it is necessary for them to start drinking early, and that is their plan.

They step down the short arched tunnel, into the vaulted cellars, below the house, where the stone walls are whitewashed, and the rock floors scrubbed clean. Each of the alcoves, off the main vaulted room has a scrubbed table and benches, with candles casting a flickering light, that illuminates a small bar in the corner.

Here the three brightly dressed ladies and a man wait, ready to serve them. John is used to bars in Liverpool, but this place seems strange and exotic, being completely different and very attractive to him. The only similarity to the Birkenhead pubs he knows, being the black upright piano in the corner, which is silent for the moment.

After a couple of beers, some other crew members arrive, and John notices they are drinking a dark red wine called Marsala so he tries it. The drink is sweet, strong tasting and very pleasant thus easy to quaff. What he does not realise is that it is somewhat stronger than he is used to.

It isn't too long, before he starts gazing into the striking dark deep eyes, of one of the girl's serving, and thinks about asking her if she would like a drink.

Fortunately, his friend Jim realises what is happening, and intervenes before any drinks can be ordered, and they drag a reluctant John outside.

'It's time to return to the ship' explains Jim as they walk back, with John between them, encouraging him to keep walking straight, at least until they are past the Naval Patrols.

John is not amused initially, but on learning that the girl would have asked for a "sticky green", which costs a great deal of money, and is not alcoholic, he realises that he has many lessons to learn. Now he understands that he is lucky to have such good friends to show him the ropes, and learning that sailors always look out for each other.

All 3 walk back down to the Custom's House, arm in arm laughing at John's foolishness and then catch the first available dysa back to the ship.

Returning in good time is probably for the best, because the Hood is going to sea very early on Monday morning, and this will be another first for John so he needs a clear head.

He is allocated the job of Bridge Runner, for his seagoing watchkeeping duties. This involves taking messages from the bridge, under the eyes of the Captain, and Officer of the Watch. He will need to have his wits about him at all times, especially as he barely knows his way around the ship yet.

At 5.30am on Monday, John is standing in the corner of the bridge, doing his best to look smart and awake, without getting in the way. The Officer of the Watch has told him to watch for Captain Corry, who will be coming up the hatchway, and he glances nervously at the ladder, as a white hat covered in gold braid, appears at the bottom. It is his first look at the man in command of his ship whose word is law.

When the Captain is halfway up the ladder, he stands to attention and announces, 'Captain on the Bridge' which brings everyone to attention. The Officer of the Watch actually smiles at him.

The Captain steps onto the bridge, with the words 'carry on' and John is now made up that he got it completely right, and his confidence grows.

As the ship slips the buoys at 6.00am, he watches the process of getting underway and is fascinated with how smoothly everything goes. So much so that when the Officer of the Watch gives him a message, to take to the Wardroom he barely notices, but fortunately no one else does and he heads off.

At 8.00am his relief arrives, and he has to be quick with his breakfast, because at 9.00am they will be going to General Quarters, for his first time, for a gunnery firing practice.

His quarter station is down in the forward 13.5" shell magazine, supplying the forward turret, and he needs to get into overalls and anti-flash clothing before it all kicks off.

All too soon the quarters are piped throughout the ship, and he joins the other seamen, as they climb down the vertical shafts into the bowels of the ship.

In the magazine, the Petty Officer in charge takes him to one side and explains how they will be moving these very heavy shells to the hoists. That he should watch this time, and the next time, he will be allocated one of the duties.

All is quiet and calm, until the voice pipe from the turret above, demands shells, and then they get to work, using the overhead rails and trolleys, to move the shells into the hoist, which are then lifted up to the turret, using the manual lifts.

He can then hear the gunners above, load the shells and cordite, close the breeches, take aim on the target, and the order is given to 'engage'. He is used to the noise of the guns, but the sound is awesome, and the magazine shakes, the ship lists from the force of the firing, and the smell of cordite pervades the magazine, making them all cough.

More rounds are required, and routine action takes over, as more shells are sent upwards, to follow the first. Until finally the main armament takes a break, and he hears the smaller guns having their go, as they clear up in the main magazine stowing the handling gear in its seagoing stowage. At 11.45am the exercise ends.

Two days later they are back in Malta, but only to replenish the magazines with ammunition, and to fill the bunkers with coal, as a big fleet exercise is planned. No one likes coaling which is a dirty job, worse in the heat of the day, but everyone has no choice but to help out.

Eventually, they sail for Marmaris in Turkey, and anchor in the bay, but there is no leave. The Commander in Chief Mediterranean wants to inspect the ship's company, so John assembles on deck with everyone else.

After the inspection, and when the Admiral has left, they stay behind to hear a Warrant read out, for the punishment of a sailor, who was drunk on shore and fighting with locals, before the patrol arrested him.

On return to the mess, to change into their working clothes, the older hands are discussing the warrant, and the new 1st Lt., who only joined on the same day as John did. Many of the older hands do not like him; however, sailors on the lower deck often distrust officers.

They see that this officer is a disciplinarian, and predict that there will be a lot more warrants in the future. John just listens, takes it all in and promises himself to keep out of trouble, his guess is that moral on board is about to take a dive.

The Captain may be a good seaman, he has witnessed his work on the bridge, but he is probably not going to get in the 1st Lt.'s way, because the running of the crew is his job, and John silently agrees that there will be a lot more warrants.

Settling into a seagoing routine, he soon learns to keep out of the way on the bridge, yet carry out his tasks quickly and efficiently, as they visit the strange sounding places.

As well as Marmaris, there is Navarin, and Tiguita, until they arrive at Cape Rosario, which is where they find HMS Theseus in need of assistance, and luckily he is on watch to observe and learn.

Unfortunately, she is stranded on a sandbank, and he is sent down to get the boat crews out because HMS Hood cannot get too close, or she might get stuck as well.

Whilst the boats are being launched, he listens to the Captain explain to the Officer of the Watch what should be done.

The Theseus already has her own boats in the water, with ropes attached to the ship, and Hood's boats join them in trying to pull the ship off the bank. Luckily the tide is rising, which also helps and as the sailors all pull in unison on their oars, very slowly Theseus slips into deeper water.

The Captain is very happy that his team has helped in the salvage operation. Even better for him is that he will be enjoying the fine bottle of port, which has been sent over in thanks for their assistance.

John and the other sailors, of course, get nothing, but little does he realise, that this experience and some others, would have a significant effect on his later life.

A few days later the ship returns to its base at Malta for a rest but not for John.

'Anchors away', bellows the order from the bridge of HMS Hood, in the middle of Valetta Grand Harbour, early in a sunny spring morning.

Breaking the clip holding the anchor chain in place, causes it to plummet with a large splash, into the clear blue water below.

Carving downwards through the anchor hawse pipe, the huge anchor chain also rattles up from the cable locker below making quite a noise, enough to wake all those lucky enough, to be still in their hammocks.

Driving the battleship astern, enough cable is laid on the seabed, in order to hold the mighty ship in place, for the duration of their visit.

Eventually, the bridge orders 'all stop', and the pin is replaced, holding securely the stopped cable, bringing peace and quiet again, to the mighty warship.

For our John, it is time to fall out and head below, for a swift breakfast before reporting for duty.

Going aft on the upper deck port waste, he can see the midships party, swinging out the boats, in preparation for journeys to the shore, although today John is required to stay on board as duty watch.

Hastening down the ladder, and turning forwards he is ready for a well-earned breakfast, having been up since 4 am, and on the bridge all that time, as they enter the harbour.

In the mess deck, he collects his porridge, bread, jam and tea then sits down, at the long, recently scrubbed wooden table, next to his now best friend, who is tucking in with gusto, into his own scran.

Jeremiah or Jer as he is known is also duty watch, and their muster time of 0800 rapidly approaches.

Knives, forks and spoons flash in the flickering lamplight, as they hurry to ensure they will be in good time for the muster. Lateness often results in a charge, and then attendance at Captain's defaulters, which will only result in more work, and no leave.

Making haste down the passageway to the quarterdeck, they pass the Bosuns mate piping the muster, and know they will be ok today, but wonder what job will they get, hopefully, work that is easy and clean.

No one is late today, which means the duty Petty Officer is in a good mood, standing and smiling at his group of ratings lined up before him.

Onto the quarterdeck, marches the Officer of the Day, resplendent in his naval uniform, unfortunately for them, it is the Gunnery Officer, nicknamed "grumpy", and they all know that the day could be long and arduous.

Placing himself directly in the middle of the quarter-deck, he reads out the various tasks for the day to the Petty Officer, who allocates each rating with his work.

'Quarterdeck dismiss', ends the muster, and John heads towards the steam pinnace, which is his job for the day.

Reaching out for the cable that runs along the top of the boatyard, he vaults the railing and moves out over the top of the steam pinnace.

Stepping onto the rope ladder he shins down and just misses stepping on the stoker, who is getting the engine ready, for a busy day ferrying Officers ashore and to other ships at anchor in the harbour.

Taking hold of his boat hook, John stands rigidly to attention on the bow, hoping he looks smart enough for the Captain, who is to be their first passenger.

Under the ship's stern, they approach the gangway steadily, and fortunately, John hooks the bow rope at the first attempt, as they glide to a halt in perfect position, for the waiting and watching Captain who then steps on board.

Very quickly they are on their way, puffing across the slightly choppy surface, adding their bow wave to those created by others in the harbour.

Whilst it is not easy as the boat rocks, John is able to maintain his position facing forward, as he knows the Captain will be watching, and in the Royal Navy, it is always necessary to put on a good show.

Xanthe is the first ship they pass, to the sound of Bosuns calls, announcing their passage to Customs House steps, which is the Captains destination.

'You will wait here until I return' is the Captains order, which at least means they can relax for a while, provided one of them keeps a good lookout for his return.

Zeal is only to be shown when required, and the chance to rest, during what could prove to be a very busy morning, is an opportunity not to be missed by any blue jacket.

Life on HMS Hood continues, until the Captain announces to the assembled crew, that the ship has been ordered back to Chatham. Some members of the crew will remain on station, and be transferred, to fill spare billets in the Mediterranean fleet.

On 7th February 1900 John, along with a number of other draftees, takes a final boat ride from his old ship; to his new ship HMS Theseus, the cruiser that always seemed to be busy. In fact that day 116 crew members are dispersed throughout the fleet, to other ships.

Although he is still a Junior Seaman, he now has a lot more experience, viewing the change with mixed feelings, as he leaves his old messmates, and joins a new mess full of different characters.

This active ship is much happier in fact than the Hood, the officers seem fairer to him, and 9 months later John is rated Ordinary Seaman, at a Captain's request man table. Standing rigidly to attention, in front of his Commanding Officer, his divisional officer gives him a good report, saying he is willing, has good seamanship skills and has never been in trouble.

His part of ship Petty Officer, standing at the rear of the room, considers him a reliable and conscientious worker, who will always complete any work allocated quickly and without any complaints.

Settling into this busy and rewarding life, with many friends in the mess deck John enjoys HMS Theseus, despite still being away from home for many months.

The most notable event occurs on 11th Feb 1901 when they are in Piraeus harbour, where the Russian cruiser Khrabry, has managed to run aground. The first warning John has is, when the

Bosuns mate pipes clear lower deck suddenly, whilst they are having their morning break in the mess.

Leaving their mugs on the tables, they rush up the ladders, onto the open deck and muster by part of ship, where the 1st Lt. is already standing waiting for them.

After all the Petty Officers have reported their parts of ship present and correct, they are stood at ease as the 1st Lt. informs them. 'The Russian ship "Khrabry" has requested our assistance; they have run aground by the stern, on the other side of the harbour.

We will move the Theseus over to them, and give her a tow off the rocks. Because the tide is still going out, we will have to wait until it turns, which means I can give you all a full briefing of what is required.

On board the Khrabry, their stern is hard aground and they are unable to turn their propellers. The bow of the ship is afloat and is being held with an anchor that they managed to drop, just before grounding.

They are working on her, lightening the ship, and moving materials from the stern to the bow. We will launch our boats, and firstly put a towing cable from our stern to their bow; then each boat will also be attached by a cable, to help pull her off. Any questions?' he concludes.

'Is she holed Sir?' asks John's Petty Officer.

'Fortunately, she is not otherwise they would have had to fix any hole, pump her out and then we would tow her off.'

John's first real lesson on salvage finishes and they set about the practicalities of getting the Theseus into position, lowering the boats, transferring the cables and waiting for the high tide.

That afternoon John sits in one of the whalers, keeping pace with the other seamen, as they all pull on their oars together, and tighten the cable attached to the stricken vessel.

The Petty Officer in the stern is watching the Khrabry, as he calls out the stroke timing with the word 'Pull', repeating it in a steady rhythm, as he uses the rudder, to keep the boat pulling in the right direction.

The Theseus is churning the water at her stern, and the three other ships boats are all matching John's boat's effort. John can see the stern of the Khrabry, as it starts to inch away from the shore. But just as he thinks they are done, she stops moving and grounds again just for a few moments, and then drifts clear, at this the sailors on the ships and boats, all cheer to a man, and everyone is pleased with the day's work.

Later in the mess deck, there is much discussion about the day; many of the old hands are relating tales of salvage, which John finds fascinating. Sitting quietly he listens, absorbing all the information, from the many stories, little knowing that this event and the knowledge of salvage he is acquiring, would lead him into a fascinating couple of years in the future.

The good life continues on the Theseus, and on the 14 Sep 1901 John is rated, Able Seaman. Then from the 8th Dec 1901 to 10 January 1902, he is able to take local leave in Malta, on the Depot ship HMS Hibernia, which allows him to explore this fascinating island more fully.

Returning to his ship he finally leaves HMS Theseus, when she is back in Chatham on 28th May 1902. Here he joins HMS Pembroke barracks, awaiting his next draft and hoping for some leave, he hasn't been home for a long time.

Walking down the corridor, he scans the notice board, and sees an Admiralty Instruction looking for volunteers; apparently, the Royal Navy has too many seamen and needs more stokers because the sailing ships are being replaced with steam ones.

John is missing home, and if he volunteers he will be able to join the Royal Naval Reserve, so still be a sailor although only part-time.

They are paying a retainer for this commitment, and he can go back to his beloved Liverpool. Thus on 5th Sep 1902, he leaves the Royal Navy and joins the Royal Naval Reserve, which is the forerunner of the Royal Naval Reserve of modern times.

A Civilian Ashore

John is sitting on a small wall, under the freshly budding trees, enjoying the beautiful spring weather, alongside him is a lovely young girl named Jessie. They are in a discreet area in the grounds of Whittingham Asylum, near Goosnargh, where she works as an attendant, and he is doing some bricklaying. He had noticed and smiled at her many times, whilst she was going between the buildings on her errands. Eventually, he plucked up the courage to ask her to meet him, at this quiet spot, during her lunch break. Now they have met a few times, and he is hoping that she likes him because he likes her very much, they are both from Birkenhead, and seem to get on very well.

'Why did you do leave the Royal Navy?' She enquires.

'They were looking to reduce the number of seamen in the Navy, and I had not been home for quite some time. I did join the Royal Fleet Reserve, and they pay me a small retainer, which means I have to attend weekly drills so that I will keep my training up to standard.'

'What day of the week is that on then?' is her next question.

'Actually, it is tonight, but I need to work, and have permission to miss tonight's drill, it is just too far to return just for that. Unfortunately for me, this job ends next week; I have really enjoyed being here and especially meeting you. However, I do have an interview in a couple of days, for a permanent job as a Firefighter in Birkenhead.'

'A Firefighter' she says lightly 'why that's a skilled job and I thought you were just an ordinary sailor'.

'I am a sailor and very proud of it, but we were also trained to fight fires on the ships, I am hoping that my naval training will be enough for me to be selected. What I am going to miss is our regular meetings, will I be able to see you again once this job finishes?' he ventures.

A small smile dances across her face 'well I am not sure' she teases 'I hardly know you, and my Dad who knows about these things told me never to trust a sailor because they are always going away.'

He puffs his chest out and replies also with a smile 'why would he say that we are the salt of the earth, and anyway I am only a part-time one, and next week I shall be a Firefighter, it is a really respectable job earning good money.'

'What was your longest time away from home in the Navy? She ventures.

'I spent 3 years away in the Mediterranean, and we visited quite a lot of lovely places, but I won't be doing that again.' He replies.

Jumping lightly off the wall, Jessie turns to John looking very high and mighty 'time for me to go back to work, and I don't think I would like my man to be away for that long'.

She turns and walks down the path towards the building she works in, 'can I see you again?' shouts John after her.

Without looking back, she answers 'maybe if you get that job' she teases some more, but is looking really happy, although she makes sure he cannot see her face.

With his Naval Service and firefighting training standing him in good stead at the interview, he does become a Firefighter. Now with a regular paying job and the odd hours that he works he can easily see a lot more of Jessie and take her out to try and impress her.

When he finally meets her father, Bernt at the family home, he finds that he is actually a Norwegian sailor, who is working on Cunard ships going mostly to New York with immigrants, so they have a great deal in common because they are both seamen. It also explains why Jessie had been warned about sailors, but despite this, their love has blossomed.

His workplace now is the newly built Whetstone Lane fire station, where they keep the two beautiful Merryweather horse-drawn fire engines and the horses needed to get them to an emergency quickly. Part of his job is to care for these mighty steads and his love for animals grows.

On the 6th Nov 1904, he and Jessie marry in St Mary's church Birkenhead; it is a grand day, with a big reception in the family hotel. The Westminster Hotel had been opened in 1901 by his father, who always wanted his own place rather than managing one for the brewery.

After living with his in-laws for a couple of months, they finally manage to buy a house, No 57 Exmouth Street, which is just around the corner from the Whetstone Lane fire station and settle into idyllic family life. Life could not be better for John who living so close spends more of his time looking after the horses.

Then in December 1905 tragedy strikes, because Jessie's father Bernt dies suddenly and they both miss him so much. He was a wonderful man, who took great delight in entertaining them all, with his many stories and life is pretty cruel.

John continues attending the regular Royal Naval Reserve training meetings at HMS Eagle on the other side of the Mersey in Liverpool, where he keeps his hand in as a seaman and of course life still has to go on.

Tragically, John's father Vaughan then also dies on 7th April 1909 after a period of ill health. This event was to change John's life considerably. His mother is now the owner of the Westminster Hotel but she needs help and asks John to take over as the manager.

The hotel was originally 3 terraced houses that were converted into a hotel which was quite close to the Birkenhead shipyards and was very busy. Reluctantly John swaps his smart fireman's uniform for a suit and the hotel continues to thrive under his leadership with his mother still living there.

Fortunately, he can still continue at HMS Eagle, meeting the many other ex-naval regulars, who make up most of the members of this local Royal Naval Reserve unit which is very popular.

Then to War

5 years later on 4th August 1914, John is responding to his countries call to go to war, he has been called up. The journey starts with him walking proudly in his naval uniform, his family in company, down the hill through the rows of terraced streets, towards the jetty below. The ferry across the Mersey will take him, to HMS Eagle where he will meet with all the other RNR ratings he regularly trains with, and then they will travel to Chatham barracks.

After some refresher training, hopefully, he will be sent on to a ship of some sort. His wife Jessie by his side is carrying their 7 month-old daughter, Nellie, as their three other children skip along in front, apparently without a care in the world.

Both of them are managing, this difficult and momentous change in their lives, as best they can, there has been a lot of talk of war in the papers, but they had both hoped it would not come to this.

'Do you remember when we first met, and you telling me you wouldn't go away?' asks Jessie.

John replies 'of course I do, was the best thing that ever happened to me, being a brickie's mate at the hospital, and meeting you my darling. However I don't have any choice about going, and no one has any idea how long the war will be; some people think it will be over by Christmas.' He has also been thinking a great deal, mostly about how he can improve his chances of returning if he is involved in any fighting that is. All he can do, he has decided, is to really focus on doing his work, to the best of his abilities which he hopes will help his chances. At the same time, he has hidden from his wife and children, the knowledge and fear; that he may not return, despite his best efforts.

'Please make sure you come back to me safe and sound' she says with a slight quiver in her voice and then shouts at the children. 'Hilda and Vaughan stop swinging your brother Jack so high; don't drop him and spoil your father's leaving'.

Of course, they take little notice, until John clips their ears lightly from behind saying 'do as your mother says, or it will be the worse for you, and whilst I am away, I want you to take care of her see.'

At this, they laugh because they know their dad loves them, and they will miss him as well. They don't realise just how serious the situation is, but why would they, and perhaps he will bring presents when he comes home, apparently this is what sailors do, is the rumour at school.

Once at the jetty, John buys his ticket, and they wait for the next service, as some of John's fellow Birkenhead reserves, also start to arrive, greeting each other with just a nod of the head. The ferry slices across the river, and ties up alongside the jetty, the family all hug each other.

Jessie wipes a small tear from her eye, which John notices, and he says 'Don't worry my darling I will be fine'. Of course, he can't be sure, and he also knows it is going to be difficult for her, whilst he is away.

Then the ferry gangway men start shouting 'all aboard' which forces John to take his leave. Once all are aboard, the gangway rattles over the decking on its small wheels. As soon as it is clear and the open guard rail is closed, the lines are removed; the steam engine puffs, and then the propellers turn, causing the water under the stern to agitate, whilst the gap between the jetty and ferry grows. All the men in uniform line the guard rails, waving like mad, and their loving relative's wave back, the children screaming good luck, and many of the women are weeping openly.

Jessie is made of sterner stuff, and she does not want John to worry, so she weeps inside, and hopes her John will return to her safe and sound.

They all stand watching, as the ferry crosses the great river Mersey, and then berths on the Liverpool side, where their men head off for HMS Eagle to do their duty.

The families disperse slowly, Jessie walks with a heavy heart, back up the hill to her lovely home, where she hopes to welcome back her man, sometime in the future.

Nellie stirs in her arms; she is getting hungry and growing quickly, so Jessie will have plenty to keep her busy. She hopes that she has been able to hide her fears from John because she does not want him worrying about them. He has been somewhat distracted lately but that is to be expected, you don't go to war every day.

She also reflects on their life together, since their marriage, no, she has no regrets, only a few sad events and they will all have to manage, whilst the men are away.

Its 3 weeks after arriving in Chatham Naval Base, where John and his mates are crowding around the notice board because the latest drafts have come in. Many of the men are off to the reserve battle fleet assembling in Portsmouth, but John cannot see his name on any of the typed sheets until he finally spots it on the bottom of one with 21 other names, HMS Centurion which is part of the 2nd Battle Squadron. She is only 4 years old so is quite a modern battleship and already in commission. In brackets behind the ships name is written Scapa Flow.

'You are off to Scotland then' says one of John's shipmates, continuing with 'that's an awfully long journey by train and ferry, I went there a few years ago and there is nothing at Scapa Flow at all either.'

'It looks to me like most of the fleet will be there from now on. The rumour is that the fleet sneaked through the Dover straits three weeks ago, right under the German noses' replies John 'still at least I have a ship because there's an awful lot of reservists here and no billets at all now'.

He does wonder what they will do with those remaining, but he needs to pack quickly, they are leaving in 2 hours, and the matter is really of no concern to him.

Standing on the barren, wind-swept treeless shore of Scapa Flow, on 26th August 1914; the 22 ratings can see the harbour launch, heading towards the small wooden jetty. At the same time, the collier SS Rydam is leaving HMS Centurion, which lies at anchor just off the shore, having just finished coaling ship.

The only odd sight is the debris laying all along the shoreline running into the distance, there are numerous ships boats, all filled with wooden furniture, lying abandoned as far as the eye can see. They have been left there, when all the ships prepared for war, they had to remove anything that can burn.

Many large warships are in the harbour, which is a stirring sight that would gladden any sailor's heart. Looking at his ship, John cannot help but compare it with his last battleship HMS Hood, which had two turrets, but this one has five turrets. In reality, it is like comparing chalk and cheese, although in this case, the cheese is huge and of the finest quality available.

On board he quickly settles into his new mess deck, it is lit with electric light instead of oil lamps, this is the most significant visible change since he last lived on a ship. Centurion is so different to the Hood because of its size, but John like most sailors quickly gets his bearings, the ship may have changed, but the routine wraps him in a warm cosy blanket of familiarity.

In the mess deck, he is one of the oldest because he is now 32 and his age, experience, and ability, establishes his position quickly in this environment. The talk in the mess, however, does disturb him somewhat, all is going well in the war preparations, but they are heading to sea again tomorrow, after replacing the ammunition used recently. Apparently, Scapa Flow itself may not be as secure as it perhaps should be. The threat of the new German U boats, entering through the channels, is causing the fleet to keep on the move; the thought that his new world might just explode, without warning at any moment, whilst lying at anchor is not comforting at all.

The next day however John is excused ammunitioning ship because he has to attend some training. At the morning muster on the quarterdeck, he is surprised to hear his name called out, along with a few others by the duty Petty Officer. Immediately they fall in as a separate group, under the aft 13.5" gun barrels.

'Attention' roars the Petty Officer in charge who turns and salutes a Cdr. who has come over to them, 'Director Crews ready for training sir' he continues.

'Very good, stand the men at ease please.'

'Stand at Ease' roars the petty officer.

'I am Cdr. Green the Gunnery Officer, and we have some new members of our team, who have just joined, so it is important that we do some training today, before the ship sails.' 'Which one of you is Foulkes?' he asks.

'Sir' replies John a little startled that he has been picked out.

'My director operator had an accident yesterday, during coaling and broke his arm. You have been selected as his replacement, and will be with me in the foretop Director Tower, operating the equipment up their', he says pointing up at the platform above the lookout top, sitting high above the ship on its 3 large tripod legs, 'I hope you have a head for heights and don't get seasick' he continues.

'I have never been sick sir, and going up there is no problem' says John 'I was a firefighter in civilian life and was always first up the ladder sir' finishes John.

'Excellent' says Cdr. Green, 'get everybody to their stations now Petty Officer, and I will join you up there shortly' he finishes with.

Soon after an exhilarating climb up the mast, and entering through a small hatch, John is standing beside a strange looking T shaped piece of equipment; that he recognises as a rangefinder. Being inside the Director, but able to look out all round over the Scapa Flow anchorage, he marvels at the view of the Grand Fleet.

Centurion is at anchor with the other battleships of the 2nd Battle Squadron, who are all getting ready for sea, every ship is a hive of activity, as men the size of ants, work to bring the group to war readiness.

'Right you're here' says Cdr. Green as he pops through the hatch, catching John a bit unaware, although he does not show it. John had been standing by the equipment, trying to work out what each of the hand wheels would do, and then as Cdr. Green climbs through the hatch John jumps to attention and smartly salutes.

'No need for that Foulkes whilst we are in here' says Green at which John relaxes a little, but of course, he isn't really used to such informality by an officer. 'Have you used this equipment before' asks Green.

'No sir but it was mentioned during our recent training before I joined' replies John.

'Very good' says Green,' stand here and you can adjust the equipment height to suit you'.

John then rotates the wheel in the middle, so that the eyepieces are at a comfortable height for him to look through. Then resting his chest against the breast bracket, they adjust the right armrest, so that is also comfortable.

'On the left is the altitude handle, and you use your right hand to adjust the range focusing scale, but first adjust the right eyepiece, so that you can see the target clearly' continues Green. At this, the shoreline comes sharply into focus, although it is a considerable distance away.

Green then proceeds to explain in more detail, how John will operate the equipment. 'We are the vital component, which brings all of our big guns to bear, onto the most important targets. I will tell you which targets to track and you just have to make sure that the centre of the target is kept in the middle of the crosshairs, in the rangefinder. Then you keep following the target steadily, got that.'

'Yes sir' replies John who immediately realises that he will be able to see all the action, instead of being stuck down below in the turret, or even worse in the magazine below the waterline.

Below them is the Transmitting Station, where other sailors operate a system that establishes the target future position, and this sends indicator information, visible as pointers in the turret, which the Captain of the turret follows to control the guns.

'On the top, there is a light that comes on when the guns are loaded and ready to fire; the electrical switch part of it fires all the guns in a salvo. When I say ENGAGE you will operate the switch, then I will use my stopwatch to time the shells and will say 'now' when the Fall of Shot is due. Each of the crosshairs in the sight is divided up with marks, you will spot the shell splashes and note how many marks from the centre, horizontally and vertically they appear, to give me an estimate of the fall of shot, got that?'

'Yes Sir, what format would you like me to use for the fall of shot estimate?' replies John enthusiastically.

At this, the Officer draws a telescope image on a piece of paper and marks a splash saying 'this splash is 3 left, 2 over and this other one would be 5 right 3 short.'

'Thank you sir' replies John.

'OK let's have a practice run, line up on that trawler over there' he points.

A few moments later John has the small trawler in the middle his sights, focussed and ranged 'tracking target sir' he says.

'Range' shouts Green into the voice tube.

'5600 yards' is the reply from below and Green quickly consults his time of flight table.

'For exercise Engage' he commands, but John has been concentrating on following the target, and does not operate the firing switch immediately. Taking the newspaper which is rolled up under his arm, Green smacks John lightly across the head with the newspaper and repeats. 'For exercise engage'.
John recognises his own failing, vows never to be caught out again, and having learned his lesson, presses the firing trigger immediately.

Some seconds later Green says 'fall of shot?'

To which John replies smartly '1 right 2 short'.

Standing behind John; Cdr. Green smiles as he consults his range table, knowing that he has made a good choice in this experienced sailor. He shouts into the voice tube 'Left 100 up 200' and the training continues for the rest of the day.

At the end of the day before proceeding below Green says to John, 'Well done Foulkes, you picked that up quickly, and tomorrow we will do the same again, but we will have a towed target to fire at, and get some real practice in firing live shells, did you enjoy it?'

'I did sir and when we go into battle we will have a grandstand view won't we. By the way, I hope you don't mind me asking but which newspaper was that you used' says John.

'Many Gunnery Officers carry the Daily Telegraph as a training aid, it certainly gets things moving.' He pauses and continues 'We will have the best view in the ship but remember, everyone on board is relying on us to do our job, the Germans may not have as many ships as us, but they are very efficient.'

'You can rely on me sir and hopefully, your training aid won't be needed again' says John with a smile.

As he follows the Gunnery Officer through the hatch; and down director mast to the deck far below, he is thinking that the Daily Telegraph will not be used on him again. It is time to recommit to his vow, to do his job the best he can, in order that he will see his beloved Jessie and family again.

In the mess deck below, John finds there is a letter lying waiting on the mess table; it has very familiar and neat handwriting, causing his heart to leap. Although it is 10 days old and has been to Chatham as well, any news is very welcome. That evening after eating his meal he sits down to reply, feeling content to find that all is well at home and that he feels more in control of his own destiny on HMS Centurion.

Early the next morning the battle group sails, with everyone at defence stations, John is busy with his rangefinder, practicing turning the unit with his body, managing the elevation with his left hand, and keeping whatever target he selects ranged, whilst not forgetting to think about the firing switch.

Cdr. Green, standing with his paper under his arm, watches and offers a few words of advice such as 'remember Foulkes, that you will have 5 very heavy turrets following your every move, so keep any movement smooth. Also, the firing solution is dependent on you giving an accurate and steady range, bearing and elevation information'.

These words simply inspire John, and in time he will become as one with his equipment, it won't be his fault if Centurion's gunnery is not up to scratch. Later in the day they actually get to fire, this time at a towed target. The first initial roar of the guns startles him, and then he finds out that estimating the fall of shot is a lot harder than he imagined, especially as the first shots fall behind the target, and are almost obscured. Practice, however, irons out these difficulties somewhat, and they continue to venture out to sea, rarely staying in one place for any long period.

Scares in Scapa are numerous; other ships think they see submarines inside the anchorage and even fire on them, but mostly they are just the local wildlife such as seals, unfortunate enough to surface, and then be mistaken for a submarine periscope.

What really drives them on is the real need to achieve accurate gunnery, ready for the fateful day when the German and British fleets will lock horns. The weather during this time, is also the worst possible but eventually, in August 1915, Scapa Flow is declared safe, and the Grand Fleet settles into a less rigorous phase of the war.

Now they are even able to carry out live firings, within the confines of the now safe and huge anchorage.

Occasionally they are given a few hours leave, with opportunities to stretch their legs on the barren surface of the islands, which are protecting them from the U boats.

John is taking one of these rare opportunities and passes a small group of his messmates returning to the ship. 'What's up with you' he asks of Chats Harris, who is holding his hand and wrist, which is wrapped in a bloodstained handkerchief.

'Bloody kitten' he replies 'I heard it calling just down the road and it sounded in some distress. When I looked into the rabbit hole which is 100 yards down the road on the right, just by that gateway, I could see a small black and white kitten crying, so I foolishly reached in to get it out. Just as I was about to grab it, the dam cat grabbed my hand, bit my thumb and lacerated my wrist with its claws, ungrateful is what I call it, and I need to see the doc back on board now. It can rot in hell for all I care' he concludes.

'It must be a feral one' says John 'and it probably didn't like the look of you. I will have a look when I get there and see if it likes the look of me.'

'No chance' replies Chas 'I bet you sippers you can't bring it on board' is his challenge. Now rum to Chas is sacrosanct, and John knows that no-one has ever tasted any of it, and he loves nothing better than a challenge.

He is willing to risk some of his own rum, plus he has a secret weapon in his pocket, and a couple of hours spare, there is little for sailors to do when ashore here anyway. 'You're on' says John to the challenge and Chas the rum rat, smiles and forgets his wounds for a while, already savouring the wonderful taste of another man's rum.

'See you tomorrow lunchtime and don't forget to bring your grog' he finishes with and the group walk on.

It is not difficult to find the rabbit hole, because he can hear the kitten meowing from a good distance away, and sure enough, he can see deep inside the rabbit hole, a small black and white kitten, with lovely white feet peering out at him. It's looking at him nervously, but John realises this little thing has a fire in its belly, and he knows better than to reach inside.

Instead, he slips his hand into his pocket and brings out his secret weapon. He had slipped a couple of biscuits, into his blue jacket when he left the mess, to stave off any hunger, whilst he took his walk and now he could put them to good use.

The kitten is obviously hungry and breaking off a few bits, he drops them into the burrow, close enough for the kitten to sniff suspiciously at them, and then gobble them up. As soon as they are gone, the kitten looks up and asks for more. John slowly and carefully puts the pieces closer and closer to the opening, so that in the end the kitten is probably close enough to grab. Instead of this he simply holds a piece, close to the cat's mouth, really uncomfortably close to its very sharp teeth and claws, however, it simply takes the proffered biscuit.

Once the biscuits are gone, John speaks some soft kind words and puts his hand near to this dangerous wild animal, which instead of savaging him, gives him a lick and starts purring.

Opening the front of his jacket, he coaxes the frightened creature inside, where to his great surprise, it snuggles down inside his warm coat, and he realises that he has a new member of his family, which he knows his children will love if he can somehow get it home.

It is only then that he realises he will be late back, buttoning up his coat, he rushes back to the jetty. He is actually 10 minutes late and that spells trouble for him, although he thinks it will be worth it. Back on board on the Quarterdeck, he finds Master at Arms Tate waiting for him, complete with his dreaded clipboard.

'Follow me Foulkes' and they head off for the office, where he knows he is in for a grilling, and probably an appearance at Captain's defaulter. 'Why are you late' he asks 'you better have a good reason or you are for the high jump'.

John then relates the story of the kitten, leaving out the bit about rum of course, and as he finishes a small body stirs. A head sticks out to view the new and strange surroundings.

'I have heard many excuses in my job but this one really takes the biscuit, however, I can see you are telling the truth. Luckily for you, I am needed elsewhere now, so treat this as a warning, the only one you will ever get. As I am letting you off this time, perhaps you should name it Lucky because that is what you are. One piece of advice, however, you better make sure that the ships cat Centaur, doesn't find it because he hates other cats.'

John is mightily relieved,' thank you Master Tate, Lucky it is' and hurries out, to get on with his duties.

Lunchtime the next day, John strolls into the starboard side of his mess deck, where Chats is sitting waiting for his Tot, 'have you brought me your rum' he asks when he notices John.

'I have brought you something that is dark, but you won't like it' he replies, then he reaches into his jacket, slowly revealing the lovely kitten, which on seeing Chats, start hissing and snarling, but then settles down as John strokes him.

'Lucky is his name and it looks like he recognises you, I believe you owe me sippers'.

Chats looks aghast, many might say, it is because the kitten recognised him, but anyone who really knows, realises that to lose some of his rum, is too much to bear. Eventually, after a few minutes, he finally grasps he has no choice and does honour his bet. Tentatively offering his glass with almost a tremor in his hand, John takes it with a small smile.

As he lifts the sailor's nectar to his lips, under Chas's watchful eye, he takes the smallest of sips and then reverently hands the glass back saying 'lovely'.

Of course Chas notices how little rum has been taken from the glass, and eventually, they become good friends, and even Lucky eventually grows to like him.

Lucky's new home is inside John's jacket, and they are inseparable, even up on the range finder platform, they are together, although John acquires a small wooden box with a rag in, that the cat sits on when he is working.

'That box could do with something in it for Lucky to use as a toilet instead of the rag' says Cdr. Green, who has also taken a shine to this plucky stray kitten. 'Come to the wardroom this evening, when we are back in Scapa Flow' he instructs John as they leave the platform.

Knocking on the wardroom door that evening, John says to the steward who answers his call 'Cdr. Green asked me to see him'.

The steward closes the door and a couple of minutes later his boss appears, with a pile of newspapers under his arm and says, 'I have finished with these Gunnery officer training aids, if you rip them up, you can use them in the box for Lucky, which will save him soiling the cloth'. At which he hands over a large pile of Daily Telegraphs with a smile, and disappears into the wardroom. This is before the surprised John can even thank him, also he realises that his training days are over as well, and he will thank his boss later.

A week later John has left Lucky, in his box in the mess deck, whilst he showers and when he returns, there is an almighty commotion going on, and his kitten seems to be the centre of it. Levering his way past the throng, he discovers that Centaur has cornered his pet, and is closing in teeth bared, looking exceedingly hostile.

Lucky for his part, has his hackles up as far as possible, for such a small thing, his back is arched, trying to look as big as he can, and is hissing for all his worth. Centaur who regularly despatches rats that are much bigger is not intimidated and keeps coming. But before John can intervene, Lucky strikes with his right paw claws out and lands a telling blow, right on Centaur's nose even drawing blood. Centaur just turns and flees, but they all knew that he will be back, and next time he will finish the kitten off.

Taking the shivering Lucky in his arms, John calms him down and wonders what to do. Eventually, he moves Lucky up to the Director with his box, makes sure he is comfortable, tells him to stay, and when he leaves closes the hatch. For the time being, he is safe and this is where he stays.

Of course Cdr. Green finds out what has happened, and wants to help but is not sure how. He is certain that the only solution is to get the kitten off the ship. A couple of days later he casually speaks to John, 'are you not due some leave Foulkes, surely you would like to see your family?'

'I am due a few days, but not many get any leave now, and the chances are very low sir. Also, I doubt the Master at Arms would be sympathetic, because I was late back, so I can't ask him. It would be lovely to get some leave, see my family and maybe then, I could even take Lucky home' John finishes with, his face brightening a bit at the thought.

A week later, the leave list goes up on the notice board, and John who is even more worried about his lovely pet, just glances at it on his way past, there are only 10 names on it, and he stops in his tracks stunned, the 8th name is his. This is unbelievable, and the answer to his prayers, he will be going home in 3 days.

Up on the director platform Cdr. Green finds John kneeling down talking to Lucky, 'you're going to be safe, in a couple of days we are off to Birkenhead, you'll love it there' he finishes with and notices his boss peering through the hatch.

'Sorry Sir just had some fabulous news' and tells him all, but of course, his boss knows because he has been to see the Master.

'I am however reluctant to let you go until I find a suitable man to operate the director, whilst you are away'.

'I know just the man' replies John, 'Able Seaman Harris has the ability, although he keeps it hidden, I am sure that he can do it if you will give him a trial. We have talked about this work in the mess deck, now we are friends, I know he understands, but probably needs practice, because it took me a while to get the hang of it.'

Cdr. Green is quite surprised because he is well aware of Harris's reputation, but he also knows John, so swallows his misgivings, and orders John to fetch him immediately.

During the training session, Chat's performs admirably, to the amazement of the Gunnery Officer, who thought he knew him, and John cradles Lucky in his arms, looking forward to some leave at last, not really caring how it came to him.

On the way down to the mess deck, Chat's looks John in the eye and says 'well that's you out of a job then,' trying to wind him up.

To which John replies 'you may have done ok, but remember you are only my relief whilst I take Lucky home, but no doubt one day, you may be as good as me.'

Chat's knows this but changes the subject, 'how will you manage without Lucky?'

To which John says 'I don't know, we have such a bond, but it is for the best'.

Chat's replies with a big smile, 'I have an idea that will help, come with me to the Quarterdeck, and bring Lucky'.

John is curious but soon has an answer up on deck, there is a photographer visiting the ship, and they have a photo taken of the three of them. 'Half of the picture for me to send to my home, and the other half is yours. When you come back you can look at it, and don't you dare tell anyone what I have done. People will think I have gone soft in the head.' Says Chats finally as they head together back up to the Director, to settle down Lucky, for his last night on board.

On the gangway John stands waiting for the boat ashore, with Lucky snuggled up inside his jacket, the Master at Arms strolls over to John and says 'a word in your shell-like Foulkes' and motions to the side. When they are out of earshot he asks 'have you got Lucky with you?' at which John nods, and opens his top button, to reveal a contented and happy Lucky.

Just at this moment Centaur stalks around the corner, apparently also checking that the other cat is leaving. 'Your boss came to see me, and that is why you have your leave, but I only gave it to you to keep Centaur happy, so make sure you leave it at home Foulkes.'

At which he stomps off with Centaur in tow, but of course John now knows the whole truth, and he is also fortunate to be going home on leave.

Standing outside his own front door, with his bag in hand and Lucky curled up he lifts his hand to knock when it flies open, and Jessie hauls him inside and hugs him. Lucky of course objects to being crushed, and they part as he fights his way out.

'Oh John what a lovely kitten' she says and cuddles him to her bosom. 'How long have you got?' is her first question.

'2 days is all' is his answer.

Then tells her the whole story, and explains why there was no time, to let them know he was coming home. The children are thrilled to see him, and of course, Nellie who is almost a year older is puzzled by this strange man, who appears to know her. He lifts her up and showers her with lots of kisses and hugs, his moustache tickles her face, which she likes and that settles their relationship.

Lying in bed that evening, the two of them are alone at last; John is almost overcome with love and joy to be with Jessie. She is struggling to contain her very mixed emotions. So very pleased to see him, and also dreading him going again, into dangers unknown, in such a very short time, as he tells her all that he was not allowed to put in his letters to her.

This gives her time to come to terms with her feelings, eventually, John sleeps after his very tiring journey, being held by Jessie into the early hours, before she also sleeps to be eventually woken by a hungry, black and white kitten walking up the bed.

All too soon, they are all walking down to the Mersey ferry, in a rerun of an event months ago, which is still very hard for both of them.

Saying goodbye is perhaps a little easier, and John whispers into Jessie's ear 'Lucky can take my place at home until I return, that cat and I have a very close bond' at which he takes him from the front of his jacket, and hands him over.

Jessie's eyes mist over, but she takes the cat and promises to look after him however long it takes because they both now know that this war is going to last for a very long time.

John returns to the Centurion, content that Lucky is now safe, and settles into the long waiting game of training, training and more training, mostly in the cold windswept harbour of Scapa Flow. Here entertainment is almost non-existent, but they are well fed, and at least the mail arrives regularly.

Carried in his pocket, along with a picture of his family, is the one given to him by Chats, where he is holding Lucky on board this very ship and he is as content as the threat of war allows.

Secrecy Beginnings

The First Lord of the Admiralty, Winston Churchill, sits at his large desk musing over his ideas about intercepting radio communications. Earlier in the year, remembering his visit to see Cdr. Samson, at the Royal Naval Air Service flying school, he had been impressed by that officer's efforts in fitting a radio to these flimsy aircraft.

Radio he knew would be the future, as it would allow commanders to manage the conduct of any war much more efficiently. He also realised that important messages sent would be encrypted; perhaps it would be worthwhile intercepting and decoding them, thus gaining early knowledge of the enemy's intentions.

He picks up a pen and starts writing, a memo to the Director of Education.

"An officer of the War Staff, preferably from the I.D. (Intelligence Department), should be selected, to study all the decoded intercepts, not only current but past, and to compare them continually with what actually took place, in order to penetrate the German mind and movements, and make reports.

All these interprets are to be written in a locked book with their decodes and all other copies are to be collected and burnt. All new messages are to be entered in the book, and the book is only to be handled under instructions from C.O.S. (Chief of Security).

The officer selected is for the present to do no other work. I should be obliged if Sir Alfred Ewing will associate himself continuously with this work."

Signing the memo with his normal flourish, he sets in motion the beginnings of something that will eventually be called Room 40 which will serve the country for many years, morphing into Bletchley Park and then GCHQ.

Sir Alfred Ewing is actually the Director of Naval Education but takes on this additional role and because his office is in Room 40 at the Admiralty, this becomes the generally accepted title for the organisation.

H. F. Oliver, the Chief of Security of the Intelligence Department (D.I.D.), responding to the memo, instructs Captain "Blinker" Hall also of D. I. D. to be Sir Alfred's deputy in this matter.

At the subsequent meeting between Sir Alfred and Blinker, they agree that the man who had recently broken the current German Code, associated with the codebook recovered from the German cruiser SMS Magdeburg, Fleet Paymaster Rotter be employed on this work.

Sir Alfred also discusses the work with his good friend Edward Russel Clarke, who is a Radio enthusiast, and he is also drafted into the organisation, to help improve the work of radio interception and install intercept stations which were generally known as "Y" stations.

Russel Clarke along with Captain Round start to install the extra radio intercepts stations, discovering on the way, that with some modification, they could obtain an accurate bearing from the transmitted signal. This is the beginning of Radio Direction Finding (RDF) where having bearings from different stations enabled the source of the signal to be located fairly accurately, well within a couple of miles which was quite an achievement.

Of course, as time went on, the German's changed their codebook to a new one and the Magdeburg book was no longer any use. The only option left was to recruit more staff for Room 40, as they tried to decode the messages using even machines but the codes were extremely complex.

The German's primary error was continuing to use unique unit identifiers at the start and end of each message. They had really ordered minds, so had changed the identifiers for each vessel, but not their position in the message which was a major blunder.

Now when Room 40 had reports of the same message, from more than one RDF station, simply by comparing the unit identifier and noting the direction of the transmission, they could pinpoint the position fairly closely.

Another contributory factor was their habit of transmitting on full power, even when close to their base so that the transmission was easily picked up in the UK.

To add to these errors most U-boat commanders radioed back to base, on a very regular basis, enabling the plotting of their course as well as location.

U-boats always used the 200-metre band almost exclusively which simplified the monitoring requirements because as the war went on it was the battle against these menaces that became vital for us.

Initially, stations were installed along the west coast of England, northwards towards Scapa Flow where our Grand Fleet, the mightiest in the world was waiting. It was the need to protect this fleet from the sinister U-boats that must have driven them on. Scapa Flow in the early days of the war was not secure from submarine attack although that would change as the war progressed.

Many amateur radio enthusiasts were asked to help which they did gladly. Of course, secrecy was vital because we could not afford for the German's to discover our intentions. If they changed their ways we would be in serious trouble.

It was from these humble beginnings, that the need for secrecy would grow, to such an extent that it would be many years before the truth really emerges. Even today over 100 years since this all happened we are still trying to understand what they did which is a testament to the quality of the people employed in this vital work.

The Battle of Jutland

John would regularly pass the notice board in the main passageway, usually without taking too much notice. He mostly ignored Admiralty Orders, when these appeared, but for some reason, probably the boredom of Scapa, he stops and takes the trouble to read this particular one.

AWO, Admiralty Weekly Order 2002 – Ranks and Ratings with Experience of Salvage Operations. Dated 19/11/1915 SV45/15

With reference to the newly established Admiralty Salvage section, reports should be forwarded at an early date giving the names, ranks, and ratings of all Officers and others who have had experience in Salvage operations, giving brief details of their experience or qualifications.

The reports should also state which of those mentioned desire to take up temporary Salvage employment if required to do so.

It all looks interesting, after all, he does have some salvage experience, and anything is better than staying here. The problem is he doesn't want to upset Cdr. Green, who has been so good to him and also a sailor's general reluctance to volunteer for the anything, especially something he has never heard of, like a Salvage Section.

A few days later, he mentions his interest in this work to his boss, who listens to his story, and then considers all he has been told, before saying 'as much as I would like you to stay, I think you should volunteer because you are just the sort of person they are looking for. Harris, of course, can do your job now, so get your application in ASAP, but remember you may not get the job, and it might be some time anyway. The job sounds fantastic to me and it certainly won't be as boring as being stuck here.'

The winter storms continue, with a miserable winter and New Year, with still no sign of a German breakout. A few men get some leave, and one or two are drafted, mostly because coaling and storing ship causes a few accidents and these men are quickly replaced.

On 26th Mar 1916, Thomas Moore is one of those replacements who arrives in John's mess, as they are sitting at the table, waiting for the mess cooks to bring dinner when he clatters through the hatchway.

'Welcome to the wonderful wet cold and windy Scapa Flow' says John, who then introduces the remainder of those sitting down.

A new face is very welcome in their boring existence as he replies 'You can all call me Pony, I have just arrived from Plymouth but home is Sunderland and I am a rigger by trade' as they make room for him to sit down, just as the food arrives.

'You are probably the Painter's relief' says one of the hands.

'A cushy number if ever there was one' says another.

'You also have to look after Centaur the ship's cat' says John and that leads to the story of Lucky being told, so John gets out his treasured picture. Soon John and Pony become good friends, and one day, he casually mentions his application to join the salvage section, which he has yet to hear about.

'That sounds very interesting 'says Pony, 'do you think they are still looking for people, because whilst the painter's job is easy, it's driving me nuts and I think a rigger would be useful to them.'

'I don't know, but there is no harm putting in a request, and it so happens I have a copy of the AWO here', replies John revealing a pretty scruffy but legible document.

'Why are they salvaging ships anyway?' asks Pony.

'It probably has something to do with the length of time it takes to build a ship, which is a couple of years' says John, using his local knowledge of shipbuilding in his home town, 'and they can also recover some of the cargo as well.'

Pony heads off back to work, with the document in his hand, and eventually a couple of days later he has also applied, however, the weeks drag by and they hear nothing.

ROOM 40 London Admiralty 29th May 1916

In the Central Submarine Tracking room, one of the 3 occupants Edward Russel Clarke, picks up a sheaf of intercepted messages, and divides them up into small groups, so that there are about 14 in all, lying on his desk. Written on the top of each piece of paper is a bearing, using this information, he draws lines on a chart, and where each line intersects draws a new cross.

Each of these fourteen crosses, line up with existing tracks of other plotted marks. The latest crosses are all spread down the east coast of Scotland and England, all heading west. 'Our radio tracking stations are working well, come and have a look at this, I think this is very important, the Germans are up to something. They are not heading for any busy shipping lanes' he says to the others.

'How do you know they are submarines' asks George, who only joined the department 3 days ago.

'Luckily for us, they are sticklers for routine and we know the radio frequency U-boats use, plus each message always starts and ends with the same group letter code. Each of these codes is unique to a U-boat, although we don't actually know the identity of many of them.

Without a doubt, this is an unusual activity, and my guess is that these submarines are setting up a trap for our fleet. They would be there to report and perhaps sink some of our ships, if they were to head out, to meet any German fleet expedition. It is likely in my view, that the German Fleet will leave port in the next couple of days, and we should advise our ships to leave immediately before the U-boats get in position.'

Picking up the phone, he dials a number and says into the handset, 'Cdr. Hall please, it's Edward Clarke here, I have some vital information for him, which I think needs immediate action, go and find him please.'

Ten long minutes later the door opens, and the boss of Naval Intelligence, known to them as "Blinker" Hall rushes into the room with a snappy, 'What's all the rush about?' to Clarke.

Showing his boss the progress of the U-boat courses plotted on the chart, he quickly agrees with Edward's conclusion. "I have just been in the decoding section and Admiral Scheer has sent a signal to his fleet at 10.48. We can't decode it properly because the Magdeburg codebook is no longer being used but we believe he is instructing them to sail tomorrow. Along with some additional information from our other sources, it all fits together and I need to advise the Admiralty immediately, of the suspected German intentions" and he hurries off because time is now of the essence.

Thus at 9.50pm on 30th May HMS Centurion, and all the other ships of the Grand Fleet, whether they be in Scapa Flow, Invergordon or Rosyth, set sail using a long practiced plan, which enables all the ships to be at sea, and into the clear ocean in less than 2 hours.

This early departure means that the U-boats do not see them leave and defeats the first stage of the German master plan.

As part of the 2nd Battle Group 1st Division, HMS Centurion takes her station behind HMS Ajax, who is behind their leader HMS King George V, with HMS Erin the final ship of this column. These 4 mighty Battleships form in line, on the port wing of the 6 columns of battleships heading southeast from Scapa Flow, looking for the German fleet.

Little can be seen in the dark, looking through his rangefinder, high up on the mast, so they are stood down to Defence Watches, in order to get some rest, before any action that may begin.

When the watches change, John is relieved by Chas, but despite all of their watchfulness, little can be seen until dawn breaks, and by then John is back at his station. Sweeping round through a full circle of 360 degrees, everything looks just like it has many times before, but rumours in the ship are rife, and John is keen to learn the truth.

Eventually, he asks Cdr. Green 'what's really going on sir?'

To which he calmly replies, 'we believe the German Fleet is at sea, and provided we can find them, I think we will finally have our day, so keep your eyes peeled', a comment that is directed at everyone present on the director platform.

Watches change every 4 hours, until at 5.02pm the ship goes to Action Stations, ready to fight, they have been hearing the distant sounds of gunfire for 2 hours now, and Cdr. Green is on his phone. He is checking each turret, magazine, and the transmitting station, to ensure that everyone is closed up and prepared.

Then the order comes from the Gunnery officer 'Load, Load, Load.' The atmosphere seems to change, for them all; the waiting is now over, excitement for some because this is what they joined for, the Gunnery Officer is one of those. John concentrates even more on his work, wanting to do his job, but also looking to survive. Everything looks just like it has all day, but at 6.15pm the sound of gunfire is louder and closer.

The 6 columns of battleships turn to port, 2nd Battlegroup first, one after the other, forming a single continuous line going almost to the North.

On completion of this turn, they steadily alter course to starboard, so that all the battleships form an unbroken line travelling on their original Easterly course. Now they are all steaming along, forming one column almost 2 miles long, like steel monsters belching smoke, as far as can be seen.

'All the other ships are forming in line behind us sir' says John.

To this Green nods and says 'won't be long now men, keep a lookout on the starboard side, because that is where they are.' At

6.27pm the ships behind open fire; and this indicates they can see the enemy.

'Over on the starboard stern quarter sir' cries one of the lookouts and John trains the director round.

'Can't see much sir, muzzle flashes, grey shapes, and water spouts, but nothing to focus on and they are out of range'.

'Damn' says Green 'we need to get closer, why aren't we closer'.

He sounds agitated and disturbed to John, who is concerned, and takes a quick glance behind him, prepared for the likely outcome that the paper, still held under his bosses arm will get another outing.

Green noticed the glance, and their eyes meet briefly, but the paper stays where it is. Seeing the concern in the face of the Able Seaman, is enough for him to calm down, take control, and with a slight nod that reassures John, they both return to the task at hand.

The sight of an unidentified ship sinking, at 6.50pm brings home to them the danger they are in, which really sharpens their senses. A turn to starboard towards the enemy is finally ordered, and they start to close the range.

John has the nearest target in his sights, tracking it slowly and steadily, with his boss waiting for the range to reduce sufficiently.

15 minutes later finally comes the order, 'Engage', at which John presses the trigger, and "Centurions" big guns finally get in on the action. Inside the turrets the huge breeches fly backward, due to the enormous forces generated, accompanied by the deafening noise of the gunfire, reverberating around inside the steel turret.

The time of flight is 30 seconds, and this seems like forever as they wait, 'Now' cries the Gunnery Officer, and John tries to sort out their shot from the many others, in the poor visibility.

In the turrets, the barrels are back in position, the breeches swing over, and the huge shells are rammed in, followed by the cordite bags.

'Short 2' cries John finally, and he waits for the turret ready light to go on. 'Still tracking, but the target is turning away' then the ready light comes on at last.

Loading the guns takes 2 very long minutes, and finally, the Gunnery Officer cries 'Engage'. The cycle repeats, and at the cry of 'Now', the target is hidden in huge columns of water, maybe even a hit in the gloom and John shouts 'Straddle'.

The Gunnery Officer and the others, up here in the director roar in approval. 'Target showing her stern' says John, as the enemy finally completes the turn away.

The Gunnery Officer surveys the scene, as the next shells are loaded, and takes in the fact that HMS Orion will shortly cut off their line of fire. Just before the turret ready light comes on, he shouts in exasperation 'Check, Check, Check' and John holds up his arm, this is to show that he has heard, and thus will not operate the trigger.

One of the lookouts reports, 'German destroyers are laying a smoke screen, to hide their retreat sir.'

Another says 'Torpedoes are being launched by others, at the rear of their columns sir, and we are turning away'.

As the smokescreen hangs like a pall, between the two fleets, the firing subsides, as all the ships take avoiding action from the torpedoes, by steaming away from them. As the range increases the torpedoes, run out of steam, no ships are hit, and they turn back into line.

'Were going South East, to cut off their retreat' says Cdr. Green 'the trouble is it's starting to get dark, and it will be a hell of a job to find them now, but well-done everyone, the Germans took a pasting. As far as I know, they only landed one shell, on the whole of the main battle fleet, although we did suffer some other losses. It's time for us to split into 2 watches, and get some food, as it's going to be a very long night.'

Despite many hours of searching, and some fierce but limited night actions, by other ships, Centurion along with the other battleships of the Grand Fleet, cannot find the German fleet.

Eventually, they are ordered to return to Scapa Flow, for coaling and ammunition, which is completed by late afternoon the following day and once again they are all at full readiness.

Following the coaling and a very short ammunitioning, most of the sailors are then able to catch up on sleep and reflect on the momentous events they had been involved in.

The feeling down in the mess deck is one of relief, mostly at surviving unscathed, along with pride in a job well done, but as news slowly leaks in of the losses in the battlecruiser squadron, they became more subdued.

Writing home about the battle is banned, and the newspapers, when they arrive are not very complimentary, because the public expected a crushing victory. Those who took part now know how unrealistic this is, after their experience as battle-hardened veterans. They also know that the Fleet is ready to do its duty, and fight again if required, as they were ready almost immediately.

At the beginning of November, the ship relocates to Invergordon, because some of the engines and the weapons are in dire need of repairs.

Pony and John are sitting in the mess, enjoying a morning cup of tea when the leading regulator brings in 2 pieces of paper instructing both of them, that they have been selected to join RFA Racer, in Portsmouth and become part of the Salvage Section.

Things move pretty quickly, and they are soon ready, and happy to leave, although they are not exactly sure what lies ahead. At least they can go home on the way, for a couple of weeks of well-earned leave, so John heads to the wardroom, for a parting word with his boss.

'I am sorry to see you leave Foulkes, and I hope all goes well for you, please take this last Daily Telegraph that I have with you for Lucky's litter tray. I have no use for this damn paper anymore, it says we did so badly at Jutland, and I have cancelled my order for it, by the way how is the kitten.'

Surprised John says 'Lucky has grown sir, big and bold and looking after the family for me, whilst I am away. Funny thing is

Jessie tells me in her letter, that he jumped into her lap, about the time of the start of the battle, and would not leave her until late in the evening.'

'Excellent because I did like that kitten, by the way, do you have a suggestion for someone to replace you, up in the director at Actions Stations?'

'Harris is your man sir, seems to have changed his ways, although don't tell him I told you, he still likes to portray the image he had before, but he will do well'. John then hands the paper back saying 'perhaps you should keep the paper as we don't want him slipping back into his old ways'.

'Yes, you are right and thank you, Foulkes, for all you have done. Enjoy your new job and keep up the good work, I can see that the U-boats are becoming a real menace now, and recovering some of the damaged ships will help. I would love to join you because the war front is changing but we need to keep the Grand Fleet ready, just in case their fleet sails again.'

At this, these 2 men, who are from such very different backgrounds, but who completely respect each other, shake hands, and then John turns away down the long passageway.

The Gunnery Officer watches him walking down the passageway, sees a proud and capable Able Seaman depart and thinks to himself, with men like that we will win this war, then closes the wardroom door.

As the ferry across the Mersey whisks him over the river to the Birkenhead side, John on the final leg of his long journey home; can see a black and white cat sitting on the jetty. Surely Lucky can't be waiting for him, but right enough as he steps off the boat, the cat jumps into his arms and tries to get into his jacket. Of course there is no room now because he has grown so much, but instead, John strokes and cuddles the purring cat, puts him down, and they set off side by side together towards their home.

In the house, Jessie is beside herself with worry, because Lucky has disappeared, which is completely out of character, and is staggered when John appears with him in tow. Holding her man tight, he explains that Lucky was waiting for him, and whilst it is beyond belief that he could know that John was coming home, the facts speak for themselves.

The two weeks of leave pass in a whirl of visiting families, seeing friends, and making up for so much lost time, as they reaffirm their love for each other. Nellie has grown and is walking now, but she quickly takes to this strange new man, who has the time to pick her up and play with her.

At night they get some peace, to be in each other's arms and do what is natural, 'what if I should become pregnant' asks Jessie.

'Our children are wonderful, and another one would be lovely. Another girl is my wish, and she should be named after you my love' says John, little knowing that he would get his wish, and of course the youngest daughter, is always the apple of her father's eye.

Just before the final day, he gives her the picture of him and Lucky taken on Centurion, 'I want you to keep this safe for me please' and she reluctantly takes it, because she feels that it is his lucky talisman, but how can she refuse the man she loves so much.

Sailing Ship Carl

In the Victory mess deck in Portsmouth, John turns to his friend Pony Moore, who has also had 2 weeks leave on the way south saying 'it's time we mustered up on deck with the rest, and hopefully we will find out what sort of mess we have got ourselves into this time.'

Pony replies 'can't be as bad as sitting waiting in Scapa Flow, we both wanted to get involved in this damn war, but I must admit, that it's not in my nature to volunteer either' at which they both head up the nearest ladder to the quarterdeck.

Under an overcast sky, on a cold early December morning, on board HMS Victory, afloat in Portsmouth Dockyard, the salvage riggers drafted to RFA Racer muster at 0800, under the watchful eye of the Bosun John Meek.

'Salvage Riggers Attention' roars the Bosun who turns smartly to the Foreman Thomas Pearce, '14 Salvage Riggers present and correct Chief'.

'Stand them at ease Bosun' replies the Chief, whose rank is actually the Foreman Rigger.

'Aye aye chief' is the reply followed by 'Stand at Ease' at which all the men relax, and then look expectantly at the Chief waiting for him to tell them what is going to happen to them.

'Welcome to the Salvage Section, all of you men will sign on as Salvage Riggers on T124 forms next, provided none of you have changed your minds since volunteering, in which case step forward now and I will arrange your return back to where you came from.'

No-one moves and so he continues, 'RFA Racer is the salvage ship you are joining and she is in refit here in this dockyard, however, the refit is not going as well as we hoped. This is because Portsmouth dockyard is so busy with other work on the main fleet and we are not a priority to them.

In the meanwhile after signing on, you will all proceed to the ship, and familiarise yourselves with her layout, under the charge of the Bosun here. This afternoon we will assemble in the classroom, and start with some salvage training, and then hopefully we can then sort out some suitable work, in order to keep you occupied until the refit is completed. Before you go, as I pass down the line, state your name and any salvage experience, so that I can assess what training needs to be done to get you up to a decent standard.'

As John listens to his future shipmates, he realises that they are quite an experienced bunch of sailors, 5 of them are even from Liverpool, and all have considerably more salvage experience than he has. Hopefully, something like a real adventure is about to start, as he gives his name and experience in a clear loud voice. Finally, the Foreman dismisses them and they muster ashore and then march over to see RFA Racer for the very first time.

At 970 tons the partially converted sloop, is lying quietly alongside the dock basin wall, as the Bosun described the changes, 'the engines have been removed and larger ones fitted, the fore and aft sailing masts have been converted to derricks plus there are holds and store areas, for the large amount of salvage equipment that we will need.

A brand new Marconi radio and aerials will be fitted, along with 4 ship's boats, one motor, 2 diving boats, and a lifeboat.

Inside there is accommodation for the crew, plus an extra 20 spaces for additional hands if they are required at any point, during a salvage operation. Come on board and we will look around, but be careful because most of the fitting out is yet to be completed.'

Once aboard it is clear that there is a great deal to do, and to make matters worse, the only person on board is the duty watchman who is only keeping an eye on the ship.

After lunch back at the Victory, they all muster for the promised training.

'You may all be very experienced and well recommended able seamen, but your salvage experience is actually quite limited.' Starts the Chief and then continues with. 'The work is dangerous, we will be striving to recover damaged ships, in all types of weather, close to the shore, and there will be the risk of mines, also there may be German submarines in the area. This work is vital, for the country and the future of the war, so we must all work together as a team, this will help to keep each of us safe, and get the damaged ships back to a repair yard.'

Little by little the riggers all start to grasp the enormity of the task ahead, that it will not be easy, but their country needs them.

At the end of the room there is a large blackboard, which the chief moves towards, picking up a piece of white chalk, he writes as he talks, 'Our boss in London is Captain Frederick Young, an ex-admiralty diver who works for the Liverpool Salvage Association as Chief Salvage Officer. The Royal Navy has hired him to put together this section, along with 2 commercial vessels from the same company, the SS Ranger and SS Linnet, which are crewed by salvage professionals, perhaps one day you may be as good as them. The Salvage Section was originally created to save just warships, after battles with the German High Seas fleet, but all that has changed. Since the Battle of Jutland, they have been using their U-boats to sink many of our merchant ships, which they continue to do even now, so we have started salvaging those as well, which is why we need more salvage ships, and that is why you are here, any questions?'

The riggers nod and look at each other because this is all news to them although the loss of merchant ships has been mentioned in the newspapers.

He continues 'Other ships we are converting are the RFA Mariner, RFA Melita, RFA Reindeer, RFA Ringdove and RFA Thrush, which are all similar to or slightly smaller than the Racer. Each of these ships has a complement of riggers, like you, along with quite a few Motor Engineers, whose job it is to maintain all the equipment you will be using.

As well as this, there is a crew to sail the ship, seamen, cooks, stewards, engineers, and stokers, along with a sparkie for the radio on-board, any questions now?'

John sticks his hand up and asks 'what equipment will the motor engineers be maintaining?'

The chief replies 'on each ship we will be carrying quite a few different pumps, steam driven, oil-driven and motor driven, also we have cutting, burning and welding equipment along with drilling equipment.

There is also some diving equipment, such as air pumps and 4 boats. We also carry two divers, who I forgot to mention, and you will act as diving attendants when required. Who is the trained rigger?' and at this Pony holds up his hand.

'Salvage also requires many anchors, wires, ropes, purchases and winches, some manual and others power driven, you will be our expert on these.'

'Now for the work, all ships have been instructed on Captain Young's orders, to head for shore when they are attacked, because we can only normally work in shallow water, although we are developing lifting barges, designed to recover small wrecks from the seabed provided the divers can reach them, which is no more than 120ft.'

He then sketches a scene with 2 ships; one is aground on the shore and alongside is a number of small boats.[2]

---

[2] *Figure 5 shows a typical salvage scene like the one the chief draws but this is actually a photograph of the salvage vessel RFA Thrush, which was driven ashore in a storm and a number of the crew lost their lives*

'This is the stricken vessel grounded on the shoreline, and beyond is a salvage ship, such as ours. The small boats we have are used to carry the divers and riggers, who are inspecting the ship, in order to assess the damage, prior to any salvage attempt. Every salvage job is carried out under the direction of an experienced Salvage Officer who will be appointed by Captain Young. He will either be there already or will travel with us depending on the situation; we don't carry our own salvage officer, each one is appointed depending upon the type of work expected and his experience is matched to the salvage job.

Other vessels that can assist, such as tugs will be obtained from dockyards, etc. and we have room for some other men on board, should we need additional riggers.

The simplest way to describe our operation, is that we will repair or plug as many holes as possible, pump water out of the ship's hull, and then move the wreck as far up the beach as possible, so that we can carry out better repairs, until we can then re-float her, for return to a dockyard, for permanent repair, any more questions?'

'Do we have to prepare our own food, as we do on an ordinary Royal Navy warship?' asks Pony.

'You will be required to clean the mess deck, but the chefs will do all the food work including the preparation. You will also have the standard naval uniform that you know, but most of the time you will be wearing overalls, these are working ships, and much of the time you will be working very hard.'

'What about leave?' is Pony's next question?

'Unfortunately leave is unlikely to be granted, even for the best of reasons, we are hard pressed, and have more work than we can cope with, but there is nothing to stop you asking, just don't expect to get any.'

Pony's final question is 'what is an RFA Chief?'

He replies 'The initials RFA Stands for Royal Fleet Auxiliary; it was started in 1905 as a civilian-manned fleet, which is owned by the Royal Navy but is generally manned by civilians. Their job is providing support, all over the world to the Fleet, and

it is not a fighting force. Because we are not fighting, we will be
flagged under the RFA, which is what you will come to know them
as. That's it for today, it's time to stop?' he finishes with this and
they all leave the room, for many of them, the change in working
pace will be huge.[3]

One week later, the Chief breaks the welcome news, that
their training is over for now, and they are instructed to proceed to
their very first salvage job.

The 2039 ton SS Carl has been lying on the beach, in
Freshwater Bay on the Isle of Wight, since the beginning of
November, and was surveyed by Lt. Kay RNR Salvage Officer
shortly after. Lack of resources had been the problem but a local
General has been creating a stink about it being left there.

The Chief then reads out Lt. Kay's report.

Report:

*I yesterday (10th Nov 1916) made an examination of the
above vessel ashore in Freshwater Cove, IOW and found her lying
broadside on to the beach, having a list to seaward of 7 degrees.*

*She is exposed to the sea from SW to SE. The rudder is
broken and for about 30ft amidships on the fore part of the main
hatch, the bottom is set up slightly. Otherwise, the hull appears to
be intact.*

*A reef stretches right across the mouth of the bay with only
8 to 9 feet of water over it at HWS. The vessel in light condition
draws 7 ft. 6', but would be unstable with masts up.*

*I should therefore recommend that masts and yards be
taken down, leaving lower masts only.*

*The ballast could then be discharged and all possible
weight taken out of her.*

*The shingle will have to be removed working from the
inshore side, and weight of vessel held up on shores bored down on
chalk foundations.*
The report ends.)

---

[3] *See. Appendix A. Salvage rating duties and RFA Racer
conversion detail*

'Cdr. Gracey the RNR Salvage Officer, is already on site and we have been detailed as his salvage crew, so don't let me down.' These are the final words from the Chief, as he dismisses the Salvage Riggers.

They head below to collect their kitbags, which are then packed with everything they think they will need for what they expect to be just a short visit.

The journey to Freshwater is quite enjoyable if a little slow, involving first a paddle wheel ferry from Portsmouth to Ryde Pier and then a local "chuffer" train to Freshwater, which even reverses direction at Newport station.

Once the train reaches the end of the line they muster outside the small station and form up into columns of three. They are after all navy men through and through and amongst civilians now. The chief brings them to attention, turns them to the left and they quick march down the lane passing many small cottages, each with its own stone wall and small garden.

Fifteen minutes later as they breast the small rise, the top of three masts appears in the sky. Slowly the whole of SS Carl comes into view, lying tilted over, like a white beached whale, high and dry on the shingle beach, and John wonders to himself, how on earth they are going to manage to move this monster.

Finally, they halt round the back of the nearby Albion Hotel, where they wait, whilst the Chief goes inside in search of Cdr. Gracey.

A few minutes later the Chief returns, with the old hotel manager, who has apparently sorted out their accommodation, which is mostly in local houses, they are to receive 2/8p per day lodging allowance. Once they have paid for a bed and keep, there will be enough left, for a couple of pints in the evening as well, when time allows, so the men are very happy.

John and Pony are to stay in a local cottage, just down the road that they marched along, which they soon find and settle into, with instructions to report promptly back at the Hotel, at 0800 next morning, ready to start when Cdr. Gracey will personally brief them.

Following a very acceptable and well-cooked dinner, in their new temporary home, they settle into their comfortable beds for a good night's sleep. The room they are in belongs to the two sons of Alice and George who are away serving in France. They may not have travelled far, but the journey through the lovely countryside; has been very slow, with a great deal of waiting, which is probably more tiring than hard labour.

At 0800 next morning under a grey, calm but cloudy sky, Cdr. Gracey introduces Lieut-Colonel Pike, who commands the local Golden Hill Fort, and will supply any working parties as required. 'You are all very welcome here and we are really pleased to see you. You should also be aware that General Seely owns the land we will be storing your equipment on. He has taken a great interest in this job and although I am sure he will be happy to see you, it was him who complained to the Government that the ship was not being worked on. He regularly rides down to this bay on his horse Warrior and then makes the animal stand in the surf.'

'Right men' continues Gracey, 'to shift the Carl we need to lighten her because there is a shallow reef offshore that she must float over. The topgallants and topmasts will be taken down first; this will reduce her weight which will reduce her draft a little. Then we will create anchor points on top of the cliff, to which we will rig holding purchases between the remaining mast tops and those anchors points.

Shingle on the beach will then be removed, all along the shore side of her hull, and all of her ballast will also have come out. Once that work is done, we will haul her almost upright.

A couple of divers are arriving today, and they will check out the hull, both inside and out and carry out any necessary repairs. On completion of these repairs, we will empty out the hull with the pumps I have ordered from the dockyard.

Then more shingle will be removed on the sea side, and we will dig 3 tunnels under the keel, which will allow cables to be run under her.

The dockyard tug Steady is acting as our support vessel and will bring over 3 anchors from the dockyard, which will be dropped onto the seabed, and hawsers connected to the anchors. The hawsers will run under the keel, through those tunnels, and up onto the deck, where they will be attached to the ship's winches.

Then at a spring high tide, we will haul on the ship's winches, and drag her off the beach, reeling out the mast purchases as she goes, so that we keep her almost upright.

Sounds simple doesn't it, however, there is a huge amount of shingle and ballast to be removed, and I have no doubt the weather will not be as kind as it is today. Carry on Chief and detail off the men to get started on the masts and gallants.'

'Yes Sir' replies the Chief, 'divide up into 3 groups, 2 of 5 and one of 4, you 4 take the foremast and the other groups the main and mizzen masts.'

So John and Pony find themselves with William and Henry, climbing the foremast and trying to remember between them, how to carry out this sort of work. It is many years ago that they had been instructed on sailing ships. Needless to say they soon get the hang of it, they are after all very experienced sailors, and of course, Pony is a rigger by trade.

The big problem is that it is winter; despite the relatively good weather, it is still very cold and windy. Being exposed high up on the mast, their hands and fingers soon get numb. To drop the masts involves removing rigging, adding support slings and undoing any securing bolts. All of which means that just one slip of a spanner; could result in dropped spars, and trapped limbs, making the work very dangerous.

By lunchtime, as they all sit on the shore, in the lee of the vessel attempting to eat their lunch, which has been provided by their lodgings, but there is an obvious problem. Everyone is fumbling with the packages, and some are even dropping food on the floor. The men start grumbling in unison, as they struggle just to open the food papers, and the Chief realises as he listens to their mumblings, that something needs to be done.

After a quick discussion with the Cdr., it is agreed to suspend work on the masts, and erect some canvas shelters ashore, complete with fire braziers. Then the teams can divide up, and take spells in the shelter getting warm until they can feel their fingers again.

By nightfall, which at this time of year is 4 pm, the shelters are up and braziers are in place, ready for the morrow, so it's off to the digs for supper, followed by a couple of pints in the hotel bar. In the bar, they meet Herbert, who is enjoying a well-earned pint, and they sit with him.

The conversation naturally, of course, turns to the job in hand, and its Herbert who starts, he has been detailed off to assist the 2 dockyard divers, who had arrived in the afternoon. 'Those divers are not happy. I heard them talking this afternoon, whilst helping them dress apparently, they did not want to come here, and it's their pay that is a problem. They get paid 4s an hour whilst diving, and they don't think they will get much actual diving work on this job, so want to go back to the dockyard. Their diving attendant Fryer, who also came with them, reckons he needs to go home to collect his pension from the Post Office. I think they are just lazy skivers, which the dockyard has dumped on us, and can't see Gracey liking this at all.'

'Gracey seems to be fair, but he is a typical Naval Officer' says John, 'I doubt the dockyard will be happy when he tries to sort it out, you know they don't always see eye to eye and some of them can be quite tactless.'

The next day the wind has strengthened, which will be a regular occurrence during this job. Freshwater Bay faces the English Channel, and the North Atlantic weather runs straight into the small unprotected bay.

Lowering the spars and mast continues, despite the steady blow with the shelters and braziers getting a lot of use because it is now even colder. Balancing on the foremast spar John notices a rider and horse standing in the water, the waves are rougher today and keep rolling around the horse's legs but it stays very still. The rider is also sitting tall in the saddle and together they are almost like a statue. This must be the famous General Seely but he turns his attention back to his work as the wind gusts past him, wouldn't do to fall off now.

Also down below the divers who should be fixing the leaks in the hull seem to be in animated discussion with the Salvage Officer.

Groups of local men from the Fort; have also set up a wooden walkway, from the ship to the base of the cliff some distance away. They are now busy on the port side, loading wheelbarrows with shingle and running it up the beach, then dumping it well out of the way.

An hour later, it's John's turn to warm his hands, and as he rubs them furiously to help the blood flow and ease the pain, the man who had been on the horse appears around the corner of the shelter leading his horse. Now John can see how magnificent the horse is and he just stares at it.

'I am very pleased to see you all here saving this ship but what took you so long?' asks General Seely for that is who this obviously is.

John quickly gathers his thoughts whilst still looking at the horse; he is not really sure how to respond, he is only a rigger and Gracey should be the one to answer.

'Well did you hear my question?' the General says.

Thinking fast he replies 'I am sorry sir, yes I did hear your question but the sight of your magnificent horse distracted me somewhat, I looked after the horses that pulled our fire engines in Birkenhead. I loved them but this is one has a look in his eye that almost unnerves me.'

'His names Warrior and he has been with me in France, under fire, my lucky talisman so to speak'.

John walks over to the horse and offers his hand to show he is friendly and then strokes the horse whilst he answers the question. 'The salvage section is very hard pressed at the moment, far too many ships to rescue and not enough men. We only arrived to do this work a couple of weeks ago and are still learning our job, but we will manage especially with all the local help which has been excellent.'

'Where have you come from?' is his next question and John tells him about HMS Centurion, the Grand Fleet and the Battle of Jutland.

At the end of his tale, he asks 'why do you make Warrior stand in the waves?'

'I believe it prepares him for sudden shocks, in the battles, there are many instances where the horses are frightened but he now knows to stand still and ignore them, and this is a great help to those around him, he is quite famous in my regiment. Surely you must have had similar experiences with your horses when you went to put out a big fire?'

'When a new horse arrived we would take it into the yard and build a bonfire nearby, as the flames take hold we would hold the horse and stroke it, as I am doing now and it would learn to trust us and become familiar with the noise, heat, and smell of the fire.'

'I can see that you love animals and know how to handle them, what is your name?' asks the General.

'Able Seaman John Foulkes Sir' is his confident reply because he realises they have something in common.

The General and then takes his leave after hearing the answer. From then on during the course of the salvage General Seely would quite often ride over to see the progress and always say hello to John, Warriors also seemed keen to meet him as well. Of course the other riggers soon caught on to this activity, and John was to suffer some ridicule about mixing with the Upper Class, but in reality, they were only jealous.

The next morning sees the diving attendant Fryer missing, and Gracey is furious, so much so that he also sends the two Divers home, the vital work of fixing the holes in the hull on the starboard side, is falling behind the rest of the team's efforts.

It then takes a couple of days for the Divers, and the attendant to be replaced. The next crew is considerably better, and this confirms the Riggers opinion, that the Dockyard had just dumped their worst workers on this job, but Gracey has sorted it, and they have been replaced. Of course, this is only right in their opinion and the salvage officer moves up in their regard.

Once the masts are reduced to just the 3 main lower stumps, and everything else is lying on the cliff, the riggers turn their attention to digging 3 pits, for the anchor points, which are then concreted securely in place.

The tug Steady arrives with more materials, including the pumps, and with great difficulty, these stores are landed onto the beach. Many of the Riggers end up being soaked because they have to wade into the sea in order to collect the equipment. Then when the tug turns to head back for Portsmouth, they all hear an ugly crashing noise, as her propeller smashes into the shingle seabed, but luckily she is able to keep going.

By the 4th January, the riggers have completed the purchases that run between the mast and the anchor points; the shingle removal down the port side has also been completed. It is then a relatively simple task, to haul on the purchases, and pull the Carl into a more upright position. This work is done slowly and carefully, ensuring that each purchase holds its own share of the load.

This sort of work is bread and butter to the salvage riggers, who are very encouraged to have completed the first stage, and Cdr. Gracey is in very good humour, saying 'I must admit I was not sure if that would really work, but you have all done an excellent job, and I think that about 600 tons of shingle have been moved. Tomorrow we start to pump out the ship, and remove as much ballast as we can'.

They all return to their lodging, for a well-earned dinner. Removing the ballast is not difficult, as they load it into baskets, slung from what's left of the masts. Hauling them up and dumping it onto the beach, is a bit like coaling ship in reverse, and of course, this sort of work is standard for sailors. The soldiers from the fort continue to help by then moving the ballast to the base of the cliff where it is out of the way.

Removing the shingle on the starboard seaward side, and digging the tunnels for the anchor cables, can only be done at low water, so when the tide is in, they go back to removing the ballast.

On the 12th the repaired tug Steady arrives, with the 3 anchors on board and the necessary wires, to lay them out in the bay, before the riggers run the wires under the Carl. The positioning of the anchors is supervised by Gracey personally, as it is necessary to have them in the right place so that the pull will be straight down the beach. Once each anchor is lowered to the seabed, it is then backed up, so that it takes a firm hold in the seabed.

The riggers row a light wire to the shore, feed it under the hull, and using the ships hand winches, pull the main cable into place, adding coir matting between the wires and the ship's hull. Three days later all 3 anchors are in place, complete with wires and everything is ready, however, they have just missed the spring tide, and will have to wait a few days until the next one.

The salvage riggers now have a couple of days, with little work, apart from keeping a weather eye on the Carl, so the Chief borrows a room in the hotel, and continues with their instruction.

Early on the morning of 27th January, a few hours before the top of the spring tide, the salvage riggers are positioned; ready to start the final chapter of their first salvage operation. Each mast purchase is manned by one man, whose job it is to release the cable slowly, as the ship slides down the shingle bank.

On board the remaining riggers, are positioned at each of the ship's winches, ready to heave on the anchor wires. Cdr. Gracey is on deck, orders them to take the strain, and then to heave with all their might. The wires slowly slide up the matting on the side of the "Carl", as the anchors take a final hold, and then they feel the ship shudder slightly. Soon she starts to slip down the beach, into the water with shingle rattling and tumbling, in a cascade of noise, as the hull pushes it along, and back into the sea.

By 1100 the Carl is afloat, and under the charge of the tug Steady, the riggers buoy the wires, so that the Steady can come back to recover the anchors, and those on board take passage back to Portsmouth.

The 3 riggers left on shore, take the train and ferry back, and that evening they all meet up on the Victory, to enjoy their tot of rum, and celebrate their efforts.

Waiting for the men on board their accommodation is also the mail, which has been held for their return.

One of John's 3 letters gives him some further news, which requires an additional celebration.

It read *'My Darling John, It looks like you may get your wish for a daughter, who can be named Jessie because the doctor has confirmed that I am pregnant, and the baby will be due in August. All is well at home and Lucky has now taken to spending more time with me as if he is keeping watch. I hope your new work is going well, and wish you were home with me, keep safe, and come back to me as soon as you can.*
Your loving wife Jessie. xxxx.

'Right boys' he declares, 'the drinks are on me tonight, we're going out celebrating, once I have written to my wife to tell her how happy I am, that we will be having another child soon.'

Pony slaps him on the back, causing John to almost choke on his rum and says 'well done matey, now we know what you were up to, during your recent leave'.

John's face turns a bright red, which is probably due to the rum, chocking his throat. Of course, all the riggers claim it is because he is embarrassed. Only John knows the real truth, and he knows better than to say anything because it will only make matters worse. It is however obvious to him, that the riggers are becoming a team and he is very glad to be with them.

<u>The following letter was sent to thank those in Freshwater who assisted in this salvage work.</u>

The sailing vessel Carl an interned German ship, employed on Government service, has lately been salved after being ashore at Freshwater Bay, IOW for nearly 3 months.

Cdr. Gracey RNR Admiralty salvage officer reports that General Seely rendered valuable assistance in allowing his land to be used for the purpose of salvage operations, storage of spars, digging of anchor pits, etc.

Also that Lieut-Colonel Pike, Commanding 3rd DCLI, Golden Hill Fort, IOW rendered very valuable assistance in providing working parties to assist in the discharge of about 1000 tons of ballast, removal of shingle banks around the wreck and allowing valuable stores and equipment from the wreck to be stored in safety.[4]

---

[4] *General Seely was a senior politician in the government before the war, until he was sacked but he knew who to speak to about SS Carl and did so. He was the owner of Warrior which was a very special horse and the real War Horse. Taking Warrior to the waves was his way of training him which was why he saw the ship and raised the matter of the vessel being left on the beach. Warrior was posthumously awarded the Dicken Medal for ALL the animals of WW1.*

HM Torpedo Boat 24

Stepping down from the railway carriage, in the late afternoon under a cloudy sky; on 19th Feb 1917, John and the rest of Racer's riggers huddle together, on the platform at Dover Priory. The bitter winter wind causing them to pull their greatcoats around themselves. 'Even Liverpool docks were never that busy' says John, as he looks out over to the harbour down below, where every berth is filled with ships of all sizes, many of those berths being 4 ships deep.

'There's huge army over there that needs to be supplied' says Pony 'and that's why they need so many ships, this isn't the only port they are using but the crossing here is so much shorter'.

'Stay here men' says the Chief,' I will go and find the Naval Provost, to sort out some accommodation, we need to find where the work is and where Cdr. Gracey is' then he heads down the platform looking for the station office.

On the platform the Station Master, who has looked to make sure all the train doors are closed, blows his whistle twice loudly, which causes the engine to puff vigorously, its wheels to spin and then the whole assembly slowly clanks away, hauling the carriages still with many passengers on the way to their next destination.

All the noise slowly abates as the train fades into the distance and John says 'Listen, be quiet all of you', then they can all hear the faint background noise, which is a bit like the rumbling of thunder far away. Of course they all familiar with the noise of guns, which are firing far in the distance, 'do you think that is from the front line?' he asks and no one answers, they all just solemnly nod in agreement, it is a sobering thought, that each of those many thumps could be killing and maiming men and animals. But for the grace of God each knows that they could have been sent to join the Naval Division and life in the trenches.

As the chief returns, he has a list of accommodation addresses, which he uses to detail them off, finally saying and pointing 'If you look out over the harbour south mole, you can just see the top of the wreck, which is lying on the outer side; Cdr. Gracey has been here a few days. Some work has already been done, so we are to meet there, early tomorrow at 0700 on the mole.'

The next morning, standing on the south mole, the riggers can see unfortunate motor torpedo boat HMTB 24 lying on the huge limestone boulders which had been used as foundations for the harbour outer sea defences. Nowhere near as big as SS Carl, almost as long but much narrower, she looks a sorry sight, with her 2 funnels slanted away from them, waiting for their urgent help. The two 8 pounder gun barrels are pointing upwards at odd angles, and her 3 torpedo tubes are out of line, because of the winter gales which have been blowing down the channel, hammering her relentlessly against these huge white blocks which are trying to completely wreck her.

Cdr. Gracey climbs out of the hull, and crosses the small gangplank to greet them, 'Good to see you all again, we have another challenge on our hands, but this job is very different from the last one. Some support timbers have been placed inside, to strengthen the damaged hull but we need to fit a lot more, and today a lifting camel[5] will be arriving. The plan is to put four 8" wires around the hull and attach the wreck to the camel, however running the wire between the hull and the wall is going to be very difficult. In the meanwhile I want you to get the camel ready.'

[5] The lifting camels were grain barges modified to allow the various compartments to be flooded or pumped out thus providing buoyancy for lifting wrecks. There is a picture of a lifting barge alongside UC-44. See Figure 7 UC-44 in Dunmore East.

'Where will it dock?' asks the chief.

'At Granville dock which is just down there, where the mole reaches the shore, do you know if your men have used a camel before?' questions Gracey.

'They haven't Sir, but I know how to use one' says the Chief, 'none of these men have any experience of these vessels, but they will soon learn, and you know they are keen.'

'I do 'says Gracey and with that, they all set off to continue their vital work.

Standing on the main deck on board the camel, after it has arrived; the chief takes them on a guided tour. 'These were grain hopper barges that Captain Young has had modified to provide a lifting capability for smaller wrecks. All of the compartments are sealed from each other and can be filled or emptied with seawater. At each end of the barge are winches which are used to handle the lifting wires. On the deck, we have the pinning arrangements which are used to clamp lifting wires securely once in place. The 2 fore and aft derricks along with the winches mean we can also lift objects on an off the vessel. In that way, we can transfer pumps to a wreck or remove cargo when required'.

He then goes on to explain the valve arrangement for flooding or emptying the hull. As the hull rises the barge will then lift anything attached to it up from the seabed. The riggers are quite happy with all of this, but the chief looks a bit troubled.

'What's up Chief' asks John.

'This camel is actually the Buffalo, and the other one I worked with was called the Alligator. That one had been modified so that the side ballast tanks can also be flooded. For situations like this one where we are doing a lift on one side only, the camel will need to be modified. Can't see Gracey being too happy about it and I will have to tell him.' At that, the Chief heads off to see Gracey and give him the bad news.

Fortunately, there are other problems with the wreck, which will give them the time needed to modify the Buffalo as Gracey tells him. 'We are having trouble cutting the 4 holes through the blocks and under the ship so that we can lay the cables under the hull. It looks like we will have to manually drill down through many feet of limestone block. We are going to need a diver working in each hole and I fear this will take many days.'

'Can't we use explosives? Asks the Chief?

'Unfortunately, there are at least 2 live depth charges nearby, and quite a number of live shells lying around, so we dare not use them.' Replies Cdr. Gracey.

A week later the Buffalo lifting barge has been fitted with the valves and deck openings, which are required for flooding or pumping out the wing compartments. Portable pumps are sitting on her deck, and the slings required for lifting the wreck, have been doubled in size to two in number 8" wires, at each of the 4 points.

The weather then takes a turns for the worse and they have no choice but to leave the wreck to the mercy of the sea. When they return to the wreck, it has moved 2ft deeper and is now resting on the seabed. This means they have to drill through hard seabed rock as well, in order to get the wires underneath, and this requires the loan of specialist drilling equipment, which can only be obtained from the local collieries.

On top of that, the divers keep getting recalled to assist in other problems in the extremely busy harbour. Dover is working flat out, and that work is an absolute priority, for the war effort. The riggers are also now assisting the divers and acting as diving attendants, which does at least release other labour back to the docks.

Finally, on 15th March, the four channels are completely drilled under the hull, and then the four slings are run from the barge, under and around the wreck, and then back to the barge.

Before tightening the cables on the lifting barge, lots of coir matting is placed under the wires, which will help to protect the hull.

In addition, the bad weather continues and the wreck is still being hammered by the waves, the hull now has a large split in it, between the funnels, although Gracey is confident that they can still lift her and move her away from the harbour mole.

On 25th March all is in place at last, and on a high tide, the Buffalo is pumped out, which lifts the wreck from the seabed, allowing it to be towed away from the wall, and taken slowly inside the relative safety of the harbour by a local tug.

Unfortunately, the only dry dock that is available is not very wide, and will not accommodate both the barge and the wreck as a unit, so the assembly is grounded, in the shelter of the harbour wall. Now the riggers and divers set to patching up the many holes in her hull. When she is pumped out after this work, she finally floats on her own, which allows them to tow her into the dry dock, to await proper repairs.

On the 28th March, the riggers are finished and depart on another train journey back to Victory.

As John sits in the railway carriage, with the other riggers, on their journey back to Portsmouth, he reflects on a job well done but he has some misgivings. Will RFA Racer's conversion have been progressing he wonders, he has his doubts because the dockyard has the Fleet as their main priority and each time they go back there is actually little progress.

But it is the rumbling sound of distant guns, which have been an almost constant background to their work, which troubles him most. Occasionally there is silence, and he knows that this is the moment when men, climb out of their trenches, to march across no man's land, with many going to their death or being injured very badly. Whilst they have been here, they have seen the wounded being returned to Dover and then being either carried by stretcher or helped from the ships into the numerous hospital trains that come to take them away.

The number of ships they have seen at Dover has been vast, with almost constant traffic, taking men, animals, and materials over to France to feed this awful war.

Ironically, he thinks that the work they are doing is simply feeding this vast war machine, with more and more ships, and he is not sure whether it is all really worth it.

Of course, he knows that he has no choice, and as the banter starts in the carriage, with Pony of course taking the lead, he joins in glad to take his mind off these troubling thoughts.

Some consolation is that he is amongst a professional and happy group, which is developing into a strong and resourceful team. This job has introduced yet another part of salvage work and he can see that the camels really do work. He has learned so much about salvage these past few months and it is a really satisfying job bringing a ship back to life.[6]

---

[6] *After this event all the lifting barges were renamed LC etc. Alligator becomes LC1 and Buffalo becomes LC2.*

HMS Q19 (Churchill's special ships)

Once they are back in Portsmouth, the riggers are not pleased to learn, that the dockyard has still done almost nothing, whilst they have been away. The Chief sets them to work on Racer doing what they can, by clearing the storerooms and maintaining some of the deck equipment.

Meanwhile not far from Plymouth on 12th March PYRAHZIOPU, otherwise known as Q19 (a disguised merchant ship fitted with guns), has been in action against a German U-boat U85. They manage to sink the submarine, but not before the U-boat gun almost sinks them as well, the many shell holes flooding her engine room.

The destroyer HMS Orestes arrives to assist and takes her in tow, managing to bring her into Plymouth Sound at Cawsand Bay, opposite Picklecombe Fort. Here she comes to rest on the bottom, although at high tide the water is lapping right over her cargo hatch covers.

Salvage attempts are made locally by the dockyard, but on 9th April the Salvage Section are asked to assist and send Captain Metcalf, to take charge of the salvage.

He immediately requests assistance from the RFA Racer riggers (word has been spreading amongst the salvage officers of the availability this group), realising that the job is going to be extremely difficult. In the meanwhile, all the accessible parts of the hull bottom have been made watertight by the divers.

Cofferdams (these are watertight extension walls rising upwards from the hatch combings) have also been constructed around the hatch combings, such that at half tide, these are standing well clear of the sea surface. This will enable them to pump out the vessel holds whenever the tide is below that level, such that the vessel will then float before the tide returns and flood the holds again.

He plans to use 2 lifting barges, which is why he needs to use experienced salvage riggers, instead of the current dockyard workers doing the job. Using experienced hands makes the job safer and easier, he knows that the Racer crew is available and will fit the bill.

So it is on Thursday 12th April, at noon that the riggers arrive in Plymouth dockyard, accompanied by Sub Lt. Durston. Unfortunately, they find that the naval barracks are full, and that accommodation ashore is in very short supply. The price of rooms in the port is now sky high, which means that the standard living ashore money that they are given; is not enough to cover their expenses.

In response to their complaints, the Chief says,' sorry lads but we will have to sort this out later, we need to get out to the wreck first thing in the morning, so just get some sleep and I promise it will be sorted.'

At first light the next morning, they are all embarked on the tug Hughli, which also has lifting camels LC3 & LC4 in tow. As the whole entourage proceeds out to the wreck, they see that Captain Metcalf is on board with them as well.

'How come we have a Captain salvage officer for this job' asks Pony, 'look over there, it's just a small steamer, there's more to this than meets the eye.'

'True enough' says John, 'and all we can see is the central superstructure, sticking out of the water, with a couple of masts standing up at either end, I guess its high tide.'

They moor up near to the wreck and then Captain Metcalf briefs them, 'it is high tide now, but as the tide goes out, you will see that we have already fitted wooden walled cofferdams to the hatches. These have been run from the superstructure, towards both the bow and the stern hatch combings, which will be visible shortly. Divers have also been down and stopped all the shell holes they can find.

The ship is actually lying on 2 rock ledges, but there is a gap in the middle. We have already laid 8 in number 9" lifting wires through the gap and up onto the ship's deck. Your job is to put LC3 and LC4, on each side of the ship, and then connect the lifting wires to the pinning points, but leaving them slack.

After that, we will have 4 pumps sitting on each lifting camel deck and drop their suction hoses into the hold areas. Space on the decks of the lifting camels will be tight, I would like to use more pumps but that is all we can manage on the deck area we have. Hopefully, we can pump enough water out, for the vessel to lift before the tide returns. Are these men familiar with the lifting camel Chief?'

'They are sir; we have just done a job in Dover, with a craft just like these.' 'Excellent, there should be time to get ready before the next half tide and then we will start pumping out as fast as we can.'

Working really hard, they manage to achieve all that is asked of them, and as the tops of the cofferdam appear, they start running the pumps at full speed and see the water level inside the holds start to drop.

Pony leans over the side, staring into the hold, and motions John over, then whispers in his ear, 'what's that shadow down in the hold' and as they stare, the outline of a 4" naval gun mounting, starts to take shape inside the hold.

'Well I never' says John, 'I have heard some rumours about special Q ships, and this must be one of those, a decoy to be used against U-boats'.

'Now I understand why we have a Captain in charge of the job, and we definitely need to get this one up' says Pony, at which John nods his head in agreement.

As the tide ebbs and then returns to its half tide height, they tighten the lifting wires on the camels and pin them in place. The wires start to sing and take the strain, grunting and groaning as they stretch, but there is still too much water inside the ship and it is clear that she not going to float, despite the pumps still running flat out.

Captain Metcalf orders them to release the wires before it gets too dangerous. 'Damn' he says to himself 'and we don't have room for any more pumps' he mutters, 'this needs a rethink'.

John overhears him. 'Could I suggest something Sir? He asks.

'Name please'

'Rigger Foulkes Sir' John answers respectfully.

'Do you have an idea?' asks the Captain.

John picks up a wooden round 4" stopper and says 'we could drill some 4" holes, along the bottom of the cofferdam, and water will run out of them as the tide drops. Once the water stops running, we will bung the holes up, and that way we will get a lot more water out.'

'It's worth a try' says the Captain, and for the rest of the day, holes are drilled along the bottom of the cofferdam, by the divers. 'Just take care not to weaken the structure' and he shows the divers exactly where he wants them to drill.

The next morning the process is repeated, only this time as the extra holes stop gushing out water, they quickly hammer in the wooden stoppers. The water level in the hold, is now considerably lower than it was yesterday at the same point, but is it enough?

Captain Metcalf is pacing up and down, encouraging the riggers to get the most out of the pumps, but they actually don't need any motivation. 'This is the telling point, pin the wires, 'shouts the Captain, as the tide rises, and the wires grow tighter and tighter, 'keep those pumps running' is his next command, and just as he thinks they may have to release the lifting wires, the groaning reduces, much to his delight. 'She's lifting, well done Rigger Foulkes' he declares, and the riggers happily slap John on the back because they now know that their efforts will be rewarded.

Captain Metcalf is then free to move on to other work, and leaves the job in the hands of the Racer Riggers, along with Lt. Davis who had relieved Sub Lt. Durston yesterday.

Before the Captain leaves he gathers the riggers round, congratulates them on an extremely well-done job, and although he doesn't mention John's idea, he does smile at him to thank him.

Finally, the wreck is towed into Plymouth dockyard on 17th April.

Without any other immediate work, the riggers wait in Plymouth, still living in their expensive accommodation. Each week they go into barracks and collect additional money to cover the difference between their allowance and what they have to pay, which is paid in arrears.

Eventually, on 24th April, Lt. Davis and the Chief muster them. 'We are going to Harwich by train, where a sunken British submarine awaits our urgent help'.

'We are still owed one week's extra money, for the expensive accommodation,' says Pony, can we go and get it now.

'We need to leave immediately and catch the next train which leaves shortly, but it will be sorted, I assure you', is all Lt Davis has to say on the matter.

Of course, the Rigger's are not sure whether to believe him or not, but they certainly won't forget about them being owed the money.

HM. SUBMARINE C16

On 16th April 1917, the small British submarine C16 is returning to her base at Harwich after her patrol.

'Periscope depth' orders the Captain, Lt Harold Boase to his planes man, who is controlling the submarine depth.

A few minutes later there comes the reply 'At periscope depth,' and the Captain reaches down to grasp the handles, then slides the periscope vertically up to his eye level. He needs to check that all is clear before they finally surface. They can only transit up the estuary and back to their base on the surface because the estuary is quite shallow.

'I can hear propeller noise astern' shouts one of the men in the control room.

Swinging the periscope round, the Captain just has time to see a huge bow, bearing down on them from the rear. A destroyer has come steaming up unnoticed on their blind stern, and there is nothing he can do apart from shout 'Oh my god'. The periscope is then ripped from his fingers, and the boat heels over sharply. This throws them all sideways and the scream of metal on metal, above their heads, pierces the calm. The conning tower is forced to one side, and the pressure hull cracks where the two are joined, due to the force of the collision. All the lights go out, and water starts to spray into the control room, drenching them all.

On the bridge of HMS Melampus, the violence of the blow throws her off course slightly, and they wonder what on earth they have hit. Looking out over the bridge side towards the stern, the officer of the watch just catches a glimpse of a damaged periscope, sliding aft as it slowly slips out of sight.

Turning to the captain he stammers 'I think we hit a submarine sir' is all he can get out.

Taking charge the Captain orders 'all stop' to the wheelhouse and as the destroyer slows, they turn to investigate, but all they can see is a trail of bubbles coming to the surface.

Inside C16 the captain takes in the scene, as the emergency lights come on to reveal some of the damage, 'quickly into the forward section all of you' he commands, and once inside, they close the watertight door to the control room. As the rear section floods, the submarine stern drops, and they sink towards the seabed. At 60ft down her stern hits the sandy sea floor, and as she settles they are finally lying almost level.

Up above they can now hear the propellers of the destroyer, circling slowly above, waiting to see if any of them can escape.

'Send me out through the torpedo tube to get help' volunteers Samuel Anderson as he vents the tube, opens the door and climbs in head first before anyone can stop him. Once inside he takes a deep breath, and holds on whilst the door is closed, the tube is flooded and the outer door opens. As the outer door opens, he sees a dim light at the end appear, and they fire him out using compressed air. Pushed quickly forward, his clothing, unfortunately, catches on the outer door mechanism, holding him fast, and despite kicking for all his worth, he cannot free himself, slowly his struggles weaken and eventually he runs out of air.

Inside the stricken submarine, his shipmates listen to his struggles and realise that he will not be bringing help.

'Does anyone else want to volunteer to use the other tube' asks the Captain. Of course, no-one does as he continues 'mind you I doubt we have enough air left to do that again anyway. OK, we will have to flood the compartment, and then open the forward hatch going out as the compartment fills with water'.

The hatch opens quite easily and water starts to pour in but for some reason, it will not open fully, there is something blocking it. Then when they try to close it, they can't, whatever was stopping them opening the hatch fully is now stopping them from closing it completely. Despite their frantic attempts to seal the gap with rags etc., water continues to leak in no matter how hard they try.

The Captain realises that they are now doomed, the compartment is slowly filling with water, and there is no way out. Taking a notebook from his pocket, he quickly writes down what has happened. Once that is done he grasps a small bottle, empties its contents and then seals his words inside, so that others will at least know the facts.

On the surface, the trail of bubbles slowly reduce to nothing, and despite many hours of waiting, their prayers on the surface are not answered, and the destroyer's sailors fear the worst.

Back in London at the salvage headquarters 5 weeks later, Captain Frederick Young (Fred) is reading the salvage report, which he has just received from Lt. Davis in Harwich about C16.

Great Eastern Hotel
Parkeston Quay
Harwich
14 May 1917
Lt. George Davis.
Tug Hughli, Anchorite
Sir, I have the honour to report on the salving of HM Submarine as follows:-

1. C16 was lying sunk in 7½ fathoms to the westward of the Ship Wash Bank heading N by E (mag), 3½ points across the mean direction of the flood and ebb stream. She was slightly by the stern and has a list of about 3 degrees to port.

2. April 24th:- Using the HUGHLI and the VANQUISHER proceeded to the wreck and started sweeping 9" wires under the bow and stern but both wires fouled the rudders and bow hydroplanes. The wires were cleared and hauled up again; this took all day as the vessels have no facilities or deck space for handling large wires.

April 25ᵗʰ:- The stern wire was swept underneath and buoyed. An attempt to run the bow wire was unsuccessful owing to the swell making it impossible for the tugs to keep in position.

April 26ᵗʰ:- The weather moderated and the bow wire was placed in position and buoyed.

April 27ᵗʰ:- Weather unfavourable. Divers got down at L.W. and reported that both wires were clear.

April 28ᵗʰ:- Weather unfavourable. Both vessels returned to port and filled up with coal and water. One of the camels was towed out and anchored near the wreck. It was anticipated that difficulty would be experienced in keeping the lifting wires in position on account of the shape of the hull, and the following plan was adopted and proved satisfactory:-

Two points were selected on the hull about 72ft apart and at such a distance from the bow and stern respectively that on the wreck being lifted, the wires would have approximately an equal load. The bow position was found to coincide with the junction of the sand and hull and when the camel was moored over the wreck about an hour before L.W. this wire was hauled taut. The stern wire was then partially hauled in, taking care to leave it hanging slack. 5" wire bridles 72ft long were shackled to the bow and stern lifting wires on each side of the camel; the bridles were then released and ran down the lifting wires to the bottom, and on heaving taut the stern lifting wire, it slipped aft along the hull until checked by the bridles. Before finally pinning, the divers examined both wires and found them in their proper positions. The wreck was drawing 54ft when she was lifted and it was carried 2 ¾ miles to the North Westward.

April 30ᵗʰ:- Pinned at a.m. L.W. and ran a reeving wire at the bow and stern. Before p.m. L.W. the 2ⁿᵈ camel was placed alongside and 2 additional 9" wires were hauled underneath with the reeving wires, and both camels were pinned at L.W. The mooring lighter ANCHORITE was in attendance from 29th April until the lifting operations finished and was employed picking up and running the 4 anchors and wires for the 2 camels now in use every low and high water. A vessel capable of doing this is essential in every case where lifting is in progress.

During lifting operations, destroyers and other craft passed at speed causing a heavy swell and on one occasion the camels rolled so violently that the wreck turned over in the wires with a list of 90 deg. to port and altered the fore and aft positions of the wires.

May 1*st*:- Pinned at am and pm LW's and carried wreck into Woodbridge Haven.

May 2*nd*:- Pinned at am. LW and carried wreck up the harbour, drawing 24' and beached her at Glutton Bank. The lifting wires were slipped from the outside camel and she was moored to a buoy clear of the wreck.

May 3*rd*:- Parbuckling wires were rove under the wreck and the bight was then dropped over the conning tower. The "Anchorite" was moored bow on to the wreck and the hauling parts of the parbuckling wires led over the bow horn to her 30-ton capstans. After several attempts, she succeeded in rolling the wreck over until it was within a few degrees of being upright.

May 4*th*:- The camel at the buoy was towed to the wreck and at LW both camels were pinned in their original positions and at HW the wreck was hauled up the bank to 8' LWS. At pm LW she was partially pumped out and three bodies recovered.

May 5*th*:- Strong NE wind and choppy sea. Work was only possible at LW when she was again pumped out sufficiently to recover eleven bodies.

May 6*th*:- The bad weather continued and at pm, LW the remaining bodies were recovered.

May 7*th*:- The fore hatch was the only opening in the pressure hull except for the conning tower hatches and as the wreck was down by the stern some difficulty was experienced in draining the water because the smallest pump available was 6". At am, LW the camels were pinned to the stern only and at HW it was carried further inshore until the wreck was lying 3' by the head. On the pm ebb, the water was almost entirely pumped out. A submarine berthed alongside the Hughli outside the seaward camel and connected up air leads to the wreck. All the ballast tanks were blown except Nos

5 and 6 which were found damaged and it was decided not to empty the petrol tanks or oil tanks for the present. On the pm flood tide, the wreck floated in good trim and with a margin of buoyancy. The lifting wires were slacked up 6' to 8' and then clamped and both camels and the wreck were towed up the river with the intention of docking at 8.30pm. Whilst towing, the stern of the wreck gradually sank until it rested on the after lifting wires at a draft of 26'6" the bow remaining afloat. Under these conditions docking was impossible and the three vessels were moored up between 2 buoys near the floating dock.

May 8th:- Preparations were made to try and pump out the water in the after end of the wreck and the lower Conning Tower door which was warped and out of action was cut away with oxy-acetylene burning plant. Both the steam and motor pumps failed to lift the water owing to the excessive height of 28'6". A 4 ½" wire was then passed under the stern, and the ends carried through the after inside quarter castings on each camel and shackled up to 3 fold purchases with the hauling parts taken to the forward winches. In this way the stern was hauled up about 9' and most of the water pumped out.

May 9th:- The remainder of the water was pumped out and all the ballast tanks blown afresh, the stern was still inclined to float at an excessive draft but it was found that a 5-ton pull would support it. Blowing the fuel tanks would have delayed operations as it was not considered safe to pump the petrol overboard and a vessel would have to be detailed to come alongside and receive it. The submarine was then tied up to one side of one camel with the stern hanging in the 4 ½" wire and the 4 – 9" lifting wires were slipped and hauled to on the other camel. The two vessels were then warped into the floating dock and after the submarine was on the blocks, the camel was towed out.

This completed the salvage operations.

I have pleasure in stating that from the time the submarine was beached on Glutton Bank until she docked I received valuable assistance from the following submarine Officers of H.M.S. Maidstone:-

Lieut. Cdr. Bower R.N.
Engr. Lieut. Cdr. Bury R.N.
Lt. Barry R.N.
   3. General remarks:-
The main cause of the sinking of C.16 appears to have been the damage sustained in collision to the upper Conning Tower hatch which was torn open.
The seating of the base of the Conning Tower was slightly started on the starboard side and the pressure hull was indented on the port side. The force of the collision warped the sliding door at the base of the Conning Tower and put it out of action. After the accident, the Conning Tower apparently flooded immediately and water was admitted into the hull past the twisted lower door until partially stopped by clothing and wedges. The fore hatch was found to have been unclamped from the inside and the reason none of the crew succeeded in escaping through the hatch is possibly explained by the fact that a fender was found inside the casing above the hatch and it bore evidence of chafe as if it may have jammed and prevented the hatch from being thrown open. In regard to additional evidence which has been collected from observations inside the submarine, I beg to refer you to Captain (S) HMS Maidstone.
   Suggestions
Lifting eyes and standard connections for air inlet, outlet and food pipe plus a buoy for supporting a telephone cable which can be released from inside.

   Just as he puts down the report, the 2nd Sea Lord walks in and takes a seat and says, 'We have a meeting today, about using Convoys to protect our merchant ships, and I hope they will, at last, approve it. Lord Fisher is against the idea because he is concerned that all a convoy will achieve, is to line up the ships for a turkey shoot, this is because we can't locate the U-boats. Those Room 40 intelligence bods seem confident that they can track them, using their direction finding equipment when they transmit their radio messages.

We now know approximately where most of them are but are having trouble decoding their signals. It would be nice to understand what they are saying, but it is really difficult to decipher them, still enough of my problems, what were you reading?'

Fred replies 'funnily enough Lt. Davis and the Racer riggers have just completed the salvage of the British sub C.16. That team is really coming on and you have set me wondering, perhaps we could salvage a German U-boat and recover their signal codebook.'

'That sounds like a really good idea to me; I will propose it at the meeting. What about RFA Racer's refit?'

'It's just been completed at the Thorneycroft yard in Woolston which is near Southampton. As soon as the riggers get back, they can carry out their trials and then I will send them to Queenstown because there are many damaged ships there.' Replies Fred.

'Great, the Admiral at Queenstown has been causing a stink because we can't help him, so that should quieten him for a while' at which he departs for his meeting.

RFA Racer then completes her trials successfully and starts her salvage work at Queenstown, helping with, SS Quantock (Q5) and the SS Arlington Court. No more working ashore in lodgings for the riggers, but they soon settle into their new mess deck. Having all the necessary equipment on board with them makes life a lot easier for the riggers.

Another piece of good news for them is that Cdr. Gracey puts in a report, about the missing payments at Devonport.

Date unknown: Done at Berehaven, related to TB 24 & Q19.

From Cdr. J W Gracey c/o SNO Berehaven to Captain Metcalf DNE

Submitted that 5/- per day subsistence, Vide Art 1506, be granted for six days to the men mentioned hereon, for the reason stated hereunder,
Thos Pearce Salvage Foreman, Riggers Ernest Coom, JJ Jones, Thos Moore, Geo Reavey, John Tremble, Thos E Robertson, Henry McDonald, Wilfred Kennedy, TC Coale, Henry Turley, Herbert Redgrave, John Foulkes, W Hall, Firemen W Connor, TH Bower, David Hardie, Chris O'Rourke, CC Abrams, 19 men in all.
This party while engaged at Dover salving TB 24, were instructed to proceed to Devonport, for Salvage Duties, the party arrived at Devonport, at 11 pm April – and Salvage Foreman Pearce, reports no accommodation was available for the party at Barracks, so arrangements, to sleep the party, had to be made at this hour, as best could be done, which much exceeded the 2/8 rate which the men afterwards drew from "Victory".
On completion salving operations on the "Q19", the men were instructed, by yourself to await orders, living on shore, on day by day arrangement, for four days, Foreman Peers reports it was not possible to get accommodation, for the party, for day to day on 2/8 it is therefore submitted, that from the time the men left Dover, to the time the men arrived at Southampton, from Devonport, (6 days) the 5/- subsistence, may be granted, less 2/8 already received, in order to meet actual expenses incurred.
J B Gracey Cdr. RNR Admiralty Salvage Officer.
On the 4th Aug, 1917 approval is given to RFA Racer for payment.

Back in London, a Sea Lords meeting is convened, about the submarine threat on 20 July 1917.

Chairing the meeting is Sir Eric Geddes, who has very recently been appointed First Lord of the Admiralty.

Also in attendance is the 1st Sea Lord, Admiral Sir John Jellicoe, the 2nd Sea Lord, Admiral Cecil Burney, the 3rd Sea Lord, Admiral Sir Frederick Charles Tudor and the Director of Naval Intelligence, Rear Adm. Roger Welles Jr.

Other attendees are the Director of the Intelligence Division, Captain Reginal (Blinker) Hall from Room 40 and the

Salvage Section Head, Captain Frederick Young who is in charge of the Salvage Section.

Sir Eric opens the meeting with 'Gentlemen, we are here to discuss the U-boat threat, which grows by the day. The government is finding it difficult to understand the Navy's reluctance, to institute a Convoy system, so that we can protect our hard-pressed Merchantmen' and he turns to Jellicoe, 'what is your opinion, John?'

Jellicoe is fully prepared for this, knowing in his heart of hearts that the Government will get its way. But he still has concerns, 'the protection of the convoys system is difficult, because we still don't have any way of finding these damn U-boats, and we are very short of destroyers. I need to be convinced, that we can steer the convoys clear of them before I will agree,' as he turns to Admiral Welles.

He, in turn, looks at Captain Hall, who replies, 'this information must go no further than this room, and in fact should not be recorded,'

Sir Eric gestures to the secretary, who leaves the room and Hall continues.

'At present, we have completed all our planned signal tracking stations, which are working well. Fortunately, the U-boats are still transmitting on full power, which makes the tracking so much easier. What we can't do is read the messages because they have changed their coding book. We have not had a coding book, since the one given to us by the Russians at the start of the war, but they still start and end their signals with a unique identifier. We even know a few of their submarine identifiers, from collecting other intelligence information, and can guess some of the rest. I believe we can route the convoys away from most of their submarines provided they don't change their routine, so I am in favour of convoys.'

'Does anyone else have anything to add,' says Sir Eric looking around the room, and seeing Captain Young nod says 'Captain Young I believe'.

'Yes sir, I head the Royal Navy salvage section and believe we could help. We have recently salvaged one of our own submarines, C.16 from 7 ½ fathoms down after an accident. The salvage enabled us to identify what had happened on board to the poor crew. I believe we could salvage a U-boat and perhaps recover a codebook for you.'

Everyone around the table mutters their agreement and Jellicoe says,' Excellent work, I also believe you want all our future submarines, to have some modifications so that air and food plus communications can be provided.'

'Yes sir, my salvage teams are doing fine work, and full of good ideas', Replies Captain Young.

'I will authorise the changes to our submarines to be done, and I believe you are recovering many merchant ships as well,' says Jellicoe.

'We are salvaging many ships, but we can only recover a proportion of those attacked. However we will continue to do our best, but reducing the numbers attacked is essential,' is Young's final comment.

'Gentlemen, thank you for your input, it has been most enlightening, please put in a place a convoy system immediately Lord Fisher, routing to be directed by the Intelligence Service. The Salvage Section is ordered to prioritise the recovery of a U boat, complete with its codebooks. We must stop the losses in shipping, or we will lose this war. Officially I will tell the government that we are diverting destroyers to do this work, they must not know what we are really doing'. At which, they all leave having finally received some clear instructions, and everyone is happy.

The arrival of a Telegram in wartime quite often bears bad news, but the one that arrived on board the Racer for John in August is very welcome. As John read the few words quickly, after ripping the envelope open, his face beams.

Pony who is looking on realises that it is probably the arrival of a new-born, to the Foulkes household. John's mind had been elsewhere for the last couple of weeks and it seemed like good news, 'everything ok?' he ventures.

'A baby girl who is going to be called Jessie' responds John happily and with great pride, 'I must write home immediately, because I doubt very much I will get any leave, even for this'.

'I am sure that you are right, but at least we can celebrate now' says Pony and offers his glass of rum with the words 'Gulpers?' and John takes the proffered tot to his lips, and drinks the correct amount which is, of course, a good mouthful.

Everyone else also offers rum but John says, 'Could you wait 20 minutes whilst I write home?'

To which everyone nods in agreement because they all know that John will soon be incapable of writing if he is to drink all that is on offer. 20 minutes later, in traditional naval manner, a party breaks out in the mess deck to celebrate Jessie's birth.

Capitan Kurt Tebbenjohanns & UC-44

31st July 1917

Kapitan Kurt Tebbenjohanns stands on the ammunition loading jetty, with his commanding officer Lt. Cdr. Pasquay, and a civilian technical expert Mr. Goedhard. They are discussing mine laying techniques, as his crew and the shore side staff, load UC-44 with her 18 mines, 4 torpedoes and plenty of ammunition for the deck gun.

In his hand, he holds a report on possible reasons for the minelaying operation going wrong. 'I have heard the rumours from some of the other Captains, but we have never had any problems with the system on board this boat during our 5 missions' says Kurt.

The civilian replies 'The only difference between a Class 1 and a Class 2 submarine is the number of mines held in the delivery tube, it is now 3 instead of 2, and perhaps that may have something to do with it. It's very difficult to find a solution when we have so little evidence, but it does seem likely that some of our submarines may have blown themselves up with their own mine. Problem is you can't get real evidence because the submarine doesn't return, unfortunately.'

'I see that you have listed the likely causes in order and that you think the salt timer plug is the most probable cause' says Kurt.

'Yes' says Mr. Goedhard' The solid salt plug in the mine release mechanism disintegrates after time in contact with salt water, once it has dissolved, this allows the mine to deploy from its launching frame.'

'I see' says Kurt 'and when we deploy a mine the arming wire opens this to the sea'. 'The 3rd mine does take longer to drop down the tube.'

'Exactly' replies the expert 'and maybe the mine is released from the delivery frame before it reaches the seabed'.

'What I can do is make sure that everyone is aware of your investigation, and gather as much evidence as possible for you Mr. Goedhard' interjects the base commander.

'We must inform everyone' is his reply and at this the 2 men take their leave, heading for the other U-boats, whilst the Captain of UC-44 carries on supervising the loading of their weapons.

By 8.30 all is completed, the crew then start checking the submarine's systems, prior to departure, and so at 9.10, they finally cast off to start their next mission. The submarine eases out of the harbour, and into the main channel with the trawler Obotrit as an escort.

The Captain standing inside the conning tower, orders a test dive that will last for one mile, knowing that they can use the escort as a guide to stay in the channel. He can hear the diesel engine on board shut down, and as soon as it does, he closes the hatch, on his way down to the control room. 'Periscope depth' is his order to the planes man, whilst he checks on the escort, and reports come in from forward and aft, that all is well with both his command and his crew.

20 minutes later the submarine surfaces and they settle into cruising watches, whilst the Captain opens the safe and then reads their orders again, now it is time to tell the crew.

There is a knock on the wardroom bulkhead and signalman Chandler's head appears, 'Can I have the code book please sir, it's time to report the start of our mission' he says.

'Yes' says Kurt 'and don't forget we have to fit in some random codes to stop the British decoding our messages, I have a list here for you to use, just fit them in as we agreed.'

'Aye Aye Sir and I will return the book as soon as I am done' is his comment as he heads for the radio.

In the control room, all of the crew of 29 who could be spared, are gathered together and the Captain starts, 'this is our 6th trip and we are ordered to southern Ireland via the English channel, where we will lay our mines as our first priority. We will then head back via the North, taking any targets of opportunity, as we travel home. On the journey out we will attack what we can, however, they will need to be good opportunities, we can decide at the time.

During the next day and a half, we will settle into a routine, but we must be prepared at all times. As you all know fleet orders do not allow the wearing of lifebelts when down below, so ensure you comply. Carry on now and pass the word to those not here.'

ROOM 40 London Admiralty

In the Submarine Tracking room, one of the 3 occupants Edward Clarke, moves over to the large chart on the wall, and picks up a flagged pin and writes the date 31 July 1917 & U-boat on it, before sticking it in a position, just off the North Sea German coast. 'One more to keep an eye on' he says before sitting down and telephoning the Convoy Control Room, about this new threat, which is heading into the North Sea.

Just as he finishes his call, the door opens and Blinker Hall, the boss of Naval Intelligence Division, pops his head around the door, and says 'how's it going, any news?'

'I have just flagged a U-boat which is on the move, direction finding shows her in the North Sea, but her messages appear to be full of random codes, and that makes decoding much more difficult. This particular U-boat doesn't make many mistakes, unlike some of the others, I have however passed on the location to the Convoy Co-ordinator, Henderson' is the answer.

'Very good' says Hall, 'we need to get our hands on a codebook, and the naval Salvage Section has been told to prioritise the work of salvaging a German U-boat. We haven't had a copy of the codebook since 1914, when the one from the German cruiser SMS Magdeburg, was delivered to us from Russia by HMS

Theseus, and that one is no longer in use. Being able to decode the signals, as well as knowing where these dammed U-boats are, would be brilliant but keep up the good work' and with that, he departs, to continue his morning rounds.

On UC-44, once she is into the main deep channel, 2 minesweepers take over the escort duties. They sweep ahead, ensuring that there are no British mines lying in wait, and they will do this until they are well out into the North Sea.

Midday the next day, the 2 escorts depart, and after lunch, UC-44 dives to 7.5 fathoms, for the rest of the afternoon. This is to ensure that their departure would not be tracked by any unseen observers, as they head towards the Dover straights.

Once darkness falls, they are able to pass through the straights on the surface, thus avoiding the nets which have been laid across the channel; these nets are supposed to deter any German submarines but are useless.

A number of patrolling destroyers are sighted over the next couple of days, but by diving immediately they are easily able to avoid them all. Finally, on the afternoon of the 4th August, they find a 600ton steamer in their sights and dive to prepare for an attack. Realising that she is only lightly loaded and that they are very close to the mining destination, the attack is broken off.

Eventually, at 10.42pm, the sub is in their designated position, ready to mine the entrance to Waterford harbour. Just before midnight after a quick cold meal, the work starts and the Captain Orders 'hands to mining stations', whereby the submarine is closed down into its sealed compartments.

The Captain, Warrant Officer Schleuter the navigator, Petty Officer Pabsch the Bosun Mate and the helmsman take up their positions in the control room, and the small submarine glides silently along its chosen path, staying at periscope depth, preparing to lay its deadly cargo.

The hydrophone operator is at his station, listening for the noise of other craft in the area, but all is quiet in this normally busy sea lane, little is to disturb their planned progress.

In the Mine Room Sub Lt. Bendler, with 5 other crew members take up their positions, ready to launch the mines as directed by the Captain.

In the Engine Room Warrant Officer Seifarth, manages the U boat's propulsion and other engineering systems, with his 9 section members.

The rest of the crew are split between the forward and aft torpedo compartments, ready to fire these should it be absolutely necessary.

Running slowly and silently into the bay, they head towards Waterford with Kurt checking through the periscope occasionally. When they were almost level with Creadon Head, which shows up clearly in the moonlight, they are able to come about and start the mining run.

At the point where the seabed starts to drop, is where they commence laying a line of mines, going down the channel, towards their original start point.

Speaking to Bendler on the telephone, the Captain quietly orders 'lay mine No 1'

'Lay mine No 1' repeats Bendler and the 3 crew members, standing by the forward mine tube, each turn one of the three handles which release the bottom mine of the three in the tube, into the sea. As the mine drops out of the tube, the arming wire attached to the tube pulls the waterproof plug out. Once the timer salt plug dissolves, the mine will be released from its delivery system. At the same time, the mechanism will arm the contact horns, fitted on top of the mine.

The salt timer plug dissolves slowly, allowing enough time for the mine to sink to the seabed, and for the minelayer to leave the immediate area.

At the end of its timing cycle, the tube guide arms holding the mine in place will open out onto the seabed. This frees the mine so that it can float towards the surface, only connected by a wire which tethers it to the sinker weight which is now sitting on the seabed.

At the bottom of the mine, is a hydrostatic valve, set to a depth of three meters, which will keep the mine at this approximate depth. The length of cable is adjusted by the valve, so that even as the tide ebbs and flows, the mine stays just below the surface, waiting for its victim.

The next two mines from tube No 1; are added along this line, leaving a row of three mines in a line on the seabed. Staying on the same course, the submarine lays a further line of three mines from Tube No 2. Then they add another final line of three, so that the mines form a continuous stretch of danger, almost reaching the mouth of the estuary.

All is proceeding normally, but as the top mine from tube No 3 slides down the tube, the men in the Mine Room all hear a louder than usual scraping noise. Bendler moves over to the tube to ask the three men in a hushed voice 'Any problems with your handles?'

'No sir' is their replies and he puts his ear to the tube, to see if he can hear anything else. No other unusual sounds can be heard, so he steps over to the telephone and picks it up, to report to the Captain.

'Sir there was some extra unusual noise, as we released the top mine from Tube No 3, but we think it has been laid and is clear'

At this moment there is an enormous and violent explosion, which rips through the stillness, and the submarine is tossed about like a toy. The hull pivots bow downwards, whilst at the same time rolling hard to starboard, throwing him across the mine compartment, and hard up against the deckhead. The lights go out in the mine room, whilst pipe joints crack spraying water everywhere, all over the crew who are all lying in untidy shattered heaps.

In the control room, the situation is no better, although some lights stay on, and the Navigator is lying in a crumpled heap. His head is lying at a very strange angle, caused by his contact with a protruding brass valve wheel; that he struck, as he was propelled across the control room.

The after end of the submarine; is a complete mess of twisted steel, because the hull has been completely breached. This allows seawater to pour quickly into the compartment, drowning the few at the stern, who survived the initial explosion.

Stunned by the ferocity of the explosion, it takes the Captain a few moments to gather his thoughts, and then pick himself up. He is still holding the telephone receiver, but it is no longer connected to the system, and he throws the useless instrument down.

Dazed but slowly getting his bearings, he frantically starts opening air valves, which will blow the ballast tanks and hopefully this will bring the crippled submarine to the surface.

At first, his efforts seem to be successful because the bow comes up to level, but the submarine is still lying almost on its side.

The depth gauge, despite its missing glass, tells a sorry story, as it shows they are still sinking towards the seabed, many feet below and there is no more air in the gas bottles. Then the deck tilts, as the bow comes up again.

Lying on its side nose up the stricken vessel continues to sink, and it is obvious that there is little they can do, so the Captain orders abandon ship, to his remaining crew.

Opening the conning tower hatch is quite difficult because of the 70-degree list, but eventually, they manage, and once the sea has stopped entering the compartment, there is still a pocket of air for them to breath. The three survivors in the control room escape through the conning tower hatch, up to the surface, whilst the U boat settles towards the seabed.

Leaving the stricken submarine last, the Captain takes a final deep breath and passes through the conning tower, striking for the surface. Up through the dark murky muddy water, he swims up as best he can in his full clothing, but fortunately, it is not too far.

At the moonlit surface, he gasps for breath, then he steadies his nerves again, he looks for the other men and perhaps a rescue boat. He thinks he can see and hear the other survivors for a short while, but they begin to drift apart, it is not easy staying afloat without lifejackets, and it takes all his attention just to stay buoyant, as the cold seeps into his battered body, even though it is summer.

At 10.20pm local time, the Dunmore East coastguard station, which is sitting on the cliff next to the harbour, notes a loud explosion to the southwest. Nothing is seen, so they send the guard boat out along with some local fishing boats to investigate the noise.

Richie (Jos) Power, Jack McGrath and Ray McGrath, have just returned from a successful evening trip, catching the Mackerel that run at this time of the year. Their 3 hand Curach was just about to be put away for the night when they hear the explosion and after checking with the coast guard, set off as part of the search party.

Not knowing what had really happened, and who might be in trouble, they know it is their duty as sailors, to help any mariners who might be in trouble. It takes them the best part of half an hour, rowing for 2 miles and then spreading out from the other boats, to search the probable area for survivors. There is no debris at all and they start to guess that a mine has exploded, but that no ship has been involved.

The sea is relatively calm but as time wears on, Kurt finds himself tiring with his efforts, simply to stay alive, and then he remembers that he can use his jacket, which is now sodden, to trap some air. With difficulty, he buttons it up to his neck and then scoops air into the front. This gives him some respite, however, this is only temporary, as the air leaks out, and the cold starts to bite even more because he is then moving less.

Almost at the end of his tether, after what seems like hours, he thinks he can hear voices. Suddenly a hull appears at his side; he throws his arm up hitting the outside and calls out weakly.

On the boat Jos, Jack and Ray, are talking amongst themselves, considering giving up the search, when something hits the hull of the small fishing boat, giving them quite a surprise. Recovering quickly, Jack who is sitting at the front, near to the location of the noise, leans over the side and sees the head of a man, well within arm's reach.

'Give us a hand Jos, we have found someone and keep the boat steady' he instructs Ray who is manning the third set of oars. Taking an arm each, they lift and drag the survivor aboard, and lay him down in the bow. Quickly they remove his sodden top clothing and wrap him in blankets, whilst he lies there shivering uncontrollably.

'Get your flask out Jack he needs a drink' says Ray.
Kurt finds a bottle is pressed to his lips and a fiery liquid, almost like Schnapps slides down his throat, warming him from the inside and breathing life into his aching body. Later he was to discover that this magic liquid is called Poteen, which is an illegal spirit distilled from potatoes.

As the shivering reduces he is able to say 'Kapitan, U-boat Boom' and then waving his arms around in a sweeping gesture, and showing a couple of fingers, he tries to make them understand, that others are in the water.

The three men with the strange accents shake their heads, to show that no one else has been found, and then they man the oars. Rowing as quickly as possible, they head back to their harbour, to make sure this man gets the attention he obviously needs. They know he has been in the water for an hour and a half since the explosion, and he is lucky to be alive.

Kurt is absolutely distraught inside as he realises that his beloved U-boat is finished and that many fine men have given their all for the fatherland, simply because the delivery system had somehow failed. Now he also realises that the order not to wear lifejackets was wrong. Despite the likely difficulties, he knows that he must inform his superiors of the details of the accident. It must be done in such a way that his captors won't know, and in this way, he can make the sad loss of life a little more acceptable.

Once in the small harbour, he is lifted gently from the fishing boat and carried quickly on a stretcher, to a local house, where the open door releases a draft of comforting warmth. He never thought he would ever feel anything again, and strangely the air has an odd peaty smell, which seems to come from the fire burning in the kitchen range. In front of the warming range, he is stripped of all his clothing and led to a tin bath, which is lying in the middle of the room filled with lukewarm water. It is obvious to him that these people are used to rescuing men from the savage sea. Eventually bathed and sitting in clean clothing, with a blanket wrapped around his shoulders, he sips a warming drink of cocoa, whilst his clothes are washed and hung to dry in front of the range.

Jack who appears to be the leader of the men who has rescued him turns and asks 'Kurt Tebbenjohanns Captain U-boat German Navy?'

To which Kurt replies 'Ja', they have found his name inside his clothing, and another of his rescuers leaves by the front door, no doubt to inform the authorities.

15 minutes later a policeman arrives and he is arrested, now he is a prisoner of war, but for the time being he is left in the cottage and they help him upstairs, where he is soon asleep.

He wakes from his disturbed and nightmarish slumber, to find himself in a very comfortable bed. Wondering at first how on earth he got there, he then remembers all that has gone before. His German uniform is on a chair, clean and pressed, and the man in the bedroom gestures towards it, wanting him to get dressed. Downstairs the policeman from last night stands drinking his tea, whilst a wonderful breakfast is laid before him. He is amazed that food is in such good supply, it's not like that at home is his first thought.

Feeling much better after eating the feast, he is given more food, which is wrapped in greaseproof paper, and then taken to the police station, where a man in Naval Uniform is waiting to meet him. The stranger is a Royal Navy Lt. who will escort him back to London, for interrogation, and then to a prisoner of war camp, the war is over for him.

His escort speaks passable German and produces handcuffs, but because Kurt gives a promise not to attempt to escape during the journey to London, they go back into a pocket, but the Lt. warms 'any attempt to escape and I will use them'.

Kurt confirms that he is the Captain of U-boat UC-44 and that they had laid a number of mines, at the mouth of Waterford port, just before the explosion.

Kurt also wants to know where he is, 'What place is this?'

'Dunmore East, just south of Waterford and a local fishing port' is the reply.

'I would like to express my gratitude to the people of Dunmore East who rescued me, and have shown me such great kindness, war is so strange, here I am trying to kill these people with my mines, and yet they show me nothing but kindness.'

'It's a fishing village and these people care for those lost at sea, plus they are also Irish and have a wonderful outlook on life, you are lucky.'

He also finds out that one of his crew was discovered alive, but died on the journey back, and they have not yet found the other one who escaped with him, his body is found later.

Once he has been formally handed over to his escort, they depart for their journey to London, by train and ferry which passes uneventfully. The journey gives him time to think, about the tragic accident, and to formulate a plan on how to tell his superiors what happened. His escort, of course, leaves him to his thoughts because as a naval officer he realises that to lose ones command and all of his men, must be the worst thing that can happen to any captain of a ship or a submarine.

In London the very next day he meets his interrogators, who introduce themselves as Naval Intelligence officers, formalities over they then question him for the next two days, but in a quite civilised manner, accepting his reluctance to answer specific questions about German methods of operating and laying mines.

He is, however, happy to give details of his lost crew, as far as he can remember, and they also discuss many aspects of the war. At opportune moments, he suggests that he would like to write to his parents and ask them to collect his belongings, from his base port. Of course, this means he must write also to his commanding officer, and all this is agreed to, with the warning from them, that all letters will be censored, to which of course he must accept.

The letter home is not too difficult, apart from the need to write down the facts, which involves reliving the dreadful events of the past week, but of course, he will have to live with that for the rest of his life.

The letter to his commanding officer is somewhat shorter but requires much more thought, because in this he must do his best to tell them the facts, without revealing the information to his captors.

Eventually, he settles on the following (*I have requested my parents to arrange to collect personally, if possible, the things which I left at Brunsbuttel. May I ask you to see that great care is taken in unpacking the box, so that there is no accident, as there are some eggs at the top. I have not yet thanked Messrs Goedhard for the gift of books. Can this be done from your end?*). Finishing with (*trusting I may hear from you some time*) he signs off and hopes his letter will be sent.

Of course, the vital words in the letter are, Accident, Eggs at the top, Messrs Goedhard and book, which he is sure his Commanding officer Lt. Cdr. Pasquay, will understand.

Hopefully, he will pass the information on, in an attempt to resolve the mine laying problem, and with that, he settles into a life of captivity, which will be until the war ends. Little realising and he would never ever know, how far-reaching would be the consequences of the disastrous accident, to his beloved UC-44 and her crew. She would unwittingly be of great assistance to Britain in its fight against the deadly U-Boats.

Back at Brunsbuttel, some weeks later Lt. Cdr. Pasquay is sitting at his desk, reading and puzzling over Kurt's letter and the strange wording, when suddenly his face lights up, and immediately reaches over to pick up the phone 'Connect me to Mr. Goedhard immediately' he tells his secretary, having realised that the loss of UC-44 and its crew, may yet save other crews from a similar fate.

HMS Haldon & UC-44 Salvage

Not long after Kurt has fallen into his fitful but deep slumber in the cottage at Dunmore East, the Royal Navy system swings into action. Queenstown orders an immediate response, both to the threat of the mines released by UC-44 and the possibility of other survivors.

Motor Launch ML478, which has been anchored for the night in Dungarvan harbour, and has lowered her hydrophone listening system, in the hope of hearing a submarine attacking the harbour, quickly recovers her equipment and sets off to the nearby estuary to look for survivors.

All night they sweep the bay with their searchlight, running up and down in a search pattern, despite the risk of mines because they are hoping to save someone. The sea is calm, which makes the task easier but the estuary has a fierce tide, creating rip currents and waves that can easily be mistaken for a head. All of this is in vain and they know that any survivor; could be carried many miles away.

However, as the dawn breaks, they do find the tell-tale evidence of an oil stream, which they follow until they can see it emerging from the depths below and believe this is the location of the sunken U-boat.

Their first job; is to rig and launch a small buoy attached to an anchor and chain. This will mark the spot for others and once they know that it has taken hold on the seabed, they head for Dunmore East coast guard signal tower, to report their find by signal lantern.

Tired and weary after a very long night of searching, their hopes for rest are quickly dashed, when the reply gives them further orders. They are to proceed with the Racecourse class paddle minesweeper, HMS Haldon, to assist with the clearing of any mines lying in the swept channel.

Closing HMS Haldon, the Captain of ML478, passes the positional information over, in order to assist them in deciding where to sweep. Then he agrees to lay off with rifles ready, to help destroy any mines released by the minesweeper.

The Haldon paddle wheels groan into action, turning slowly at first and dipping into the reasonably calm seas, moving her forward. As she clears the motor launch, she turns to starboard, away from the stationary vessel, whilst the crew on her stern, drop the Paravanes and towing wires into the water, using her aft derricks to launch them.

As she reaches her normal sweeping speed, the Paravane takes up its position, to the side of the ship. In this way, the wire will guide any mine tethering wire, into the attached wire cutter and so release the mine which will then float the surface.

The riflemen; positioned at her stern will then try first to detonate the swept mine, by firing at the horns protruding from the top.

The motor launches job; is to follow and destroy any mines they miss, so they also get underway, following at a safe distance and out of the likely line of fire.

Once at the marker buoy, the Haldon sweeps the stretches across the mouth of the bay, between the marker buoy and both shores without finding anything. Eventually, they come to the conclusion, that the U boat had been dropping its deadly cargo in a line down the middle of the estuary.

As the Haldon sweeps the suspected area, moving away from the submarines marked position, towards Waterford, the mines start bobbing to the surface. Haldon rifle fire destroys the first two and misses the next, so the launch moves in firing from her bows as they sail closer. Ultimately, there is a massive explosion and the sea erupts, with such force that it rocks them from side to side somewhat but the little motor launch takes it well and there is no damage, although the riflemen lying on the bow get a drenching.

Four more mines are destroyed in a similar manner and just as they are thinking that the job would soon be over, there is another deafening explosion and the stern of HMS Haldon disappears, behind a huge plume of water. When the spray clears, it is clear she is badly damaged close to one of her paddle wheels.

Fortunately her great paddlewheels; keep turning and the Captain of HMS Haldon alters course, towards the nearby Creadon Head, which is the nearest shallow water. Despite the mine going off under the aft stokehold and aft boiler room, she still has a head of steam. There is enough steam available from her undamaged forward boiler room and eventually comes to rest, near the shore in a couple of fathoms of water. ML 478 comes alongside and they load the half a dozen casualties, along with the medic and a senior officer, before heading for Dunmore East harbour to report.

On board HMS Haldon, water fills the after boiler room and stokehold, entering through the holes in the damaged wooden hull. Once they have the minesweeper stabilised, the hands are mustered for a roll call, which reveals that the deckhand John Gowans is missing.

After a long and wearing train, ferry and car journey Lt. Davis RNR, who has been appointed Salvage Officer for HMS Haldon, arrives at the Dunmore East Coastguard station, in the afternoon of the 7th Aug. Here he requests transport so that he can inspect the damaged ship.

The armed trawler "Morococala"; has been detailed to guard the Haldon, whose crew have returned to Queenstown, leaving just some watchkeepers on board.

RFA Racer arrives in the Waterford and Suir estuary late on 7th August 1917, after her short trip from Queenstown and docks in Dunmore East harbour. She has been working in Queenstown, helping to deal with the large number of merchant ships lying in the harbour which was her first work since commissioning at Woolston in May. The urgent move to Dunmore East means that much of her equipment, either needed some repairs or was still on ships in that harbour.

It is midnight, when Lt. Davis who has been waiting on the jetty, steps aboard, just as soon as the gangway is secure, where he meets the Captain and the Salvage Foreman Thomas Pearce.

The salvage riggers and senior hands from the other ships departments are mustered quickly in the empty spare accommodation to sort out a plan of action. This space is quite often used as a conference room, where he does his briefing. 'HMS Haldon is beached on Creadon Head in 2 fathoms of water. The mine breached her aft boiler room which is now full of water. The bulkhead between the engine room and the boiler room is struggling to hold the water back. We will need to shore up this bulkhead and patch up any holes in it before we can start pumping out the water in the bilges. Bosun, what materials do you have on board for this shoring up?' he asks.

Very little' replies the Bosun, 'we used most of what we had at Queenstown, but we have enough to make a start in the morning.'

'Very well' replies Davis, 'I will look at what you have and order what we need immediately, at least we can start at first light.'

'Did you say 2 fathoms of water?' asks the Captain.

'Yes,' he replies.

'Unfortunately we will have to anchor off; otherwise, we will ground as our draft at 14ft which is greater than 2 fathoms.' States the Captain.

'We can use the Morococala as a work platform, she is able to go alongside and then we can ferry whatever we need, using the trawler and your ships boats' answers Davis. With all this decided, they all head off to prepare for a very early start in the morning, which would not be long in coming.

John and the rest of the riggers, spend the next morning transferring a 12" steam pump and what little shoring materials they have available, onto the armed trawler. This vessel then ties up alongside the Haldon and by the afternoon, they are on board starting to shore the engine room bulkhead. It is bowing and creaking alarmingly as the waves wash against the ship's side; it looks like failing completely at any moment.

Admiralty Salvage Section Headquarters

The 3rd Sea Lord Admiral Sir Frederick Charles Tudor, steps into the office of Captain Frederick Young who runs the Salvage Section for him. 'We appear to have a submarine UC-44, which has sunk in Waterford bay in Ireland that we must try to salvage her; you know that this is an absolute priority, as we must try to recover the radio Code Books.' Waving a signal in his hand, 'I have just come from a meeting at the Admiralty with the other Sea Lords'. He continues, 'The battle against the U-boats must be won and this could give us the edge we need'.

'Of course sir,' replies Fred in his normal unflustered manner, 'we are in luck because RFA Racer is already on site, salvaging HMS Haldon which was probably damaged by a mine from that U-boat.

You might remember the salvage riggers on board Racer, salvaged our submarine C16 a few months ago. I will also instruct the delivery of the 2 lifting barges they will need and they can start immediately. Lt. Davis is the salvage officer on station and he is very capable and he knows the men.'

At which the Admiral leaves wondering if anything will ever faze this remarkable individual, who is always calm no matter what the situation.

A knock is heard at the Wardroom door on Racer, which is then answered by a steward, who is handed a signal message by Sparks the radio operator with the words 'this has just arrived from Sunhill headquarters for Lt. Davis and it is urgent'.

The officers gather round, whilst Lt. Davis reads the short message, who then addresses the Captain, 'we have to leave the Haldon and start work first thing in the morning recovering the German U-boat UC-44. I will stay with the "Haldon" and hand the job over to her skipper, with some guidance he should be able to manage. Meanwhile, you head down to the sub's marked position and get some divers down to do a survey, by the time you have done that I should be back on board.'

'No problem' replies the Captain. 'Go and find Bosun Collins and ask him to report to me ASAP,' the Captain instructs the steward who leaves immediately.

As the morning light breaks through the darkness, RFA Racer drops anchor near to the marker buoy and the two diving boats are lowered into the slight swell. As each boat is brought alongside, it is loaded with the diver's air hand pump, wires, ladders, buoys, a single diver and half of the salvage riggers.

The first boat which includes Diver Precious and John rows over to the marker buoy, where they secure the dive boat to the buoy.

Finishing dressing the diver in his suit and helmet, connecting him to his airline and telephone line they are eventually ready. The deployment ladder is laid over the side of the boat, and then he can climb over and walk down into the water. As he moves to the ladder, 2 riggers move to the other side, in order to balance the small boat. 2 others man the manual air pump and John who will keep in contact with him on the telephone, handles his recovery line.

Fortunately, it is almost slack tide with very little current. This should give them enough time to find the wreck, and attach marker buoys to the bow and the stern. The marker buoys will be used as guides when they are towing lifting wires under the stricken submarine.

John watches as the diving helmet sinks below the surface and soon he can only see the trail of air bubbles rising to the surface. He will use these to monitor the diver's position. 'Keep turning those handles' he tells the men who are manning the wheels on the air pump 'and keep that air hose from kinking' he instructs the rigger in the bow.

Pony is slowly and carefully uncoiling the hose, which is attached to the recovery line in the front of the boat.

As diver Precious is lowered slowly down, he uses the buoys tether wire as a guide, until he finds himself standing on the seabed. John can hear the diver breathing on the telephone and eventually he says, 'I am on the bottom and there is a hard sand and shingle seabed'. 'How deep am I? 'Is his very first question because he knows he has gone down quite a distance.

'90ft' replies John who looks at the marks on the recovery line.

'That's almost my limit' replies Precious 'and it will take quite a while to return to the surface. I will need to stop on the way up to acclimatise so be prepared and remind me as I come up' warns the diver.

'No problem' says John,' are you ready to move over towards the sub yet?'

Turning slowly, he eventually sees the shadow of his target, in the gloom with its pointed bow nearest to him. The U-boat is lying on its side, at an extreme angle, with most of its belly showing and the mine delivery tube apertures like circles, receding into the gloom. 'I can see the submarine' he says' make sure I have plenty of slack on my line as I am going over to it now'.

On John's reply of 'Roger', he leans forward towards the submarine and plods along leaving a trail of bubbles in his wake. Each step creates a cloud of sand as his heavy boots clump onto the hard seabed.

Halting at the bow, he removes his diver's knife and holds it vertically whilst he faces the hull. 'I am going to knock on the hull 5 times and then listen for any response, so keep quiet up there' he announces, at which he raises his arm and brings the hilt down, with a resounding thump, which sounds loud and clear in the stillness. Once he has completed the 5 blows, he waits patiently for any reply from inside, but it is deathly quiet.

He was not actually expecting any response from the unfortunate sailors still inside, they would have run out of air by now but he had to try. 'No reply' he tells John. 'Next, let's attach the bow marker buoy to the wreck; you can lower a wire down using my recovery line as a guide.'

On the boat, John grabs a large shackle, to which he attaches a wire and then closes it around the recovery line, before sliding it over the side.

Down on the seabed, the diver can feel the wire moving down his line, which he is holding in a loop in front of him. When it arrives he unscrews the shackle, wraps the wire around the submarine bow cable cutter and then locks it in place using the shackle.

Moving away from the bow, he instructs those in the boat to attach a buoy to the wire, whilst he inspects the wreck.
He can see the mine delivery tube holes, as dark ovals stretching along the sub into the distance, there are 6 tubes and as he passes he realises that 3 of them are empty, but the other three are still loaded.

At the stern, he can see the awful twisted hull damage caused by the mine, but can also see, that the central part of the submarine is relatively undamaged and that it is a UC2 class of submarine. 'Tell the other boat that I am standing by the stern and they are to get Diver Keen down, to attach another buoy to this part'

'Roger' says John who turns to the 2nd boat with the instructions. By this time the other diver is already in the water so he says 'Diver Keam is almost with you'.

At which Precious says 'time to start my ascent' and moves away from the hull and John slowly pulls in the safety rope, until it is almost vertical.

'You are under the boat now' says John.

Precious stops walking and replies 'start hauling me up and don't forget the stop'. At the 15ft stage point, there is a wait for 15 minutes, for the diver to acclimatise and then he reaches the surface. Eager hands help him back into the boat and his helmet is removed. 'It's always nice to be free of that helmet and be able to breathe fresh air' is his first comment.

An hour and a half later all the team is back on board, both boats have been recovered. The 2 new marker buoys, attached to each end of the submarine, swing in the current, which is now getting stronger. The original marker buoy has been removed, it will be returned to the motor launch when possible.

Lt. Davis has returned from the Haldon and is being briefed by the 2 divers. 'And so to sum up your reports, the submarine is lying 90ft down, on a hard sand and shingle bottom, with a 70-degree list to port. She still has half of her mines on board in the 3 aft tubes but these are not in the way. The bow is clear and should be easy to sweep under but her stern is damaged, which may cause some problems. We are therefore ready to start sweeping under her.' He concludes. 'All to the good, that is excellent work but I fear the weather is worsening. Added to that she is very deep, is lying across the tide, which is very strong and this is going to make for an extremely difficult job.

As the Racer returns to harbour, the powerful screw tug Goole No.7 arrives with the lifting barges LC1 and LC2, ready for the job of raising the sub. The LC's are tied up inside the harbour and the Goole No.7 comes alongside Racer, for another conference in the spare mess deck.

'The tug is to remain here and help Racer to tow lifting wires under her' says Lt. Davis. 'First, however, I would like the divers to try and enter the submarine, through the conning tower' he continues.

Divers Precious and Forsyth turn to look at each other with a grimace, this is not the sort of work that they are happy with. Going inside a cramped narrow conning tower at 90ft depth with almost no visibility is not to their liking, they shake their heads at the prospect.

Diver Keam is made of sterner stuff and sees it as a challenge if others can do it then so can he.

Lt. Davis notices the two Divers faces and realises that they are not that eager. He is not surprised and says to the 3 divers, 'We are expecting 2 very experienced divers late tomorrow, they have been inside a similar submarine UC5, and so all I ask tomorrow is that you give it a try. One of you will be retained and the other 2 can go to Berehaven, to assist in the salvage work that you were doing there before you came here.'

'Very good Sir' says all 3 and this appears to lighten the atmosphere as the crew departs to grab some food and sleep ready for the next day.

At low water, the next day Racer is back where she was, with a dive boat attached to the bow marker buoy. Diver Keam is on the seabed, standing by the conning tower, with the bent submarine periscope angled above him. 'Slowly lift me up 10ft and I will take hold of the periscope' he instructs those on the boat, shortly after he is hanging down and looking inside conning tower at the small open hatch. 'Lifting my legs up now and I will attempt to swing them inside the hatch opening, do not let go he warns'. With a clang, he manages to get his 2 feet, which are encased in his heavy large diving boots, inside the hatch but he is now almost horizontal. Although the lower parts of his legs slide inside, he finds it impossible to drop any further inside, each time he moves, his suit catches on a protrusion and he fears that he will either snag and tear his suit or he will get stuck. 'I cannot drop inside' he announces 'and I will need your help to remove my legs from the hatch as they seem to be catching on something, pull me up 2 feet only' he instructs.

After a couple of lifts and drops, he eventually pulls his feet out of the hatch, which is a great relief. 'I am free he announces, that was not easy and I would love to wipe the sweat from my brow if I could because it is running into my eyes'.

That evening, Divers Gohm and Eaglestone, arrive from Harwich and intensely discuss with Keam his efforts that day. 'The problem is that the sub is lying over so much, I couldn't get a clear drop down through the conning tower hatch, which is at least open but very small. The ladder down into the submarine is lying almost on its side, so that gives no help at all' says Keam.

'OK' replies Eaglestone, 'we will try again tomorrow but it sounds like you are right, however, we can also try the forward hatch by the gun'.

'Excellent' says Lt. Davis 'it's vital that we get inside and recover whatever there is that is inside, but we should not take extreme risks, get some sleep now and we will see what happens tomorrow' as he departs to report progress to the Admiralty.

The next day Eaglestone and Gohm both go down, where they suffer the same problems as the other diver. They also try to open the forward hatch, which despite huge physical efforts won't open and they are forced to give up.

Lt. Davis decides to send divers Precious and Forsyth to Berehaven, where they can continue the salvage work that Racer had been diverted from but promising them, that they would be able to return once the salvage of UC-44 has been completed. He tells them that he needs divers with the greater experience for this job and that Diver Keam would be retained as the spare diver on board.

Lt. Davis is standing on the deck of Racer which has anchored near to the diving boats and is surveying the sea and the coastal area. Turning to the Captain of Racer, Lt. Horace Gauld RNR he says 'I don't like this location, the estuary is quite wide open where we are and although we can see both shores 2 miles away, there is a huge amount of traffic heading in and out. Mostly they are smallish ships but it is no wonder that the German's wanted to mine this area.'

'Yes' agrees Horace 'and I have no doubt they will come back and try again and we are not armed so could not defend ourselves from attack.'

'On top of that this place is quite exposed to the Atlantic weather, which I am sure will play its part, but there is little we can do. This job must be done however and I will see if we can get some sort of naval guard' at which he heads for the radio room to request help.

A few hours later, back in the harbour, they are in the wardroom having their evening meal when Horace asks 'Any luck getting a guard from the Admiralty?' as he tucks into a lovely pie, made from a gift of fresh fish received that morning from the local people.

'The Admiralty in London didn't want to know but the Admiral in Queenstown is sending ML478 to us tonight and she will stay until the U boat is recovered. They have a 4pdr gun and 2 depth charges available. Also, she was the boat that marked the wreck originally, so we can give her back her buoy.' Replies Davis who then tackles the rest of his fish pie remaining on his plate and calls for more of the same.

The Captain mumbles his acknowledgment, as he makes sure he gets his share of this wonderful food. At the end of the meal, the Captain beckons the steward to come over and says 'Do you know where the fish came from?' he asks.

'No sir but I can find out' he replies.

'Make sure you do and give a bottle of Port to whoever is responsible, we may be here for some time.' says Horace.

'Certainly sir, the locals are very friendly and I will make sure that they know how grateful we are, our meal in the mess deck is just as good.'

Their armed lookout ML478 has arrived and lies to the seaward of the salvage team guarding them against U-boat attack. The wind is getting up and as the waves start to increase Lt. Davis halts all diving, it is their final attempt to gain entry and he orders Racer back into port.

Once alongside the riggers start to prepare the sweep wires on the after deck, along with the necessary buoys, which will hold them in place as each wire is swept underneath, 4 wires forward and 4 wires aft have been ordered by Lt. Davis.

On the 13th they are finally able to try and start the sweeping work. Divers have been down in the morning, making sure that the marker buoys are secure and removing any large debris from the path of the sweep wire. Once this is done they are ready to start sweeping but the weather forecast predicts it will worsen from 3 pm.

As well as ML478 there are 2 trawlers and 2 drifters patrolling 2 miles away because the location is very open to attack from German submarines.

The tug Goole No7 is alongside Racer as half of the prepared 9" sweep wire and one marker buoy, is passed over to her afterdeck.

Horace confers with the tug Captain, who is very experienced in ship handling but has no experience of this type of work. 'This is not going to be easy' says Horace, 'we are crossing the tide, with the wind behind us and we will have to stop as we reach the submarine so that the divers can go down and make sure that the wire is in the right place.' He continues. 'We will take up station, 300 yards apart, 300 yards from the stern marker buoy and then lower the wire until it lies easily on the seabed.' 'Initially, 4 of my salvage riggers will be with you because they have done this before' he finishes with.

'Good' says the Captain of the Goole, 'my crew are happy to have the assistance and I will watch your bridge for orders, this is your party and you have the experience' he finishes with.

As the 2 ships slowly drift apart, the teams on the aft decks pay out some wire, using the steam winches and then the ships slowly motor towards the start position. The first attempt at lining up fails, because the drag of the wire, the wind, the tide and the lack of experience all add up and the tug only just misses hitting one of the marker buoys.

Hitting the buoy would be a disaster because it would likely sink and then it would need to be replaced before they could start again. Another problem is that going astern too hard could pull the sweep wire into the propellers causing considerable danger and damage. Only slow astern is to be used which also restricted the available manoeuvrability. After 3 attempts, they finally get to where they need to be and the wire is lowered to the seabed 90ft below. Once this is done, they move forward in unison, until the wire starts to straighten out, which indicates that it has caught on something. Hopefully, they have caught the stern of the submarine and both ships stay at very slow ahead holding everything in place.

Now the dive boat rows to the stern buoy and despatches Diver Gohm to the seabed. The heavy swell is making his life difficult, as the dive boat moves up and down 'try and use your arms to reduce the movement' he asks his dive attendant over the phone,

'OK' is the reply and the movement reduces.

'That's excellent' says Gohm and his descent continues. As the bottom comes into view, he can see the wire wrapped around the stern but it is caught in one of the propeller blades and won't sweep under. 'Damn' he says 'tell them that the wire is caught on a propeller if they give the wire some slack maybe I can move it over the blade.'

'OK, walk away from the submarine and I will instruct them' replies his attendant.

Moving well away from the stern and the sweep wire, he turns to watch. Some minutes later, the wire lowers to the seabed on one side but the other side is still caught up. When his dive attendant gives him the all clear he leans forward and plods over. Grasping the large wire in both hands he leans back and pulls, it moves slightly but not enough and he is concerned that it will drop onto his legs. 'Can't shift it' he says 'drop me a 6ft wire strop and a crowbar lever' is his next message.

'On its way' and shortly after a line drops next to him, with the tools he has requested. Taking the wire strop he loops it around the sweep wire and then stands next to one of the other propeller blades, where he wraps the wire strop around the lever, in such a way that he can pull against the other blade in safety. At first, the arrangement keeps slipping off the polished phosphor bronze blade, so he asks next for a metal file.

Using the metal file, he manufactures a groove in the blade edge, which will hold the lever in place. Now when he pulls, the sweep wire slips over the edge and onto the floor creating a cloud of sand which soon clears. 'Done it' he shouts, returns the tools to the surface and turns to walk away.

He doesn't want to be near the wreck when they start towing but he will have to go back again and make sure the wire is in the right place under the hull.

On the ships, their propellers rotate faster and take up any slack on the lifting cable. Now they have to work even harder, pulling the wire under the submarine. At first, they do not appear to be moving, but then very slowly the forward marker buoy appears to drop astern. When Horace thinks it is far enough, he orders very slow ahead and instructs the diver to check the wire position.

'They reckon the wire is in the right place now, so can you go and have a look' says the dive attendant.

'On my way' replies Gohm, who leans forward, into the current which is starting to increase, clouds of sand from his footsteps are swirling behind him. The sea is also murky from the debris disturbed from the seabed under the submarine, as the wire was pulled under. As he draws closer it clears and he can plainly see that the wire is halfway down the submarine with one leg, almost touching the side of the leaning conning tower. 'Tell them that the wire is in perfect position and they can buoy it up where it is' he says.

'OK' says his dive attendant, 'time to get you up as the tide has turned and the swell is worse, that's probably it for today I think'. He signals the Racer to buoy the wire and starts to haul in the diver from the seabed.

Back on board, after recovering the dive boat and making their way into the harbour. Lt. Davis is talking with Diver Gohm, who is undressing from his diving suit, on the upper deck and the salvage riggers are all gathered around. 'The submarine is lying in a nice clear area, but the wire on her port side caught on a propeller blade, which I just managed to shift it past. It would be easier if the tug could be positioned farther away, which would lower the angle to the surface and hopefully then miss the blade' says Gohm.

'Ok, we will do that for the next wires' replies, Lt. Davis. 'Also we will have to tow the forward wires from the submarine bow because the wires won't go past the conning tower either which is leaning over so far, it will get in the way' continues Gohm.

Jack turns to the salvage riggers next to him and whispers 'this job is going to take a long time, everything is against us but we won't be beaten' as they are all dismissed and return to their mess deck after a long and difficult day.

After the evening meal the three friends John, Pony, and Chas, who was originally an engine room man on board, but has been recently promoted to salvage rigger from stoker, step ashore for the first time in Dunmore East, ready for a few beers to celebrate his promotion and some much-needed relaxation.

'Howay man for five days we've been waiting for the weather to clear' says Pony 'and I wonder what delights this place has in store for us like' he continues.

'That's right but at least HMS Haldon has been taken to Queenstown and the lifting barges are almost ready, so we have not wasted all of our time' is John's comment.

They walk along the long narrow sturdy stone mole, with the harbour wall on their left, protecting them from the sea. Their destination is the small town, nestling on the low cliffs to their right, overlooking the small but crowded harbour. There are still fishermen working on the many boats they pass, who nod and smile which is very encouraging. 'Where are we going' asks John?'

'I heard on board there's a place called Butchers Bar, which is the nearest place just over the hill' replies Pony 'but it's an odd name for a pub'.

'I don't care what it's called, provided we can find it and the beer is good' replies John. Five minutes later the three friends have climbed up the hill and round the incline, which exposes them to the gale which is blowing into the bay. Now they can now look down into the harbour, where RFA Racer is lying alongside with Goole No 7 and the two lifting barges nearby, along with dozens of fishing boats.

'Give over admiring the scene' says Pony 'it's along the road we need to go' and they turn up the road and round the corner past the houses, which then provide some protection from the wind. 'No sign of a pub, only some shops' he continues but as they walk on, they pass a small shop with meat hanging in the window, the last in the row on the left.

It's Chas, who is very eager to celebrate his promotion and pay rise with an evening of drinking; that puts two and two together. 'Ey up' he announces in his broad Teesside accent, 'are you coming in here, there's a bar at the back of the butcher's shop and it's heaving in there'.

Trooping through the shop, where pieces of salted meat are hanging on hooks from the ceiling, they pass into the dark smoky confines at the rear. It's actually called Powers Bar but known locally as Butchers Bar, for obvious reasons.

'Come in lads, the boozer's full but you're welcome' shouts the landlord Peter from behind the bar, 'what's your bevvies, is it shorts or three jars of plain?' he adds.

The level of noise drops, as the locals notice the strangers and the Geordie and Teesider look bemused, but of course the Scouser John is used to the Irish and says 'three jars of Arthurs please'. Then turns to his friends with his explanation,' they only sell Guinness in Ireland which is either called plain or Arthurs, after the founder of the brewery, get your dosh out Chas it's your round first.'

The locals make room for the three sailors at the bar, as their very dark beers with a white creamy top, are reverently placed in front of them.

As the noise levels return to normal, they grasp the glasses and swig back a mouthful. Although the taste is different to their normal beer, it slides easily down the throat and they are soon keeping up with the locals.

Standing next to them is a man who introduces himself,' Richie Power is my name, although everyone calls me Jos and my dad is the landlord here. I was one of the three men that rescued the Captain from the German Submarine. Are you three from the ship that is working on it?'

'We are' replies John, 'we hope to bring it into the harbour but so far the job has been far from easy. We did salvage a British submarine a few months ago but that was in a sheltered estuary, unlike here which is open to the Atlantic although perhaps I shouldn't be telling you that.'

'Don't worry' says Jos,' The Royal Navy is very welcome here and we won't be telling anyone what is going on.'

'I thought as much' replies John, 'We have been given some lovely fresh fish during our stay and that was a fine thing that you did, rescuing the Captain from the U-boat'.

Jos is pleased with John's reply, 'it's the sailor's way, you would have done the same and of course, everyone here is very happy to have the British around'.

Having settled in with the very friendly locals, the celebration of Chas's promotion could not have gone better.

As the three friends stagger back down the hill to RFA Racer, they know that they will enjoy their time in Dunmore East and will even grow to like the unusual taste of the Guinness. Nearing the ship they smarten themselves up until they have entered their mess deck, where they create a bit of a stir getting their beds ready and finally climbing into them for what was left of the night.

The next day they complete the maintenance work on the lifting barges and John is instructing Chas, on the finer points of using it despite them both suffering almighty hangovers. 'Each lifting barge is fitted with 7 watertight compartments, each of which be emptied or filled using the oil-driven 6" pumps, These can also fill and empty the 4 buoyancy compartments at each side, which we use to keep the barge level. On deck, we have 2 steam-driven winches at each end and these are used to tighten the lifting wires so that it can then be pinned into the clamps. The clamp has rollers designed to increase the hold as they take the strain during lifting. We can also use the winches and the derricks to lift pumps, hoses or other equipment on or off any wreck during recovery,' states John.

'Champion' replies Chas' and you say the forward hold is a storeroom plus the aft hold is now a small mess deck, they seem to have thought of everything, it's canny all that is'.

After this they both grab a bucket full of grease and get to work, ensuring that the pinning equipment on deck is free and easy so that it's ready for the lifting which is due any day. Chas lifts his head and looks out over the harbour, 'Ey up, all the fishing boats are leaving John, the pubs gonna be empty.'

'I think they are closing the harbour, to give us room to bring the U-boat in, we have most of the wires in place under it', replies John and they both get back to the greasing which is a messy dirty job.

A couple of days later LC1 is positioned hull down, directly over the sub, this is because its lifting tanks are now full of seawater, so the waves are lapping onto its deck and all the riggers are getting somewhat wet.

Four anchors have been carefully placed at each corner, in order to hold the barge in place and one of the Racer's boats is running around the barge, passing ropes to the riggers on board, each of these is attached to the buoy on the end of a lifting wire.

One team consisting of John, Chas, and Pony manage to lift the heavy dripping wire on to the deck, and then they lay the buoy that was supporting it to one side.

'Right' says John 'let's place the wire into the pinning mechanism and wind it around one of the winch drums.'
The other end of the lifting wire is also placed in a similar position, by another team, on the other side of the barge and John calls 'stand clear and take up the slack slowly'.

Chas who is now driving the winch drums, slowly and gently hauls the wire up from the depths, until it starts to straighten.

At this point, LC1 swivels slightly, aligning itself over the submarine and John's next command is 'keep it there and steady until the second wire is in place.'

As the teams at the other end of the barge, accomplish the same with their wire, it is clear that the sea is starting to worsen and the waves are now surging over the deck, soaking everyone's boots even more.

The Chief who has been monitoring the situation decides that enough is enough. 'Release the wires slowly, this is getting dangerous, we won't be able to pin all the wires today'. Taking up some strain on the winch, allows the pinning mechanism to be freed, and then the wire is free to slide over the side, using the winch to control it.

'Make sure the buoy doesn't take you with it as well, as you finally drop everything over the side.' Is the Chief's warning to them all. 'Once we have all the wires pinned on the barge and the load is lifted off the seabed, it is not safe to release the load, until we have it lying steadily on the seabed.' The Chief continues with, which of course is mainly for Chas's benefit because everyone else knows this already.

The two wires are dropped over the side with their buoys, and then the pumps started up, in order to empty the lifting tanks. As the barge rises up at least the waves stop breaking onto the deck. The anchors are lifted and LC1 is towed back to harbour after another fruitless day.

Two days later they are out again and this time manage to put half of the wires in place before they have to abandon the lift yet again. It's the end of yet another frustrating week for the riggers, who are changing into whatever dry clothing they can find, when there is some banter amongst them, 'So you reckon it's those dam Irish Leprechauns 'replies John to Chas.

'Of course it is; I think they want us to stay here for the rest of the war, and keep spending our money in the bars ashore'.

'The only problem with that theory is we are not actually getting ashore often, because we get in too late' replies John.

'The rumour from the boiler room is that we will need to return to Queenstown to coal soon' adds the ex-stoker and at that moment, the Chief opens the mess door and announces that they will be going to Queenstown tomorrow to coal ship. Of course, this is a right dirty job and it will create even more washing, but the men hope that the change might bring them better luck.

Early the next morning, as daylight is breaking and RFA Racer prepares to come alongside at Queenstown to coal ship, the 3 friends are up on deck because Chas wants to watch a port entry.

'As a stoker, I was always down below in the hot and smelly boiler room, and rarely had the chance to see us coming into harbour' says Chas. He stands there gazing in awe, at the approaching jetty and the surrounding countryside, which is just starting to appear, through the lovely morning light, which is slowly brightening on the horizon.

John and Pony have seen it all before, but are prepared to humour their friend, and they remember their own excitement at entering a new port for the first time.

Looking round in all directions, Chas notices a grain elevator, attached to the jetty side storehouse, which is hanging directly overhead and it is getting perilously close to the wireless aerial spreader on the foremast.

He yells 'Bridge, watch that elevator by the foremast' but as the Captain looks up the two items come into contact. Horace immediately orders 'Full astern' into the voice pipe to the engine room and the ship slowly moves away from the elevator. Fortunately, the damage is only slight and after waiting for an operator ashore, who hauls the elevator out of the way, Racer finally berths.

The Captain, of course, is very pleased to have averted major damage, to such an essential piece of salvage equipment and shouts down 'well done Rigger Abrams'.

A broad grin lights up Chas's face and his friends heartily slap him on his back. They don't realise the main reason for his happiness, is because the skipper has called him a rigger, rather than a stoker.

The rest of the morning is taken up with coaling one side of the ship, until they repair below for lunch and immediately after, the ship is swung around so that they can coal the starboard side. During this swinging process, all the lines to the tug and jetty parted which causes the Racer to bump the schooner, William Gilmore of Fleetwood, damaging her stern and upper works quite badly, although Racer is almost unharmed.

'The bad luck continues' is all John can say.

Back at the submarine the next day, it is immediately noticeable that some of the buoys, holding the lifting cables are missing. Lt. Davis appears on deck and says' apparently the steamer Farnborough was towed in, whilst we were away and they sank some of our buoys in the process. The divers will have to go down and attach new buoys to the lifting wires'.

'Will do sir' says the Chief,' ok lads, get the boats ready and I will get the divers up top'.

Lt. Davis finishes with 'I will send instructions out to all vessels to keep clear, and at least the weather seems to have improved.'

Finally, on the morning of the 9th September, the barge is finally hull down with all the lifting wires pinned to it, ready for a lift and it seems like a miracle to the riggers.

'Start the pumps 'instructs John to Chas, who always seems to be ready by any technical equipment.

'Smashing pumps on' replies Chas. Water starts pouring over the side from the barge lifting tanks, as she slowly lifts to take the strain. Added to the noise of the pump and the water discharge, is the creaks and groan from the wires, as they stretch and settle into place. The barge seems to shudder as well, but nothing stops the lift and the deck resounds to a great cheer. All on board can hardly believe their change of luck.

The tanks are empty, the pumps silent and even the wires have stopped moaning, 'why have the wires quietened' asks Chas.

'Always happens when the load is clear of the seabed' replies John, 'it's a very good sign but towing the barge, with the submarine hanging 90ft down below us won't be easy, it's still dangerous.'

The anchors, which have been holding the barge in place, are then lifted clear and the tug starts pulling the heavy ungainly load, slowly towards the western shore.

As they move forward, the wires scrape as they swing slightly to the stern 'Steady with the tow' shouts the Chief 'not too fast' and slowly the submarine moves in unison with the barge.

At the front, the Racer's steam launch is taking soundings of the seabed and they drop a small anchor attached to a buoy, at the position they guess the barge will ground. As the lifting barge approaches the buoy, the tug slows then stops, just before they reach the buoy, because they know that the submarine will ground soon and this must be done very slowly.

'Open the flood valves' shouts the Chief and as the barge settles down into the water; the wires sigh as the strain is taken from them. 'Tanks full' is his next words, 'Close the valves and we will tighten the lifting wires'.

John and Chas attend to one of the pinning points, 'See how the wire can be released now the weight is off' says John, as he turns the release pawl with a spanner, 'we couldn't do this if the wire was under strain'.

'OK, and I will get on the winch and take up the slack' replies Chas.

As evening falls the barge and submarine are settled, the anchors are in place and the lifting cables slackened off for the night.

All of the riggers return to Racer but John, Chas, and Pony have been detailed for anchor watch on the barge. After a quick meal and their rum ration on the Racer, they row over to the barge with their bedding, to take over for the night watch. 'We will take it in turn, 3 hours about, but let's get settled in first with a cuppa and some rest before we turn in' says John. Pony takes 3 pieces of paper and they draw lots for watches, whilst Chas brews up. Warmed from the small stove, good food, and the rum, they relax away from the hustle and bustle of the mess deck, sipping a good brew.

Chas is keen to know something about his new friends and turns to John, 'what did you do before the war apart from being in the Royal Naval Reserve' he asks.

'I was firefighter first, which I loved. My parents had started the Westminster Hotel in Birkenhead, but when my dad died I became the Manager for my mother' is his reply.

'That's very grand' says Pony.

'The hotel does very well' says John, 'it's actually 3 houses they bought, that have been converted to a hotel. The best part is it's just up the road from the Shipbuilder's Cammel Lairds. This keeps us busy all year but the war has increased the work, so hopefully, they are managing without me'.

'Now it's time to clear the table and get some sleep, you've got the 1st watch Pony and I've got the 2nd one, Chas the 3rd' says John 'make sure that you do rounds every 30 minutes, after all the trouble we've had so far with this salvage job, we can't afford to mess up now' he concludes.

The other 2 murmur in agreement and quite quickly all is quiet, apart from the slap of waves on the side of the barge and the gentle sounds of contented sleep, coming from the bunks in the little mess deck.

The next two days see UC-44, eleven cables closer to the shore, which will at least give them some protection from the prevailing westerly weather.

Admiralty Salvage Section Headquarters

The 3rd Sea Lord Admiral Sir Frederick Charles Tudor, calls into the office of Captain Frederick Young, looking for an update on the submarine salvage.

Captain Young answers his request as follows 'Lt. Davis has just requested the attendance of a mine expert.'

'Why is that?' asks the 3rd Sea Lord.

'They have finally started lifting the submarine and there are 9 live mines still on board, which will have to be removed, its great news and I shall send Cdr. Heaton over immediately.

'Excellent but I had hoped that it would be brought to the surface somewhat quicker than this though.' adds the impatient 3rd Sea Lord.

'I am not sure that you understand just how difficult this job is' replies Fred, 'that submarine was 90 ft. down and weighs about 500 tons. The weather has been very difficult and she was sitting right in the middle of a tidal estuary run. We have one of our best salvage teams on the job, and I am very hopeful that they will succeed, now that they have brought her closer inshore.'

'What about the other submarine UC-41 being salvaged from the Tay estuary in Scotland, we desperately need to recover one of them?' enquires the Admiral.

'That one is also progressing and we are devoting all we have into both jobs, even though there are many damaged merchant ships that we could be working on. However, I do understand how important this work is.' 'I have another notion about recovering documents because I am sure that you can see that using salvage teams in this way, is not that productive.'

'What's your idea then?' replies the Admiral.

'Why don't we set up a specially skilled diving team with the express purpose of getting inside a sunken submarine and finding those important documents?'

'Great idea and then we won't have to worry so much about the German's finding out what we are up to. I will bring it up at our next meeting and it will free up your salvage teams as well. Put together a proposal, including anyone you think suitable and I will get it approved.' continues the smiling Admiral.

'I know just the right people for that job' replies Fred who has already selected a few names, including those working in Ireland. 'I also plan to stop the salvage of the other submarine, once we get what we are after, I hope that is OK?' says Fred.

'Fine, I don't know what we would do without you.' Replies the Admiral as he departs.

Ten days later UC-44 is lying, just underneath the barge and is quite close to the shore of Dunmore East, just to the south of the harbour, in a small sandy bay ringed by low grass topped rocky cliffs. The riggers can even see the shadow of the U-boat, with the conning tower sticking out to one side. Cdr. Heaton has visited them, but there is little he can do because Lt. Davis and the riggers are coping very well. He has gone to Queenstown to wait because the salvage is going well.

John and Chas are standing on the deck of LC1, as LC2 is brought alongside, for the next stage of this delicate operation.

'What's the plan now?' asks Chas, who is always keen to learn as much as possible.

'We are going to sling the submarine between the two barges now. By lifting with only one barge, she should rotate until she's upright. Then we can bring her up between the barges and out into the air, it's called parbuckling'. 'Away man that's grand' replies, Chas.

'First, we will transfer the wires on this side over to LC2' Johns tells Chas 'That will be the easiest part, then we buoy the other wires and move this barge out and round to the other side. Finally, we pick up the wires again but on the other side, it's all complicated because the lifting wires are now a lot longer'.

For the rest of the day, they drop the huge cables over the side, which is heavy backbreaking dirty and worst of all dangerous work.

These experienced sailors are however aware of the risks and finally, before dusk, the 2 barges are lying either side of the submarine, ready for the lifts required to get her upright, which will start the next day. At the end of the day Lt. Davis sends the divers down, for a final inspection, who report that some of the lifting wires have cut badly into the hull, but hopefully, they will come clear as they rotate the submarine.

The next day as only the one barge LC2 is pumped out, to start the rotation process, a couple of the lifting wires, start to sing with the strain and its obviously the ones cutting into the hull, 'Stop the pumps, this is dangerous' shouts the Chief, 'open the sea valves and let some water in to relieve the stress on the wires' is his next command.

Lt. Davis steps over to see what's happening, 'The divers need to go down, to try levering those wires out of the hull and into an undamaged section of hull' the Chief advises and that is what happens.

All the next day the divers, attended by the riggers struggle with crowbars, levering the lifting wires, away from the damaged area and eventually they are all freed. Two lifts using just one barge; bring the submarine upright enough, for the conning tower to clear the barges. The final lift of the day brings part of the submarine conning tower, into the fresh salty air and then the whole ensemble, is finally towed into the relative safety of Dunmore East harbour.

UC-44 is now lying close to the shore, opposite the long mole, underneath the harbour cliff walls.

Lt. Davis surveys the wreck with the divers, 'Do you think you can get inside now he asks?'

To which the divers respond with 'we are happy to try again sir' and off they head to get ready. Unfortunately, the submarine is still lying at about 15 degrees and is full of water. Getting inside, wearing full suits with helmets is still impossible.

They report to Lt. Davis after their efforts and he says 'OK we will do another parbuckling lift and then a final lift so that she can be pumped out properly, which will allow us to enter without helmets. In fact, at low tide, she should be grounded, and the water will also start to drain out of the holes in the hull.'

The next day after some pumping out, the divers are able to climb down the conning tower, dressed only in their diving suits but no helmets. Carrying some portable electric lighting, it reveals the very shadowy, confined and dark interior of the control room, with one crumpled body lying in the corner. 'Send down a body bag' calls Eaglestone to the riggers who are waiting above.

When the bag is lowered to them, both he and Gohm roll the stiff body into the bag and close the ties. 'Drop a lifting rope down' is his next request and he attaches it to the rings on the bag. Then they manoeuvre the awkward package until it is under the conning tower hatch.

Up on deck, the riggers swing the barge's derrick out, until its pulley is over the conning tower and then drop the rope over onto the pulley. John looks down the deck towards the winch, where of course Chas is standing at the controls smiling and ready as always. 'Haul away slowly' he instructs Chas. As the body bag is then guided up and out into the open, the riggers all remove their caps and bow their heads.

It is a sign of respect for a fellow sailor, who has given his all, but he is also an enemy and the first one that most of them have seen. The mood has changed, and very reverently the body bag is laid onto clear deck space. Someone will have to try and identify the corpse; all are hoping that the job will not be given to them.

Down below the divers open the hatch and move into the mining compartment, remove the bodies from that area and the row of body bags mounts during the day.

The following day Cdr. Heaton returns, and takes over responsibility from Lt. Davis, although he remains to carry on his good work. Finally, the submarine is cleared of all the bodies they can find, 29 in all.[7]

It is only then that Cdr. Heaton, Captain Gauld, Lt. Davis, and the Divers start searching the interior, looking for items of importance, especially intelligence information.

Lt. Davis is the unlucky one who ends up searching the bodies, each one is tagged and any documentation or items of interest noted.

'When you do the search, please let me have any keys that you find, it may save us a lot of trouble' says Cdr. Heaton.

'Of course sir' says Davis, knowing that he is looking for the safe keys, and eventually he is able to hand over a set of keys, that look like they will do.

The riggers are sent off to the Racer, to do other work but they are well aware that their bosses are looking for intelligence, and Cdr. Heaton has briefed them not to tell a soul anything. In his briefing, he only mentioned things such as the torpedoes, mines, and periscopes, etc. Of course in the mess deck there is much talk,

---

[7] *The number of bodies recovered is very confused, John says 30, the salvage report gives 19, a website for U-boats another number etc. This type of submarine had a normal crew of 30, however occasionally they carried men for on the job training. I believe that at least 2 extra were carried on this voyage for training, which would give 32 less the 3 who escaped which leaves 29. Perhaps John's 30 includes the body of one of the escapees.*

and Sparks the radio man speculates that they are really after the German signal codebooks.

Down in the submarine they locate the safe, it's in the very small space used by the officers, and fortunately, the set of keys fit. Once open, they find inside lots of documents, and luckily there is only a small amount of water lying at the bottom of the safe, so most are only slightly damaged.

The Captain takes all of the documents to his cabin, where he and Cdr. Heaton carefully look through them. 'What are we actually looking for' asks Horace whose grasp of German is quite limited.

'Funkspruchbuch is the title they will use' replies Cdr. Heaton and lifting up the documents one by one, he reveals a really thick book, with that very title and announces 'this is what we are looking for, we have to get this to the Admiralty immediately. I need to stay to get the mines out safely, so you will have to go to London straight away Horace'. 'I will write you a short report and you will need to take an armed guard, select someone you know and can trust. He must be able to use a gun as well, you must protect this stuff and we cannot afford to lose it now, especially after all the hard work done to recover it.'

'I can leave in the hour; we should be in London by tomorrow if we go by ferry and boat train. My cabin steward can come with me, he's from London and is quite handy, so it won't look odd either' replies Horace.

'Put everything in a locked briefcase and do not let it out of your sight, this is that important' says Cdr. Heaton.
Horace replies 'you can rely on me, probably best to handcuff the case to my wrist as well.'

1.30pm the next day Horace with his steward is greeted at Paddington station, as they get off the train, by the Naval Provost. Along with two of his burly men, they are whisked into a naval staff car and driven directly to the Admiralty. They even escort them into the Admiralty building and down to the Salvage Section offices.

Before they go inside the building Horace turns to his steward, 'give the pistol to the Provost and go home, I will see you here in 24hrs and remember to tell no one, you're just here because I needed to visit the Salvage Section headquarters in the Admiralty that's all'.

'Aye aye, Sir' says the steward, who heads home, wondering what it's all about, he has heard the rumours on board but is glad of an excuse to go home and see his family.
At the Salvage Section office door, the Provost and his guard leave. As Horace enters the room he finds Captain Young, whom he knows well, the 3rd Sea Lord who he also recognises and two men in civilian clothes, who are strangers, all seated at the conference table.

Laying the heavy and full briefcase on the table, he removes the handcuffs, unlocks the case, opens it and removes the many documents. The civilians spread them around, pick up the big book which is marked Funkspruchbuch and huge grins light up their faces.

Nodding at the 3rd Sea Lord, they put all the documents into their own briefcase, smile at Horace and say 'Thank you so much' and leave.

'I can't say much' says the 3rd Sea Lord 'except that this recovery is Top Secret and must be treated as such, that includes everyone involved. Well done to you all and have a good trip back to the Racer, because I am sure there is much more to be learned, from that Submarine. Oh, and by the way, Professor McLennan of the Board of Inventions and Research, will visit the submarine in the middle of next week and is to be given every assistance.''

Of course sir' says Horace, as he rises whilst the 3rd Sea Lord takes his leave.

'Take a seat and please call me Fred' says Captain Young, 'a drink to celebrate, the sun is over the yardarm and you can tell me all about the salvage. I would have loved to have been with you but these days I don't get out much at all. After that, we can have a meal at my club.'

Horace spends the afternoon and evening, telling all he knows. Even when he thinks he has run out of facts, Fred will ask another telling question and more will be revealed.

Captain Young's final question is 'Did you receive the camera equipment, which we sent a few weeks ago; I think it is important that we record the work we do, to continue the learning process?'

To which Horace replies 'Yes we did and luckily one of my Motor Engineers, has some experience, so we will be able to let you have pictures from now on,'

At the end of a lovely meal, Fred bids him farewell and says 'Horace, your ship and crew are one of my best, keep up the good work and one day we will win this damn war, despite those U boats.

Back in Dunmore East, the work continues and after a couple of small final lifts, the U-boat is left resting right under the harbour cliff. One of the lifting barges remains alongside the wreck, holding it almost upright; this is so that they can use her lifting derricks, to remove anything required.

Standing next to the body bags John, Chas, and Pony wonder what will be done with these poor souls, at which Lt Davis appears, 'I have arranged for our faithful guard boat ML478, along with a Naval Padre to take the bodies out to sea for burial. You three men can go with them, to give a hand and act as burial party.'

'We had better change into uniform then' says John and they go back to Racer. A short time later ML478 slips into the harbour and the other riggers swing the body bags over onto her deck. Standing alongside the Padre, the three riggers, now in uniform, salute as they pass the Racer. On board, their ship, the gangway party on duty, pipe them out of the harbour. These are after all fellow mariners, who gave their all and they deserve a decent burial, although it seems strange to bury them at sea.

'Why are we doing this?' questions Chas.

John replies 'must be something to do with secrecy is my guess.' And all three nod in agreement.

It takes quite a time to add the weights to each of the 30 bags. As each bag is weighted, it is lifted up onto the burial board, and then covered with a German flag that they found in UC-44. They say the Royal Naval prayer over each one, and then with as much dignity as possible, consign the poor soul to the deep. Lifting the inboard end of the board allows the bag to slide out from under the flag, over the side and into the depths. Having travelled over 15 miles out to sea, before starting the burial, the sun has set and it is almost midnight before they finally return.

The sombre group of 3, stand together as they journey back, Pony saying ' I don't want to do that again in a hurry' and who could disagree with that sentiment.

Removal of the mines is started the next day, with Cdr. Heaton briefing them on what is required. This is following his survey of the sub's mine delivery system. 'The mine is carried in a cradle on these 4 arms', as he points down inside the mine delivery tube, whose top hatch is now open, 'we need to strop each of them to a lifting eye, which we will use to pull up directly. The 4 horns that you can see, must be protected at all times, the mine probably won't detonate if you break one, but we shouldn't take the risk. Who is the best man on the winch?' he asks, and of course, they all look at Chas, who nods his acceptance of their choice.

'I need 3 men to go down into the sub and operate the release mechanism' and he takes these men down to show them the levers on the side of the tube, inside the mine room. Once everyone is in place, with the davit poised directly overhead and the lifting rope attached, he orders 'take the strain but gently' and Chas operates the winch until Cdr. Heaton signals stop.

'Release the 3 catches' is his next order, shouted down into the fore hatch and they can see the small pawls, on the inside of the tube rotate.

'The catches are released' echoes up from below to the deck above.

'Haul away slowly' is his next order and gradually the mine slides up the tube and slowly reveals itself, in all its menace. Once the mine is hanging clear, the davit is swung around, until it is over the deck of the barge, and is lowered onto the prepared clearing on the surface.

'Hold it there' he orders, 'now we must remove the horns, Foulkes come here and watch' and he takes a spanner, slides it onto the hexagonal base and starts turning it. Slowly the horn is unscrewed out of the casing, and as it comes free, he cradles it in one hand, so that the now visible wires at the bottom are accessible. 'Cut those wires' he instructs John, who carefully snips through the cables with his pliers, and once that is done, the horn is put carefully to one side. 'Ok, your turn now and Moore can have the cable cutters'.

John then carefully does the same to the other 3 horns.

'You can carry on now Chief, removing the rest of the mines from the tube; the next one will be a bit harder because it's much farther down but shouldn't be a problem. If you have any difficulties, I will be in the wardroom' and he departs to leave the riggers at work removing all the rest of UC-44 deadly cargo.

John notices whilst they are working, that Motor Engineer Victor Pearson, is taking some pictures of their work. At lunch break, he manages to have a quiet word with him. 'I see you are taking pictures of our work, is that naval camera equipment?' he asks.

'It is, we are going to photograph, as much of our work as possible from now on, for training purposes.'

'That's a good idea' says John, 'will you need any help, because I have a little knowledge about photography and I am keen to learn?' and so develops a relationship, where John is able to help with the work, and at the same time, collect many small pictures of their work. It also becomes a habit, to write some information on the back of each picture, using his very neat handwriting.

By the middle of the next day, all 9 mines are safely clear of the U-boat and are then loaded onto HMS Snowdrop, along with 2 torpedoes. These have been removed, from the forward tubes, and all of this weaponry is to be delivered to the Naval Mine warfare people in Portsmouth.

The submarine is now clear and relatively safe, so a more thorough search takes place, and the items found are stored in temporary boxes, for Cdr. Heaton to review. Into one large box, he puts the most interesting parts, making a list of them and then turns to Chas, who did such a good job on the winch and says. 'These 3 items are full of methylated spirits and I believe you were a stoker on here, so you will know where to dispose of the contents. Once they are empty, put them in this box, with this list inside and seal it up, be as quick as you can, because they are being collected in an hour.'[8]

'Of course, Sir, nay problem' and Chas heads below, carrying the odd-looking brass flasks, two of which look just like brass bottles and a 3rd which is much more elaborate, having handles on both sides. The methylated spirit is soon disposed of, but as he returns from the boiler room, he slips into his mess and slides the two that look like bottles, into the bottom of his locker.

On deck, glancing around, he makes sure that no one is looking, puts the remaining flask into the crate and with a pencil from his pocket, crosses out the number three and strikes a number one.

The altered paperwork then goes on top, and the box lid is quickly screwed down tightly, just as Cdr. Heaton arrives, with a driver to collect the boxes.

'Excellent work' he says to Chas 'would you mind helping this man get the boxes into his van'.

Of course, Chas is delighted to help and is already planning how to make use of his ill-gotten gains.

That night ashore in the Butchers Bar, where the locals are always so welcoming, both Pony and John can sense that Chas is up to no good. He has ordered three pints straight away and is talking in whispers to the landlord, out of earshot, at the far end of the bar. They do notice a smallish cloth-covered package, go over the bar, which the landlord inspects out of sight. Looking very

---

[8] There is no record of who took these items ashore, but Chas was an ex stoker and would know how to dispose of the contents.

pleased, he nods his head in agreement and goes into the private area at the rear.

Chas wanders back down the bar to them, picks up his pint looking extremely pleased with himself, and takes a great gulp saying 'drink up lads, there more where this comes from'.

'Have you paid?' asks Pony.

Chas replies with a grin, 'Sort of, the beers are on me tonight' and they settle down to a long session, with many beers being served, but no payment apparently being made.

On the way back the 2 friends are intrigued, they have had a great night and everybody is happy, but eventually, Chas reveals the truth. How he stole the 2 round flasks and brought one of them ashore tonight to sell.

'But those are incendiary devices' says John.

'Yes I know but I sold it as a hot water bottle, it will work like a hot water bottle and they don't know any better. Apparently, there is a market ashore, for mementos of UC-44, so we need to find other items because we now have a great contact. 'What do you think the incendiary device would be used for anyway' asks Chas finally, realising he may have gone too far.

'My guess is that they would open the top, reverse the mesh insert, set fire to the liquid and then splash it over all documents. In this way, they would destroy them, but of course, they had no time when she sank.'

'They won't be that interested in my items then, it's those documents they wanted, so we can carry on selling without worrying' and at that, the friends relax.[9]

---

[9] *The Imperial War Museum has in their collection one incendiary device, item MUN240 which is the one he left in the box. The other 2 are still in private hands in Dunmore East Ireland. The current owner of one of these is now aware that they were not actually hot water bottles. The use of stoneware and brass hot water bottles was quite common at that time, amongst those who could afford them.*

Work continues removing any interesting parts, such as the periscopes and the deck gun along with its ammunition. Visits take place, from the Queenstown Admiral and other interested parties, but the crew of "Racer" start to get restless because no one can decide what to do with the hull.

The Sea Lords meeting, on the submarine threat, takes place in London on 17 October 1917.

Present:

Sir Eric Geddes, First Lord of the Admiralty.

1st Sea Lord, Admiral Sir John Jellicoe.

2nd Sea Lord, Admiral Cecil Burney.

3rd Sea Lord, Admiral Sir Frederick Charles Tudor.

Director of Naval Intelligence, Rear Admiral Roger Welles Jr.

Director of the Intelligence Division, Captain Reginal (Blinker) Hall Room 40.

Salvage Section Head, Captain Frederick Young Royal Navy Salvage Section.

'Could you give me an update on that most important item recovered from UC-44 please Roger' asks Sir Eric.

'We have had the codebook for a few weeks now and I am very pleased to report, that they are still using this codebook. The information we are gathering, from reading their messages is absolutely vital and extremely useful. Rerouting the convoys is also I am glad to say, working well.

In fact, the recovery of this codebook; is the most important breakthrough, in the naval war against U-boats and nothing should be done to jeopardise that. Our biggest concern is that the German's will find out that that we have this item, and I must insist that the wreck be disposed of as soon as possible, take it to sea and sink it.'

'Excellent' says Sir Eric who turns his attention to the 3rd Sea Lord and Captain Young. 'Can you take that submarine out to sea and drop it out of sight?'

The 3rd Sea Lord looks at Captain Young who says, 'We can take the submarine out and hopefully sink it, but please realise that the equipment we are using, is designed to lift wrecks up from the seabed. It is not designed to drop them at all.
We believe that it can be done, but could take quite a long time; maybe it will take longer to sink than to salvage.

Also, we are waiting for an expert, sponsored by the 2nd Sea Lord to visit the wreck, for final intelligence gathering.'

'That is Professor McLennan, who is leaving today and will probably need until the end of the month,' replies Cecil Burley.

Roger Welles, also adds some more information, 'you should be aware, that there are many other documents from that submarine, there is a complete list of U-boat Commanders, which is most useful in understanding those that are operating most effectively, lots of technical information, and much more, again I must stress how vital it is that this U-boat disappears quickly.'

Sir Roger ponders the various arguments for a while then says, 'this is a difficult decision you leave me with, but as the U-boat has already been in view for some time, we will wait for the Professor's visit, which is quite important. Then I would like you to take her out to sea and sink as quickly as possible, thank you, gentlemen.'

The intelligence men present are not happy, especially about the delay, but at least they will be taking her out to sea to dump her.

Fred also is thoughtful, as he ponders how his team, are going to achieve such a difficult task but he will find a way, and he has confidence in the Racer and her crew.

Lt. Davis has returned from London, where he has tried unsuccessfully, to get the authorities to change their minds, on the disposal of UC-44, he gathers the riggers in their mess deck. 'I know you are all just as frustrated as I am, but we have our orders now and carrying them out, is not going to be easy using this equipment. You must believe me when I tell you we have no alternative. I told them that the wreck had been in full public view for 2 weeks but this advice was ignored. Using the lifting barges in reverse, to drop the wreck will require ingenuity because as you know once we have a pin, the only way to release the wire, is to have some slack on it but I believe we can do it.' The riggers simply nod their agreement, glad of the prospect of finishing the job.

They have been waiting in the lovely welcoming Dunmore East, for too long and feel that their contribution to the war effort could be more, so it is time to finish this job for once and for all.

On the 2nd October, John's mother dies and he has been refused leave. He sits down to write, what is a really difficult letter to Jessie, who of course is very busy with their children and especially his new and very young daughter Jessie.

As the eldest now because his older brother died in 1916, it falls to him to try and sort out this mess. On his father's death in 1909 his mother had taken over the running of the hotel and now he would have to look elsewhere. His revered Norwegian Father in Law had also died in 1905, so the logical course was to arrange for his Mother in Law, Ellen Anderson to take over the hotel for him. Fortunately, she was already involved in running it and they could do the paperwork required, using the postal system.

What a mess this war creates for us all, he thinks with a very sad heart as he finishes writing.

It is the end of November, back at the Admiralty, and Fred is holding the UC-44 salvage report in his hands as he discusses the job. 'I told you, Charles, it would be difficult to do, but my men have finally got UC-44 out of sight, although it is still quite close to the harbour.'

'The intelligence people tell me the codebook is still being used, so we can now breathe easier, and the Sea Lords intend to make some awards for this work. They will be citing the recovery of the mines as the reason, the 2 officers involved plus one of the divers will get awards, but can you give me the name of one of the riggers please, for a Mention in Despatches.'

Fred looks him quizzically in the eye and says 'I will get Lt. Davis to pick out one man, but I assure you Charles, that this work by RFA Racer, deserves far more than this paltry award, listen to this.' And he picks up the salvage report, turns the pages and reads, 'I am pleased to report to you, respecting the goodwill and loyalty, in which all on board RACER have helped in this work, which at times was extremely arduous, a better crew could not be found.'[10]

He pauses so that his boss can take in his words, and then continues, 'we will leave the wreck where it is, the weather is steadily worsening as winter approaches, and I need "Racer" working on other wrecks, which is what she is doing now.'

'I know you are not best pleased, but the fact is, that this work is as secret as it can get. It is vital for the war effort and we must press on. Those men have done something amazing, but they

---

[10] *RECOGNITION OF THEIR WORK*
List of Medal Awards for the work on UC-44:-
'For skill and bravery shown in recovering mines.'
Acting Cdr. Gervase W Heaton RN bar to DSO.
Lt. George Davis RNR DSC.
Petty Officer Frank Pegrome Eaglestone DSM.
Rigger William McDonald Mentioned in Despatches.
I firmly believe that the award was for the recovery of the code books but they could not say this at the time, the mine recovery had some importance but not that much.
Lt. Davis in one of his reports, actually states that the mines were removed by the Salvage Riggers.
The photograph in this book and others that I have seen, only show the Salvage Riggers doing this work.
Medal awards for the men are quite often only given to one man, but are earned by a group of men; this was and still is the way of things, there were 2 divers involved but only one got a medal.
During WW1 the Royal Fleet Auxiliary, were awarded very few medals and something as simple even, as a Mention in Despatches was rare for this section of the Royal Navy.

will probably never know what they have achieved, which is a great shame but it must remain so, perhaps someday the facts will be revealed, but until then we must press on.'

Charles then leaves the room, content in the knowledge, that he has successfully crossed a very rickety bridge, and that the Salvage Section will continue its excellent work.

(Some Terminology used:
Pinning= Securing lifting wires to lifting barge after stretching.
Lift = Water being pumped out of a lifting barge so that it lifts a wreck, which is then towed to shallower water and then grounded again. The effect of the tide can also be used to achieve a greater lift.
Parbuckling lift = A method of rotating a wreck by lifting with one barge and sometimes dropping with the other one.)

SS Antwerpen

RFA Racer is leaving Dunmore East[11] for the final time, on her way to Queenstown, in order to pick up her own divers and some equipment. The harbour wall at Dunmore East has a big crowd on it, the locals are here to see them off and every one of the Racer's crew, who can be spared, is on deck.

'See those ladies over there' says Chas.

'What that group of three that seem to be crying' replies John.

'Yes, some of the lads have been very friendly with them, if you know what I mean' says Chas with a wink.

'Well the people here have been very welcoming and kind to us' says Pony and he adds 'whatever was going on, is none of your business Chas and you selling those mementoes was no better.'

At this, the three friends laugh, and both Chas and Pony, are happy to see that John is getting back to normal, after the shocking news about his mother.

Once berthed at Queenstown, they collect their missing divers and then depart because the local salvage company is now managing very well on their own. This area no longer needs the Racer's help so it's off to Plymouth for them.

---

[11] You may think that the recovery of the codebook is the end of the U-boats. Some U-boats however did not use their radio so much, these were always the greatest threat and of course the German's were still laying many mines. Added to this the salvage section has been concentrating on recovering a U-boat and all this time the volume of wrecks has been growing.

Alongside in Plymouth docks, there is some new pumping equipment waiting for them on the Jetty. This is loaded onto the decks, in its crates and the Motor Engineers then take over, unpacking the items and preparing them for use.

The chief then calls the riggers, 'up on deck men, Chalky White the Motor Engineer is going to explain how to use the new pumps and we can have a practice.'

On deck Chalky explains, 'welcome to the new submersible pump, it is powered by this motor generator set, which is mounted on a small raft' as he points at a small petrol engine, which is connected to a generator and mounted on a small oblong frame fitted with lifting eyes at each corner.

Holding up the cable, which is connected to the generator he displays a large plug and says,' the cable connects to the pump using this 3 pin plug and socket, it is not waterproof, so make sure you keep it out of the water'.

Pointing at the other item, a large drum-like circular pump, which is connected at one end to a discharge hose he goes on, 'unlike all our other pumps, this one is dropped down into the water until it rests at the bottom of the compartment.

The inlet has its own filter at the bottom of the pump and you simply use ropes to lower the complete arrangement into the water. The discharge hose takes the water up and over the side to get rid of it'.[12]

He pauses as the riggers take it all in and then continues. 'On the raft here is the on/off switch and gauges, which show when the generator is producing enough electricity, any questions?'

At which Chas raises his hand and says 'are you telling us, that we are dropping an electric motor into seawater, surely that is dangerous and won't work'.

---

[12] *This is one of the most important pump developments for use at sea; portable pumps are used to remove water from compartments, today almost all of these are submersible types using the same principles. See: Figure 9 Submersible pump being maintained after use.*

'This is a very extraordinary motor that has been invented by the Scotsman WR McDonald. It uses a special type of electricity, which creates a rotating magnetic field and this turns a special rotor inside the pump. You don't need to concern yourselves with that; however, there are a couple of things you need to be careful about. Do not operate the motor until this gauge here steadies on the green line.

Also only run the pump when it is in water, otherwise it will overheat and finally if the pump starts making a funny vibrating noise you are to stop it straight away. I will demonstrate the noise you may hear which is quite distinctive.'

The salvage riggers are dubious about all this, but help Chalky who they really like, to drop the motor over the side and then secure the discharge hose. 'Another attribute of this pump is that you do not need to secure it before use, which makes it so much quicker to use. Also, it will empty a compartment in one go, this is because it pushes the water up rather than sucking it up,' continues the genial Chalky. 'Start the generator' says Chalky and of course, Chas immediately steps in, starts swinging off the starting handle and the motor burst into life.

'Voltage at the correct level' shouts Chas and throws the switch to start the pump. Slowly water starts to jet over the side and quickly there is fast flow. Surprising every one of them, the entire submersible pump just sits in the water below gently humming away.

Chalky goes to the control panel and removes one of the fuses, immediately the pump emits an odd rumbling vibration. Although the flow decreases, it does continue and Chalky shouts 'that is the noise you don't want and you must stop the pump straight away or it will overheat. Now stop the motor and we can retrieve the pump.'

Once the pump is lying on the deck, the engineers start stripping it down, because the bearings need greasing every time it is used. They also check that there is no debris in the pump, and this John's opportunity to take a photograph of Chalky with everything in pieces because he is fascinated by this amazing new equipment.

Racer armed with this new pump then heads to Falmouth, but on arrival there, they are almost immediately ordered to Penzance, where the SS Antwerpen is lying beached after a torpedo attack.[13]

She is heavily laden with coal, which is destined for Rouen and now all of her holds are full of water as well. At high tide, only her superstructure is visible to them, as they arrive late in the afternoon of 22nd Nov.

Anchored just off her, is HM Drifter Moss which has been busy removing coal, from her No1 hold using a grab. They have been ordered to lighten her by Acting Cdr. George J Wheeler RNR Salvage Officer, who is in charge of this operation.

After carrying out a diver's examination, they know that the ship has sustained a large hole on her port side, 47 feet long by 17 feet deep, which even goes under the bilge keel and she is lying on a hard sandy bottom.

There are cracks to the side plating, which go through the No 2 hatch combing, with the damage extending across the deck, to 6 feet from starboard bulwarks, the ship is almost split into 2 halves.

For the next 2 days, the riggers place salvage pumps, in Nos 1, 3, & 4 holds, which at least controls the water level.

The engine room however then fills with water, because the top of the stokehold at No2 bulkhead gives way. Whilst they are pumping some more water out, during the AM low water on 24th Nov, further complications arise.

'Sir, look at this' says John and when the salvage officer comes over, he sees that the vessel appears to be flexing, 'looks

---

[13] *Guidance from Captain Young resulted in the Royal Navy, issuing instructions to all ships Captains.*
They were told to head for the nearest shallow water after an attack, where damage occurred to the ship. This is because salvage is only really possible in shallow water.

like the two halves of the ship are moving independently'
continues John.

'Stop pumping immediately' orders the salvage officer.
'We will need to support the fracture in the hull down below, by
fitting strengthening beams and probably make a shield to go
across the hole. I will ask the dockyard for a shipwright team and
in the meanwhile, our divers can fit some strengthening beams. We
can also try and remove some coal from the other holds so that
there is less weight at each end of the ship' is his final comment.

A naval working party is requisitioned from Devonport,
consisting of 1 officer and 30 men, who arrive on 25/11/1917 and
are engaged in unloading coal at low water, straight into the barge
St David and the Collier Treleigh.

Divers are down each day, checking the hull and on the 30th
Nov report that the tide has started scouring sand from under the
bow. The removal of the coal; is necessary to reduce the hull
stresses, but the extra buoyancy then creates another problem.

Any slight swell results in the ship flexing, thus other
cracks start to appear in the foredeck, on the starboard side. This
now requires stiffening with structure channel bars, which are
bolted across the fracture.

By 3rd Dec the scouring under the bows gets worse and
there is a hole in the seabed under the ship, some 15 feet deep. It
runs from the bow, extending almost one-third of the ship's length
and she is now in great danger of breaking in half.

The shield that is being manufactured, to cover the
damaged area is finally ready on the evening of 3rd Dec, with the
intention that Racer will fit it to the side of Antwerpen, the
following day. They will start pumping, the day after that but
unfortunately, the wind changes direction to SSW and then
increases during the day to a moderate gale, as the barometer rises.

The riggers are standing by the next day, in the freshening
wind ready at 9 AM, ready to put the shield in place, but they all
know it is too windy.

'Forget the shield' says the salvage officer, 'get the
pumping equipment off the wreck and stand by at the mooring

ropes, we may need to let go quickly. I fear the ship is going to snap in two and there will be very little warning.'

Chas, Pony and John, clamber over onto the deck and start to sling one of the many pumps on deck, back over to the "Racer".

'Can you feel the deck flexing?' asks John and his two friends nod in agreement.

'Look over at the crack, it is opening and closing, so we don't have long' says Pony.

By midday, they have recovered most of the equipment, apart from 2 pumps, some hoses, and electric cables. The cracks are widening and closing even more with the swell. The deck is moving and groaning in time with the motion. Significantly the wind is increasing all of the time, which will only increase the swell.

'Everybody off' shouts the Chief, 'that crack has widened to over 2 feet now and it's not safe, quickly now'. As the last man climbs onto the Racer's deck, safe and sound he shouts 'Slip fore and aft' and as the two vessels drift apart, the bridge manoeuvres Racer to a safe distance, where they can all watch. Shortly after, there is a loud 'Crack' and the mainmast on the wreck breaks and falls onto the bow, and the bow then drops down by about 10ft.

'She's broken completely in half' says Pony 'that's really done for her now.' He is looking quite sad, to see a ship go to her watery grave and all their hard work come to nothing.
A day and a half later, the gale has blown itself out and as they steam towards the wreck, it is clear that even more damage has occurred. Much of the wooden fittings, that were around the bridge and the bridge itself are no longer visible. They have been swept away, by the waves crashing over her and the bows are even further down.

Climbing over the slanting deck, towards the 12" steam pump, still sitting on her, John can see it is quite damaged, the stop valve hand wheel is completely missing and its spindle is bent. As well as that 3 of the shackles, on the pump's wooden bed are no longer to be seen. 'It's quite damaged but we can probably fix this one ourselves.' shouts John. 'Get me two slings and put the derrick top overhead, whilst I disconnect the pump from its hoses' he continues.

Meanwhile, Chas is organising the removal of the 8" submersible pump nearby, 'the cable is damaged and the connection has been under water since the mast fell, let's lift the pump out of the hold and have a look at it.'

The pump is ok but the cable needs repairing and that is a job beyond their capability. The insulation has been ripped open and seawater is now inside the cable.

'Quite a few of the hoses have been also been flattened in places' reports John.

The Chief replies, 'put them to one side because they will need pressure testing before we can use them again'.

After recovering all their vital salvage equipment, a diver carries out an examination and reports that ship has broken in two, immediately over the old fracture. The starboard side of the ship forward; also has another clean break, under the port bilge, although one or two sections of plating might be holding still. All the remaining coal from No2 hold has also been washed out.

Both sections of the vessel have dropped from amidships, about 10 feet and the decks are now covered by seawater at all states of the tide.

Extensive scouring is going on under the keel, along the starboard side and it is deep enough for a diver, to walk right under the bilge.

The salvage officer gathers the riggers together, 'to salve the after portion as it is now lying, it would be necessary to discharge some bunker coals, and in view of weather conditions, it is doubtful if this could be done. The bow portion would also require lifting, after discharging her cargo.

Taking into consideration the exposed position and the extensive scouring, it is not possible to say what would occur, whilst we make those preparations.

I think that the best thing is, either to sell the wreck or to offer salvage work to a private company, on a percentage basis. In view of the uncertainty of the weather conditions and the difficult nature of the work, this salvage operation is abandoned. You will be better employed elsewhere.'

'Our first failure' comments Pony.

But of course Chas has to have the last word, 'we saved a lot of coal, which is being rationed and I don't think anyone could have done better or tried harder than we did.'

At which Cdr. Wheeler turns to them all and says 'absolutely correct and there are plenty of other ships, needing our help' and of course Chas stands their beaming, as they all cheer up, their reputation is intact.

USS Armenia

Meanwhile, USS Armenia is torpedoed on 5th December 1917, in the English Channel but manages under her own steam, and with the assistance of local tugs, to get into Dartmouth harbour, where she is beached at Kingswear.

Her cargo consists of 3212 tons of flour in bags, along with 2566 tons of wheat in bulk, which is needed urgently to feed the British population.

Initially, Lt. Gauld RNR Assistant Salvage Officer arrives to take charge, and his first action is to borrow a twin 4" submersible pump and place it in the engine room, where it easily controls the leakage. The pump belongs to Devonport Dockyard and was being used on the SS David Lloyd George which is also at Dartmouth after salvage.

Straight away a Mr. Hosegood visits because he represents the Landed Grain Committee of Bristol. 'You must understand' starts Hosegood 'that this food is urgently needed and the priority is to unload the ship, before any salvage work takes place, if at all possible.'

'Of course, Sir' replies Gauld 'we could salvage the ship without removing the cargo, but we will do as you ask, although some work may be required, in order to stabilise the wreck, so that anyone removing the cargo is safe.'

'Excellent' says Mr. Hosegood' I am also very concerned that the water will damage the grain and flour, so removal first is the absolute priority' and he takes his leave.

RFA Racer along with Cdr. Wheeler arrives on the 9th December at 10.30pm and the next day, at first light, the divers survey the wreck.

Whilst this is going on, the riggers place a 12" steam pump, over No 5 hold and start pumping out as best they can.

The divers report that the torpedo caused a hole on the port side of No 5 hold, some 38' 0' long by 18' 0' deep, on a section of the hull, where there is a curvature of the ship's side of approximately 5' 0'. There is also only a wooden bulkhead, separating No 5 hold from the after peak stores and freezing rooms, so in consequence, these are also flooded.

The side of the shaft tunnel, which houses the main shaft from the engines to the propeller, is also badly damaged. There is leakage through this tunnel and its bulkhead into No 4 hold, with some grain in there being damaged. Leakage is also happening through a watertight door and the shaft gland into the engine room.

Cdr. Wheeler orders the necessary timber and stores for effecting temporary repairs, from HM Dockyard Devonport, which arrive on the 12th December.

Two large pitch pine beams, 12" x 12" x 17' 0" long, are secured vertically across the hole inside the hull, and attached to the ships side plating, using 1" bolts. Then 18 pitch pine planks, 12" x 6" x 38' 0" long, are worked to suit the shape of the ship's side. These are secured at each end by two 1" bolts with nuts and washers, through the ship's plating and with similar bolts, through the 12" vertical baulks. These planks are then stiffened from the inside, using vertical iron straps, 3" x ¾" x 6' 0", which are fastened with 1" bolts through the planks. The seams between the planks are caulked with oakum, filled with tallow, and then covered with strips of canvas which are held in place with narrow battens, making it practically watertight. The patch is also shored up with timber on the inside and the lower part is filled with about 3 tons of cement, to ensure complete water tightness.

The vertical beams and 13 of the planks; are fitted underwater by the divers, which means a considerable amount of underwater work, drilling holes then fitting and bending the planks.

In the shaft tunnel a considerable quantity of grain, about 20 tons, has found its way inside. The removal of two of the tunnel covering plates; that had been distorted by the explosion, enables the grain to be removed and then the plates are bolted in place using 200 new bolts. Using some wedges along with cement, they then make this watertight and also secure the spare tail shaft, which had been blown loose.

The bulkhead between Nos 4 & 5 holds; is efficiently shored with twenty 6" x 6" pitch pine baulks and made watertight.

Cdr. Wheeler then leaves because the ship is almost stable, leaving Lt. Gauld to take charge.

He gathers the riggers round for a briefing, 'the ship is now almost watertight, but we have been instructed to unload her as soon as possible, in order to save her cargo, which is urgently required.' The riggers nod in agreement, they all know that food is in short supply and they all have families at home. 'I cannot get a working party to unload her, and am hoping that you will volunteer for this urgent work, what do you say?'

'Let's get on with it, we will all volunteer' exclaims Pony and everybody is behind him, even though they have already been working as hard as possible for the last few days. They are very tired but eager to help.

'Split up into teams of 4' says the officer' one team will remove the grain using pumps. Another team will put on waders and go down into the hold to remove the bags of flour whilst the 3rd team will carry on with the repairs.'

To remove the bulk grain, they make a sieve from some wire mattresses, which are found ashore and pump the water, containing the wet grain from No 5 hold, through this contraption, in order to separate it. This arrangement does not work that well, so they then build a large wooden box, with many holes in the bottom, which is laid on top of the grain. The box is filled with the grain and water mixture and the water then drains away. Now they can fill tubs with the grain and winch it up and then ashore.

The grain is kept covered with water as much as possible, on the advice of Mr. Hosegood. To achieve this, the diver's remove 2 plugs in the patch and so the grain is turned out in good condition, although wet.

On 14th January, the patch is sufficiently secured for the vessel to be taken from the mud and to lie afloat at some buoys. During the planking up of the ship's side, the team of 4 men from Racer who have been nicknamed "the flour men"; are down in No 4 hold, with wading dresses breaking out bags of flour, doing excellent work for 16 days and 3 nights.

On the 23rd January, the other riggers are urgently called to the SS Admiral Cochrane, which has just arrived in the harbour and is looking like she will capsize, so everyone except "the flour men" leave to assist her.

On 4th February, the USS Armenia is inspected by Mr. Morgan, who is the District Superintendent of Ship Repairs, Mr. Bell the Board of Trade Surveyor of Plymouth and Mr. Parsons the acting Lloyds agent in Dartmouth. They issue a seaworthy certificate for the vessel, approving her to proceed to West Hartlepool, for permanent repairs.

A 12" steam pump along with a 2" Worthington pump, are left on board and Lt. Gauld, Salvage Officer goes with her. She is accompanied by a powerful trawler as an escort, which can be also be used as a tug if necessary. This time they have saved the ship along with her precious cargo and so another success is chalked up to the Racer.

SS Admiral Cochrane

SS Admiral Cochrane, bound from Portland to New York, via Plymouth in ballast, is torpedoed at 3.20pm on 22nd January 1918.

With the help of the Torpedo Destroyer HMS Opossum, 2 local tugs, Verne of Dartmouth and Dencade of Brixham her Master successfully enters Dartmouth harbour under his own steam.

The torpedo has struck on the port side badly damaging Nos 4 & 5 holds, fragments also being blown through the starboard side and the main deck. The hole in the port side is approximately 36ft. long by 23 ft. deep extending right under the bilge. Sitting extremely stern down, the draft of the vessel is 7 feet forward but a massive 34 feet 6 inches aft.

It is almost low water, about 6.45 pm when they enter Dartmouth, the stern unsurprisingly takes the bottom off Kettery Point and one bow anchor is let go under orders from the local pilot. The vessel then takes a list of 12 degrees to port with soundings on her starboard side being 30 feet and on her port side 66 feet. Then heavy leakage takes place into No 6 hold and her engine space, causing these compartments to become flooded, such that as the tide rises the after part of the vessel becomes covered at high water and the list increases even more.

Lt. Gauld RNR, assistant Admiralty Salvage Officer, who is engaged on completing salvage operations of USS Armenia at Dartmouth, orders RFA Racer alongside Admiral Cochrane where she is made fast on her port quarter at 9.15 pm on 23rd January.

Once all the wires are in place the Riggers gather round the salvage officer for further instructions, 'Let's get an 8" submersible pump into the engine room immediately' Lt. Gauld orders.

It is getting very dark now but using the deck lights of the Racer, they sling the pump over and down below in double time and this at least manages to control the leakage into that compartment.

'I also need a temporary wooden bulkhead built in the shelter deck, between Nos 5 and 6 holds, No 6 hold is filling with water from No 5 hold and we need to stop that as quickly as possible' is his next instruction so the remaining riggers, divers and the shipwrights get to work, but it takes the rest of the night and all the next day.

All this time the work just gets harder and harder, the deck angle continues to grow and by the time they are finished, the list is an alarming 29 degrees. Everyone is slipping and sliding on the wet metal decks, the greatest fear is that she will capsize and block Dartmouth Harbour entrance completely.

Captain Young their boss has managed to get out of his office for once and is at Fishguard in South Wales, on his way back from an important visit to the Scilly Islands. He telegraphs instructions to Lt. Gauld, to obtain barges or other craft and connect up with tackles to the mastheads; this will act as a counterpoise and prevent the vessel from capsizing.

Cdr. Wheeler has also been diverted back from his trip north and arrives back at Dartmouth at 3.45pm. Captain Young then arrives at 4.35pm on the same day, the 24th which is all much to Lt. Gauld's great relief.

Immediately they order the Racer onto the wreck's starboard side, then a 6" wire is put over the hull and connected to the mainmast. Holding this in place with a heavy purchase they haul the two ships together.

Captain Young watches as his team from Racer, carry out his instructions quickly and efficiently. There is no hesitation, only some general guidance from the Chief.

This work is very impressive; however, he is not convinced that they have done enough yet to save her from capsizing. 'OK men that should hold her for the next tide but we are not out of the woods yet. Get some rest now because as soon as the lifting craft I have ordered arrives from Portsmouth, we need to connect her to the wreck as well.'

A few hours later the riggers are called, but there are no grumbles even though most are yawning. They dress and muster on the lifting craft with the Captain. 'We will put the lifting craft between the wreck and the shore; then fill the tanks with water to hold it in place. The stern of the craft can then be anchored to the shore and we will drop anchors to hold the bow. Having created a stable platform, we can connect some cables to the ship with tackles, and then heave her upright'.

Again they rush off carrying out his wishes. As the morning light breaks, they are finally ready to start and each tackle has 2 men on it ready to pull. 'All together heave' he shouts and every man bends to the task, and slowly the wires tighten and take the strain.

'Stop heaving' is his next order and he turns to Cdr. Wheeler, 'that's enough strain for the moment, it will hold the vessel but we need to lighten the load, what else can we remove quickly?'

'How about removing the 160 tons of coal in the port shelter deck because it's safe enough to go there now.' replies Wheeler.

'Good idea' says Young and the riggers set to on the sloping deck, shovelling all the coal out and into baskets to be slung ashore. 'OK men, now we have lightened the port side we can try pulling her over, so let's get back to the tackles.'

By mid-low water, the list is down to 25 degrees and by low-water, its 21 degrees, with the main deck hatches for Nos 4 and 5 hold now clear of the water. 'Thank you, men, for your supreme efforts; please go and get some food, whilst I organise the shipwrights to batten and caulk the hatches. Then you can come back and repair the holes where fragments from the explosion have blown through.'

As the riggers leave, he turns to Cdr. Wheeler and says, 'Please could you get the Captain of Racer to clear lower deck for me when the riggers have eaten, I need to go back to London shortly and will leave you to finish off, but I would like to say a few words before I go.'

'Of course sir' replies Wheeler who goes to find Racer's Captain.

Standing on deck with almost the whole ship's company assembled, the riggers look up to see Captain Young step out onto the bridge wing and smile at them all. 'Before I go I thought I would take the opportunity to speak to you all. The salvage work you are doing is extremely important for the war effort and I want you to know that.

In my office, I read all the salvage reports and every single one about this ship is very complimentary. The quality of the work you do, the effort you put in and your attitude is all first-rate. I have now seen this for myself and I congratulate you all on doing such an excellent job, often in very trying conditions.

I am proud to be the leader of such a fine department and so should you be, well done and please keep it up.'

Everybody smiles as Captain Young takes his leave and it is the Chief who breaks the spell, 'back to work you lazy lot, we aren't finished yet, there will be no resting on our laurels here, there is, after all, a war to be won', at which they all laugh and head off back to the wreck.

It takes until 1 pm on 29th January to plug all the holes, and then empty the after peak tanks of water using some compressed air.

One 8" plus two 4" submersibles are put into No6 hold and the shelter deck. Once pumping has commenced, they return to the tackles and with some heavy strain, the list is again reduced so that at 3.30pm the vessel floats at her moorings with only an 8-degree list to port.

Now they hold the ship in this position until 5 pm when the tide will rise and they can take the vessel further up the mud to Kingswear.

The tug Aetna is made fast ahead, the tug Enterprise made fast on the port side and using Racer's engines on the starboard side, the vessel is run up on to the mud at 7 pm. Anchors are run out forward by the Harbour Master and vessel is moored temporarily until the bow anchors, which had been slipped could be recovered and then run out.

Now at low tide, the torpedo damage is more visible and after a survey, gear and stores for effecting temporary repairs are ordered from Devonport. More submersible pumps and air compressors from Racer are put on board and the work of patching commences, with sections being built on deck according to requirements.

The engine room is pumped dry, and finally, the damage to the shaft tunnel in No 4 & 5 holds (then submerged 9 feet) is made good, and the tunnel is pumped out.

On the 9th Feb at spring tides, the vessel is moved about 300 feet further up the beach.

Owing to the damage extending under the bilge and the rear quarter, it is necessary to build the various sections with quite some curvature because the hull has a twist of 5' 0" between ends.

In order to raise the bottom damage out of the mud, about 800 tons of bunker coal is then discharged and the vessel given a list to starboard so that this damage can be repaired more easily.

The vessel then finally floats off the mud at high water, and she is anchored in the harbour ready to be moved to a repair yard.

Back in London Captain Young is having his daily talk with his boss. 'Did you enjoy your trip away?' the Admiral asks.

'It was good to be at the coal face doing a little bit of real salvage work, I do miss the job you know.'

'I know you do but you are more important here, directing operations and advising your teams, how was RFA Racer anyway?'

'It is amazing to watch those men who are after all experienced but only as seaman. Watching them go about their work was a joy and I told them so.'

'That's good and I am pleased to tell you, that the Sea Lords actually think we might be winning the war against the U-boats, but we can't afford to let up.' He finishes with this and departs with a smile as Fred picks up more salvage reports and some urgent signals because there is always much to do in this very busy office.

SS Comrie Castle

The SS Comrie Castle is bound from London to New York via Plymouth in ballast; she is unfortunately torpedoed on the port side holing the engine room and No 4 hold at 8.45pm on 14th March 1918 whilst close to St Catherines Light.

Heroic efforts by the crew and the Portsmouth based tugs Pert and Enterprise enable her to be beached at 10 am the next day on Horse Tail Shoal 1½ miles from the Dean Light Vessel.

RFA Racer is instructed to proceed at once from Dartmouth on 21st March arriving early 22nd with the Salvage Officer Cdr. George Wheeler on board.

Work has already been started on the ship by a dockyard salvage party under the direction of Lt. Cdr. Damant RN.

The foreman of the shore side salvage party greets George with 'The officer in charge has fallen down the forepeak this morning, and is on his way to hospital as we speak sir.'

'How badly hurt is he?' asks George.

'He won't be back for quite a while sir, he's in a lot of pain but will be ok, I will brief you on what we have done and discovered so far anyway.'

'Very good, let me have the details please.'

'The ship has been washed up the bank bow first by the tides, and is now about 1500ft from her original position; this is because there was nothing to hold her in place. We have pumps controlling the flood in No 5 hold, which is still leaking heavily.

Yesterday we tried to haul the ship off the sand at high tide, using 4 tugs but failed, so you will probably have to haul her off manually with anchors.'

'Very good and thank you, could you now take me around the ship, whilst I see what can be done to solve the problem?'

'Certainly sir' and the two off them head off.

On his return, George issues his instructions to the assembled riggers and divers. 'Take the 3-ton anchor, lay it out astern of the wreck and rig a 6" wire between the anchor and a 25-ton purchase anchored on to her stern. You divers are to go down into the engine room and inspect the condition of the shaft tunnels, which appear to be the source of one of the major leaks. You two riggers are to try putting air into Nos 6 and 7 ballast tanks, to push the flood water out of them. We need to raise the ship up in order to pull her off the bank, and that means reducing the volume of water inside.'

A few hours later the anchor is in place and they gather again to review progress.

'The tunnel doors are broken and the bulkhead is buckled onto the shafts, with holes in it as well, so we don't think we can seal them', reports diver Keam.

'We were unable to empty the ballast tanks either' reports the riggers.

'That settles it then, we will have to get the water out of No5 hold and fix the leaks in it. That will give some lift, and we can then flood the forepeak and storerooms, which will balance the ship and lift the stern' decides George.

Pumping in No 5 hold commences, but they have to stop many times because there is lots of loose baggage and matting. This needs to be cleared from the pump inlets, but eventually, they pump enough water out.

The bulkhead between the engine room and the hold is then shored, along with some plugging and wedging of the smaller leaks.

The next day the ship floats, and they pull her astern until she grounds again, mainly because the sand they are trying to cross is uneven.

Turning their attention to No 4 hold which has 2 ft. of water in it, they pump this out and again do leak stopping, until the pump can control this leakage, this gains them another 16 ft. as they haul again on the stern anchor.

Next, they secured the tug, Pert, alongside and haul away on the purchases with Pert helping which gains another 40ft.

At the next tide, the ship starts swinging in the tide surge and turning level with the shore, so the tug is moved out to sea and she pulls the bow around so that the wreck is finally turned with the bow of the ship running straight out to seaward.

The ground tackle which was connected to the anchor is now moved to the bow of the ship and reconnected to the anchor.

Hughli is made fast alongside and using her engines they attempt to create a channel in the sandy bottom and another 200ft is gained.

The battle to drag her over the huge expanse of sand continues, with one of the ships own anchors being dropped off the bow, along with 105 fathoms of chain and this gives them another 60ft. Slowly the ship is being hauled over the sand, then another bow anchor is taken out gaining another 100ft and they think that she will only need to be dragged another 200ft before she is free.

A week of very hard work; and the end is in sight when the weather decides to intervene, work is abandoned and Racer steams into Portsmouth to get much-needed coal and water.

Two days later they are back on board, fixing the damage caused by the bad weather, plugging new leaks and more pumping out.

Overnight on 29th March they finally manage to pull her clear and early in the morning, the vessel is beached near Netley where at last they can make some more permanent repairs and finally pump her out in a sheltered location.

On completion of the repairs, all but one of the pumps is removed, the anchors left behind are picked up and at high tide, some tugs take the ship away for full repairs.

RFA Racer is then diverted to her next job on SS India in Stokes Bay close to Portsmouth.[14]

---

[14] *These are notes from the Salvage Report which show that it was not just the riggers but the whole ships company who were fully involved in this work.*
Right through the operations, Racer supplied steam to ship's winches for heaving on tackles and anchors.
It is desired to commend the work of salvage party of Racer and Hughli who averaged 20 hours heavy work per day during the whole of the operations, they fully realised that a sea from the Southward would cause the ship to break in two.

SS India

The salvage of this ship was quite straightforward taking only a couple of days to complete. The only item of interest is the two mysterious regular holes found in the bilges, which were probably drilled by crew members at some time for reasons unknown.

Of course, the salvage team found them and repaired them.

The April 1918 report on the salvage of Portuguese ship SS India by Lt. Cdr. George J Wheeler Salvage Officer.

I have to report on salvage operations on Portuguese SS India bound from London to Cardiff, having on board 30 tons of gun parts and ammunition, torpedoed in port side of engine room at 9.30pm 29th March in a position about 5' East of Owers Lt. vessel, and towed to Stokes Bay by HM Tug Pert, 2 other tugs and trawlers.

On orders received, RFA Racer and Hughli were employed on 31st March in dismantling pumps & gear from SS Comrie Castle and proceeded at 5.30am 1st April arriving at 7.15am when I took charge of operations.

Nos 4 & 5 holds had been leaking from the tunnel and one 6" Aster pump from dockyard had been put in No 4 hold. Divers and carpenters were sent down to plug and wedge to stop leaking, a 4" submersible pump being put in each hold. The leakage was reduced significantly to enable pumps to control and eventually the holds were pumped dry, the ship being brought upright by pumping out port No 4 tank.

Tugs were requested and at 3 pm HM Tugs Pert and Swarthy arrived, Pert making fast on port side Swarthy ahead and Racer fast on the starboard side, supplying steam to windlass and steering gear.

The anchor was hauled up and towing commenced, the vessel being anchored off Netley about 5.45pm.

During the night divers made good the leakage into the after holds.

It also became necessary for Hughli and Racer to work engines at 11 pm owing to the small steamer at anchor fouling the berth of the India, and the latter was manoeuvred until the risk of collision was over.

April 2nd the vessel was pumped dry by 10 am and the pumps were broken out ready for removing.

At noon, the vessel took a list to port and investigation showed that 10 feet of water was in hold No 2, although Nos 1 and 3 were dry, the ships carpenter had sounded this No 2 hold and reported it dry.

Two 4" submersible pumps were put down No 2 hold and by 7 pm had pumped down. A heavy leak was discovered in the after bilge compartment and a hole about 3 "diameter found in the margin plate of the tank. The hole was regular as though drilled out, and a leak stopper was made and fitted. The tank top was set up in the way of stanchions and all leaking slightly. These were stopped by wedging, tallow and cement, such damage to tank top was reported to have been done some months ago when the vessel was on rocks for 20 days.

By 9.30pm the whole of the hold appeared good and watertight, pumps then being broken out and got on deck.

At 10.30pm water was heard running and further investigation proved a hole similar in appearance and position in margin plate port side, the tank in the interval having filled up from the sea. A leak stopper was made and fitted over this hole, completed about 2 am 3rd April and by 4.30pm everything being in order, Racer left the vessel and proceeded to Southampton to coal.

SS Celtic

The SS Celtic was the largest ship in the world when she was built, and she is travelling up the North Sea on 31st March 1918. She is just south of the Isle of Man and heading for New York in ballast with some troops on board when a torpedo slams into her port side bringing her rapid progress to a halt.

The Captain of the German U-boat, who is looking through his periscope, is doubtful that one torpedo would do enough damage to sink a ship of this size, although he is elated that one of his fish has found its mark, especially on such a large target. Slipping round to the other side, he fires his last torpedo into her starboard side at point blank range. This one also hits the target but does not detonate and he judges it time to leave the area, because rescue ships will be on their way by now, and he needs to get back for more ammunition.

In Liverpool docks, the urgent radio messages asking for help from the Celtic, result in an armada of tugs, warships, and steamers, including the L & NW railway cargo steamer Slieve Baron heading out on a mercy mission.

The salvage section gets a telephone message about the incident and being such a large ship, urgent action is necessary. Cdr. Kay is allocated as Salvage Officer, plus RFA Racer is ordered to leave Hughli to finish off the SS India. The salvage ship sets off immediately with an escort down the channel and then up the Irish Sea as quickly as she can.

The Celtic remains afloat although powerless, because of the extensive damage and flooding in her engine room, but the tugs manage to move her to Peel, where she anchors and the troops on board are disembarked to the Slieve Baron, for onward passage.

Cdr. Kay reaches the ship first on a local tug which gives him time to assess the damage. Then the Racer arrives with its submersibles, which are immediately placed in No 3 hold, which has the most water in it. As more submersibles arrive from Liverpool etc., they are put into the engine room and other holds.

Although the Celtic has taken on a great deal of water, they get the floods under control but need to beach her, to finish the job. To do this she is moved to Carrickfergus and grounded so that the torpedo holes can be patched.

There are a total of 14^{15} pumps on board in the various compartments, and that number is reduced as the damage is repaired.

On the beach during low tide, the torpedo holes are revealed and the riggers get to work cleaning up the edges and preparing standard patches which are soon bolted in place and sealed with cement.

Leaving only a couple of pumps working, the rest of the units are recovered and sent back to their owners.

The Celtic herself is then moved to Belfast for Harland & Wolff to take over, and finally, make her fully seaworthy.

---

[15] This incident demonstrates just how important pumps were in salvaging any ship but especially such a large one. It is not just pumps that are required however because each unit will also require some sort of power and enough hoses to discharge the flood water back into the sea.

SS Anchoria

The salvage report for this ship was not found during my research at Kew. It may well be in the files, so either I missed it or it is missing.

The photographs for this ship, however, have some significance in the overall salvage story and justify some comments about what they reveal.

Figure 19 shows the ship half submerged in Lough Swilly which must have been a daunting sight for the crew of Racer.

It looks an extremely difficult job however the other picture gives a clue as to what was done because they certainly saved her despite all the difficulties.

Figure 20 shows two submersible pumps lying in hold after they have completed the pumping out of this space.

The electric cables are clearly hanging down along with the pump discharge hoses, and the men are posed in a relaxed way and so give the impression that the job was relatively easy.

The men, in their working overalls, are sitting on large pine beams that have been used to support whatever repairs they have made to the hull plating.

This hold would have been completely filled with water; however, the use of this type of pump really simplifies that part of the job because it is simply lowered into the hold and then switched on.

Today portable electric submersible pumps are universally used to remove liquids from compartments.

They also have many other uses as fixed pumps in tanks used to supply liquids. In my work with petrol pumps, there were certain installations where this type of pump was the only one that could work, and I am sure there are many more instances of this.

HM Torpedo Destroyer Magic

Fred is sitting in his office, studying the latest request for assistance from the Admiralty; the Destroyer HMS Magic is reported to have been torpedoed in Lough Foyle.

The vessel was attempting to make her home port of Londonderry under her own steam, but has grounded and now needs their help. Picking up his phone he asks his secretary to come in and dictates a signal to Lt. Hewitt and RFA Racer to attend her immediately.

On board the salvage vessel they have just finished the latest job, and after short preparations sail at 2.30am, arriving at 8.50am with their escort.

'That's the strangest looking destroyer I have ever seen' says John to the others up on deck.

'Surely there should be a 4" gun in front of the bridge,' replies Pony.

'There's no room for one now, Lt. Hewitt told us she had been torpedoed, but she is far too badly damaged, it must have been a mine,' finishes John.

Racer ties up alongside the stricken destroyer on her port side towards her stern, and Lt. Hewitt heads for the bridge to see the Captain. Standing on the bridge looking down from above at the damage he is amazed at the amount of missing deck. 'That looks odd to me; I can't believe that it was a torpedo.'

'You could be right,' replies the Captain, 'any way we were making good progress with the 2 tugs alongside, which are tied up just in front of you, but we seem to be stuck'.

'I will get my men below to assess the situation, we could do with sending Divers down, but the tide seems pretty strong here.'

'The tide here is very strong so that is probably wise.' Concludes the Captain as Lt. Hewitt goes below to instruct the riggers.

After a thorough inspection, Lt. Hewitt, the Captain, and the riggers assemble on what's left of the forecastle. 'It is my opinion that a mine has destroyed the hull structure below the gun. The deck plating, however, did not fail and the bow has folded under the ship and is now stuck on the seabed.'

'Sounds logical to me,' says the Captain, 'what do you propose to do?'

'We can burn through the deck plates on this line across the bow, which should weaken the structure quite a lot. Then we will put a wire around the break. At the same time, we will use the engines from the tugs and Racer to pull the ship away from the bow and hopefully break the two apart.'

'I have just been advised that HMS Mandate will also be here shortly to give some assistance as well, she is from the same destroyer flotilla,' the Captain tells them.

'Thank you, Captain, that good to hear, you riggers can get started now, please move the burning equipment onto the focsle right away.'

Initially, the cutting of the plate goes quite well until there is a shout of 'Fire, Fire' from John who is standing next to the welder. He immediately switches off the torch, lifts his goggles and steps back from the small inferno.

John picks up the buckets of water, throws the contents onto the burning area and the flames die back. The welder gets back to work, but in the short time that John has been refilling the buckets over the side, the fire has restarted.

'Buckets are no good,' says John. 'We need something more permanent, such as a fire hose.'

'Let's ask HMS Mandate to supply one suggests the welder.'

'Good idea,' says Lt. Hewitt who then steps over to the destroyer to arrange it all.

Time after time the fire restarts because the lagging is soaked in oil, but the permanent fire hose quickly responds and slowly they cut the plates across the deck, from port to starboard. The plates start to move apart slightly, and this allowed further cutting on the structure below until they can cut no more. Everyone breaks then for the day as the light fades.

The next day chain nippers are passed around the foremost part of the submerged deck, and also round the starboard bollard. A 5" manila hawser and 3 ½" wire is passed from them to Racer, which was anchored about a cable's length off the starboard bow of Magic. These are connected to the after winch on the salvage ship, and in this way, the damaged structure is anchored down and held in place.

Once this is completed the tug which is tied up alongside Magic attempts to tow her away whilst Racer pulls in the opposite direction.

'This is not going to work, 'says Lt. Hewitt, 'Racer is in the wrong position and it is 9 pm so let's stop now and try again tomorrow.'

The next day, Racer is in a better position, HMS Mandate also has a towing hawser attached to the rear of Magic, the tug Flying Cormorant is pulling as well, and it looks like they will succeed as the structure starts to give way. Then Mandate's towing cable fails; however they soon have a replacement hawser in place, and this time the damaged destroyer is free at last.

[16]Racer remains in an effort to try and destroy the wreckage which has been left whilst Magic is taken to Berry for major repairs.

---

[16] *Authors Note, Racer remained to make an examination of wreckage, and it was decided to try to level it. The charges available proved insufficient for the purpose and it was left with the upper most part, about 2 ½ fathoms under the surface in the following position:*
2.7 Cable 195 degrees from the ridge NE Perch
2.25 Cable 96 degrees from the Ridge Pile Lighthouse.
One cable clear SE of dredged channel on NE end of Middle Ground.
Extract from the salvage report:
I have to report the excellent manner in which the Commanding Officer, Officers and men of Racer carried out their respective duties and by so doing completed the work satisfactorily and very expeditiously, also of the valuable assistance rendered by HMS Mandate in subduing outbreaks of fire and in towing.
WW Hewitt Eng. Lt. RNR Assistant Salvage Officer.

SS Esperanza de Larringa

The fully loaded general cargo ship SS Esperanza Larringa, destined for Manchester, is torpedoed on 1st May 1918 just north of Lough Swilly.

On inspection, No 3 & 4 holds are found to be dry and the ship is loaded between decks with agricultural implements. She is also full of bulk maize in her lower holds but the engine room is filling up with water slowly.

Racer goes alongside and installs pumps in her engine room, which soon get the flood under control, to such an extent that the ship's pumps can then manage on their own.

The ships ballast pump has broken down, which makes pumping No1 hold impossible at present because all of the cargo is in the way. Instructions are received that all corn cargo whether it is sound or damp, is to be landed at Londonderry, so lighters are ordered to take away the grain.

Whilst they are waiting for these the motor engineers manage to repair the ships ballast pump and this controls the flood in No 1 hold.

The vessel has on board in addition to the corn, a considerable amount of other cargo, and much of this has to be removed to get at the vital grain. As the unloading continues the repair materials that were ordered arrived.

On the 28th Larringa drags her mooring and partly swings when one shackle on her port anchor is carried away and she drags the other one. Fortunately, the Dapper which is nearby, comes alongside, to hold her in place with her engines until high water when she lays another anchor out and the ship is hauled up to her old position.

As the cargo is removed they discover more leaking areas, such as around the tunnelling which is fixed as the holes are found. Finally, everything is saved, the ship is temporarily made seaworthy, and she is towed away for proper repairs.

I have included the list of cargo to give the reader an idea of what was carried by these merchant ships.

Cargo List:
2860 tons of maize of which 900 tons is wet.

366 tons of spelter.

681 tons of Agricultural Machinery in 194 cases.

9240 bales of twine.

486 tons various pieces of ash, poplar, spruce, fir, aspen & walnut.

1842 pcs staves.

1900 pcs lumber.

855 hardwood batons.

560 wheels.

78 bundles shafts.

88 tons of lead.

Convoy on the rocks

In Room 40, Edward is on the phone to the Convoy Control Centre as usual. 'We have a U-boat patrolling the North Channel of the Irish Sea, between Mull of Kintyre and Rathin Island Scotland, current position is midway, probably heading north.'

'Thank you for the warning' comes over the phone, 'we have an empty troopship convoy which is heading for New York to collect more American troops. It is due in that area shortly so what would you advise?'

'Tell them to stay close to the coast of Ireland, passing between Rathin Island and the County Antrim coast, they should be ok then' and puts the phone down to continue his discussion with Blinker Hall his boss.

'I can't believe that the codebook from UC-44 is still being used by the Germans, it's been almost 4 months now,' says Blinker.

On board the convoy lead ship SS Oriana, the convoy Commodore has just seen the signal instruction, which is ordering them to travel between the island and the Antrim coast. He looks at the chart, takes a ruler and draws the new course.

'Would you like me to get the Navigator to have a look sir' asks the Officer of the Watch.

'No need' says the Commodore, just head for the new course and change onto it when you reach it. A little later after turning onto the new course, they run into a fog bank, but by this time they are steady on the new course.

As a precaution, the Commodore orders the convoy speed to be reduced to 11 knots, and then heads downstairs for his dinner with a parting comment to the 2 lookouts, 'make sure you keep a sharp lookout ahead'.

On board HMS Mystic the navigator turns from his chart table to talk to the Captain, who is in command of the convoy port wing escort destroyer.

'What is it pilot' asks the skipper using his nickname for a man who has demonstrated his navigation skills on more than one occasion in the past. The Captain always reckons you could blindfold him, take him anywhere, and he would still know where he was.

'We are too close to land sir, as far as I can judge we will come very close to Torr Head, and we should inform the Commodore as soon as possible.'

'Officer of the Watch close the Oriana, signalman you get on the Aldiss lamp and pass this urgent message now' orders the Captain. As the Mystic nears the Oriana he can see the light flashing, as his signalman tries to get them to take notice, but nothing happens and the convoy sails onward.

On the Oriana, the ship's Captain, now on the bridge, notices the glint of the signal light and asks the port lookout, 'what's that?' to which he gets the reply.

'Just the bloody Royal Navy wanting attention, I'm too busy looking ahead sir, as ordered by the Commodore.'
At the same time, the lookouts on both Mystic and Oriana shout almost in unison 'Land ahead'.

This is a bit of an understatement, as a great wide barrier of rocks and land appear out of the fog and gloom, only 100 yards ahead.

Of course, it's far too late for anyone to do anything now, as all the ships in the convoy steam into this catastrophe.[17]

The Commodore, sitting at his normal seat, in the great dining room is eating his lovely dinner and then flies backward as the ship quickly slows and lurches upwards. Finally coming to a screaming grinding halt, his food lands right in his lap, covering him in gravy, closely followed a large glass of red wine.

Down in the boiler rooms, where the stokers are busy shovelling the coal into the hungry furnaces, all the men are thrown violently into the hot boiler face, causing quite a few burns.

Those on the bridges just have time to brace themselves, as the front of the ship comes into direct contact with the large granite boulders, crashing over them lurching onwards, and then grinding along the rocky shore until they come to a screaming unnatural stop.

In the ensuing silence, the Captain of the Mystic looks back, to see one of his three funnels lying at a funny angle, then looks at the pilot and says with a grimace 'right again pilot'. Then turning to the lookouts, 'get below and check everybody is ok and then I want a damage report from the Chief Engineer'. At which they scurry off because the skipper's mood is pretty black.

'What's the situation' asks the Commodore as he scrambles up to the bridge, after first removing as much gravy as possible.

'All of the convoy is aground sir' is about all the Captain can say, he bitterly regrets not checking the course set by the

---

[17] *At first glance this accident looked to me like a simple navigation error made in fog, navigation equipment then was not that accurate. Looking at a map however, it makes no sense to take this risky route. Now I believe that this is more evidence, although circumstantial, that they were told to take this risky route because of greater danger elsewhere, Room 40 again?*

Commodore and suspects that the Mystic was trying to warn them of the danger.

'Get a signal off to Command ASAP' is all the Commodore can say and let me have damage reports from each of the ships please.'

Oriana, Manora, Aeneas, and the 2 destroyers are all perched on the rocks like beached whales, a few men injured in the boiler rooms and some in the mess decks, but no one is dead' reports the Captain to the Commodore, who has changed his jacket and is down in the dining room continuing his meal.

'Very well' is the only comment, as the Commodore ponders the situation. He had been looking forward to a week of good meals, in nice surroundings with an almost empty ship, but all has changed.

He also knows that really it is his fault, but he will never admit to it and the 2 men eat in silence, as they wait to be rescued from a pretty grim situation.

Help of course soon arrives on 17th May in the form of the salvage ship RFA Racer with Salvage Officer Cdr. Kay to direct operations.

Racer ties up alongside Oriana starboard side to and the Captain and Kay meet on the bridge to survey the scene, the fog has long cleared and the weather is glorious.

'My men have split into 5 teams using our 4 boats so that I can get a survey done of all of the ships as soon as possible' says Kay as he points to each boat in turn.

'It's great to see you so quickly, do you think you will get us all off, we are well up on the rocks. It was high tide when the Commodore ran us aground; I should have insisted my Navigator check the course he laid'.

'Where is the Commodore?' asks Kay.

'He's gone back to see the Senior Naval Officer and explain what happened, but no doubt he will find someone to blame, anyway my crew is at your disposal.'

'Thank you' says Kay 'once I have my reports I will take you up on your offer of assistance, however, you will be pleased to learn that the salvage crew of Racer is very well thought of.'

'On that subject Cdr. I have told my crew to set up two dining areas, one for the officers and one for the crew which they can use 24 hours a day.'

'Wonderful, these men do work very long hours and some nice food will be an excellent reward for them, I can assure you.'

John, Pony, and Chas then appear on the bridge to report the results of their survey of Oriana.

John says to Cdr. Kay, 'both of the forward holds, No 1 & 2 have holes in them, with water to a depth of about 6ft sir, we could put a submersible pump into hold No1 because that appears to have the worst damage.'

'I agree' says Kay and by the way, the Oriana has set up a 24-hour dining room for you all. So when you have put the pump in place, get something to eat and tell everyone else you see, the food will likely be much better on here, than on the Racer.'

The 3 salvage riggers beam at the Oriana's Captain, who recognises that these men are experienced and that his idea of feeding them will work wonders.

After installing the pump, with help from the ship's engineers, the three friends sit down in the huge dining room, to white table cloths, silver service and waiters galore. On the table, there are even handwritten menus offering many delights, and of course who is already sitting down, none other than the Racer's 2nd chef Norman Weatherley tucking into a feast.

'Didn't take you long to get yourself outside some decent grub Norm' says Chas who is regularly winding up the chefs.

'We have shut down our galley to give it a deep clean' he replies.

'Good idea' says Chas 'and I am hoping your taking note of what good grub looks and tastes like as well.'

Norm looks him in the eye, notices the glint of humour, and decides to take no notice. Anyway, the food is so good, he can't really take offence now but he will get his revenge, sometime in the future.

After the meal and whilst they are waiting for the water level to recede, and the availability of a diver to start plugging the holes, John notices Vic lugging his camera equipment onto the Oriana deck. 'Do you need a hand with that, I have some time to spare,' he says.

Vic replies, 'it would be very useful if you could help me, all the boats are away doing surveys, the only way to get ashore is down that long ladder hanging off the bow of the Oriana. You can drop the stuff down on a rope and come with me because the ground ashore is extremely rough.'

Standing on the bows they can see the Manora lying on the rocks, so they take one photo of her from Oriana's bow and then 2 of the Mystic. Afterward Vic climbs over the side onto the ladder, scrambles down and eventually, they are both standing on the shore.

'We can go up the hill, taking the bows of the Oriana on the way up and then I want one of the 2 ships together, which will make a really good photograph.'

Up on the hill looking down on the Mystic and Oriana, they can see the boats alongside, with the mast and funnel of the Racer, showing behind the Oriana and Viv is really chuckling. 'I wonder what the convoy Commodore would say if he knew what we are doing?'

'From what I hear it was his fault, but luckily for us, he is away, so let's get it done and back to work' responds John who can also see the funny side of the picture.

Back down in the hold, Pony is watching to see where the water is flowing into the hold, so that he can guide the diver in his patching work, the hull resting on the rocks is not helping as the diver wriggles his way past the rocks following the guiding tapping sounds.

They also have a pump now in No2 hold and much the same is going on, although that section is easier to patch, because there is more room for the diver.

From the other holds, the crew of Oriana has been removing as much coal as possible, into a lighter. This will lighten her as well, and eventually, all is ready to try and pull her off.

Anchors have been dropped out to seaward, with wires attached to the ship's winches, the tug Flying Swallow is also cabled up.

All the other ships have been hauled off by this time, and now they have to try and move the biggest one of them all.

However despite all their efforts, Cdr. Kay standing on the bridge of the Oriana realises that she is still stuck fast on the rocky shore. 'Looks like the sea is too calm' says Cdr. Kay, 'let's get the destroyer HMS Millbrook that is standing guard over us, to try and stir the sea up and create some waves, by driving at us and turning at the last minute.'

Standing on the Oriana stern the riggers tension up the winches and the tugs take the strain, whilst the destroyer gets up to full speed driving straight towards them, turning out to sea at the last minute, throwing her bow wave into the side of the Oriana, but nothing happens.

More runs follow and finally on the 6th run, after all the practice of the previous attempts, getting closer and closer each time, there is a build-up of a local swell, John feels the deck shudder slightly under his feet and gradually Oriana slips slowly and rumbly, back into the water afloat again.

Anchoring close to shore, the riggers are then able to do some final pumping out and leak stopping, until the salvage officer is finally able to declare her seaworthy enough, for a trip to the dockyard.

Whilst they are clearing up and collecting all their salvage gear, John reflects on another job well done but tinged with sadness, because they have had a week of fantastic food and service in the dining room.

On the bridge, the Captain shakes the hand of Cdr. Kay, 'I and my crew are most grateful for the work you have done to free us. You were right when you said that the salvage riggers were a fine team of men, you should be really proud of them. Plus it was inspiring, if a little frightening to watch that destroyer get closer and closer, but it worked, marvellous.'

'Yes I am proud of them and they would like to express their thanks for the use of your dining room. I suspect the cooks on the Racer will be getting a lot of stick in the future from the men, thank you and god speed bringing the troops over.'

"Der Tag" & HMS Shirley

Room 40 Admiralty; May 1918.

Frank Clarke is looking at his U-boat movement records, flipping back and forwards between the daily records and then calls his staff together. "It looks like all those troublesome UC class minelaying submarines have disappeared; there should still be 40 of them in operation, mostly from Bruges." Of course, everyone agreed with him, but their whereabouts were to remain a mystery for a while.

Room 40 Admiralty; June, July & August 1918.

It was during this period that the location and purpose of the UC class was eventually established, they had moved to Wilhelmshaven and Cuxhaven.

Now they were regularly laying a great belt of mines to the east of Bell Rock, supposedly in complete secrecy. Of course, we still had the code book from UC-44 for most of this period and the tracking stations were monitoring every move they made.

'Blinker' Hall is looking at the tracking records with Frank and they are discussing the actions that have taken place. "As you know Frank, the German plan called "Der Tag" (The Day) is fully known to us, the intention is to lure our fleet into this huge secret minefield."

"When the German High Seas Fleet sails they will position themselves so that the Grand Fleet sails into the minefield and is badly damaged by the mines as they come from Scapa Flow" adds Frank.

"Are your arrangements with the Senior Naval Officer (SNO) at Aberdeen going well?" asks 'Blinker'.

"Captain Laird is my contact there and he has been very co-operative, he only knows part of the story about the minefield but is happy to send his minesweepers out to wherever I tell him.

They are simply given an area to sweep and that is all. We are also putting mines in the channels that the Germans think are clear if they do try their plan they will be left to run into those mines." Finishes Edward and 'Blinker' leaves.

As part of this operation to clear some of the mines, the paddle minesweeper HMS Shirley has been badly damaged on 20th August, and the salvage ship RFA Melita under the guidance of Lt. Brooks, the salvage officer has managed to beach her in the river Dee at Aberdeen.

RFA Racer is then ordered to relieve Melita which she does on the 24th August, where Lt. Brooks briefs the salvage riggers. 'HMS Shirley has been mined with extensive damage to the ship's hull on her port side abaft the paddle box, penetrating through the after part of the engine room bulkhead.

The Engine room, after stokehold and also number one storeroom aft are full of water, with all other compartments practically dry. Her decks and side are badly corrugated, plus the plates in engine room and stokehold on the starboard side are sprung which has caused the after funnel to be thrown out of position.

The after boiler was blown up about three feet and all the steam connections broken. Surprisingly the after part of the port sponson is destroyed but somehow the paddle wheel has remained intact.'

'We have cut away most of the ragged plating and repaired the garbage strake on port side, which cracked at the forward stokehold bulkhead for the side of the sponson. On the starboard side of the after part of the sponson, we found similar damage as on port side, which has been dealt with in the same manner.

The hole is forty-four feet along the hull, has a depth of eighteen feet and your main job is to repair that damage. The Keel plate in the stokehold is also damaged and the foundation of the bulkhead shattered.

We now have a number of shipwrights and you will be assisting them once we have replaced RFA Melita's equipment with yours because she is needed urgently elsewhere.'

For the next 4 days, the shipwrights and riggers shore up the bulkheads and fit heavy framing so that they can then start adding the planking to the ship's side.

On 21st September the patch is completed and HMS Shirley is ready to be transferred to Dundee for a permanent repair. A large pump is placed midships on the upper deck and as the tide rises, she is pulled off the mud bank.

The pump manages to keep the level of water inside the ship at a reasonable level, but the journey to the repair yard can only be done in good weather. This is because they have been forced to use timber that is thinner than normal and the journey will mean going out into the North Sea.

Whilst waiting for tugs, they then discover that the keel bilge area is leaking quite badly, and this requires more leaks stopping. Another storm blows in and the weather is still not suitable for the journey. Once the gale has blown itself out, they tow her out ready to depart to her final destination.

During all this waiting, one of Chas's friends, Stoker Hardy breaks ship on 3rd Oct and goes absent without leave for 26 hours. On his return, the Captain sentences him to detention, and on 7th Oct he is sent RN Barracks Portsmouth for punishment.

With rigger Foulkes as his guard, he is escorted to Perth, where he is handed over the local Master at Arms there, and John then returns to Racer.

Finally, on the 14th Oct, the tug Stormbird tows Shirley to the repairers at Dundee. She is still leaking badly and the pump has to be kept running so Motor Engineers Mr. Pearson, White, Dewey, and Doran sail with her to manage the pump.

Master Rigger Dole, Diver Keam, Riggers Coom and diving attendant Redgrave are also embarked to keep trying to patch any holes.

To look after them all on board, steward Goodwin is also taking the trip, and they all mess together for this relatively short journey. After delivering the ship it is then just a short train journey back to Aberdeen to re-join Racer.

HM Tug Oceana

In Aberdeen RFA Racer and her crew sit and wait for their next salvage job. They have collected from the station all the equipment which was used on the Shirley. It was returned once she was docked, and now they are maintaining and repairing all of their equipment.

Finally, on 22nd Oct, they are ordered to Kirkwall, which is near to Scapa Flow and of course, this is where John started this war before joining the salvage organisation. The Grand Fleet still lies there in wait, although by now it is under the command of Admiral Beatty.

A small admiralty tug Oceana has been sunk in Mill Bay just to the North of Kirkwall by the tug Stobo Castle after a collision in fog. Unfortunately for Oceana, Stobo Castle has an icebreaker bow which makes short work of the other tug.

After Cdr. Wheeler has been briefed ashore in Kirkwall, by the local Commander, they cross to Mill Bay and anchor near to the 2 small masts; they are all that is showing of the victim.

Taking the boats away, the divers go down for an inspection and on completion, they brief the salvage officer.

'She is quite badly damaged but we may be able to save her, probably we could lift her using the tide and the Racer,' says Diver Keam.

'Not sure I like that idea, but we can't get a lifting craft at the moment because they are all busy and she is fairly small. OK, you riggers get some wires ready and we will give it a try.'

After sweeping 2 wires using just the Racer which is quite difficult, the divers go down but report with some bad news, 'the tug has broken in half sir; just pulling those wires under revealed more damage so we won't be able to lift her.'

'OK, get all the gear back on board and we will return to Kirkwall to report to the Admiral, he won't be very happy, as for some reason he is insisting that we save her.'

After reporting back the Racer then returns to Aberdeen with the salvage officer telling them, 'we may have to come back, he now wants us to salvage any equipment we can from her, so await further orders.'

Back in Aberdeen, the riggers settle into some routine maintenance until a telegram arrives for John.

'You say your mother in law has died,' says the Chief, 'I am sorry to hear that, especially since when your mother died, we were not able to give you any leave. Because of that, I am happy to recommend to the Captain that you can go home, we are not that busy anyway.'

'Thank you Chief' replies John who has had more than his share of tragedies.

'But remember that I am going to say that it is your mother that has died if you know what I mean, the Captain has changed since then so he won't know the difference.'

On the 1st Nov John heads home on the train with leave until am 5th Nov.

His leave was granted and the Captain thinks it is his mother that has died, there is normally no leave for a mother in law, perhaps he is lucky but he doesn't think so.

Of course Lucky is again waiting for him on the ferry jetty at Birkenhead and this time Jessie knows he is coming home because the cat is missing.

At home, he comforts his darling Jessie and then takes over the organisation of the funeral, etc. On the 4th Nov, it is clear that the only time for the funeral is on Wednesday 6th Nov and his telegram plea for more leave is successful.

It is a sombre rigger that arrives back at Racer on the 7th Nov leaving his wife to handle the hotel etc., but there is little he can do, however, rumours are now rife that we are winning the war at last.

Monday 11th Nov the Captain clears the lower deck, 'men I am pleased to tell you that an Armistice has been signed with Germany and the war is over.' Everyone smiles and cheers, and he continues when they have calmed a little, 'It is however important to advise you, that the process of demobbing everyone now that hostilities have ceased, will take quite a time. Also please be careful tonight, I know you will want to celebrate especially tonight but take care. Before you go however I would like the ship dressed with flags to celebrate.'

Down in the mess, everyone is getting ready to head into Aberdeen after they have got the flags out in record time, 'Come on John, get changed and come with us, it will do you good.' Says Chas and everyone else shouts get ready.

'OK' says John, not really feeling like it, especially after recent events but as usual, he knows Chas is right.

Pony whispers in his ear 'you know it makes sense and someone has to keep Chas in check, or he will run riot.'

Once changed they all head off into Aberdeen where the whole town is out celebrating, every pub they go into is full but they don't buy a drink the whole night, they are in uniform and everyone wants to thank them.

By Wed 13th Nov everyone has recovered from their celebrations and hangovers, so the maintenance work continues, with the divers down repairing the ship's bottom with some copper sheeting.

Then on Fri 15th Nov in the late evening, they are ordered to proceed to Kirkwall as soon as an escort arrives.

They are ready by 7.20pm for sea and shift to an outer berth awaiting orders to proceed. Finally on Sat 16th at 7.00am they go to sea and join a northbound convoy.

By Sun 17th Nov at 10.40am they are anchored off Kirkwall and they get out the motorboat to take the CO ashore for orders. He returns with Cdr. Wheeler and after coaling ship, they eventually anchor again in Mill Bay, Eday sound on Tuesday 19th Nov.

The next week sees them visit the Oceana twice, using divers to recover what they can from the wreck. The deck gun is unbolted and hauled up along with anchors and towing wires.

On the 24th Nov, they return to Kirkwall to land Cdr. Wheeler and the recovered materials, and then they sail for Aberdeen going alongside on the 26th at the Lorry dock early in the morning to coal ship.

The riggers now settle into pretty boring a routine of maintaining the equipment, whilst the ship is visited by various RN officers, who are planning to do some badly needed refit work on the Racer.

On the 16th Dec John, Chas and Pony along with most of the rest of the ship's company are granted Xmas leave.

The journey home is uneventful, the only surprise to John is that Lucky is not waiting at the Ferry terminal and he walks home a little concerned.

'Hello, where is everyone' he shouts as he opens the front door and is suddenly surrounded by Hilda, Vaughan, and Jack.

Four-year-old Nellie walks in holding 18-month-old Jessie's hand, she is walking now and behind them is his darling wife carrying Lucky.

The hallway is awash with his family clamouring and shouting, so happy to see him and the prospect of a great Xmas beckons. After eating and finally settling his excited children into bed, he can sit in the lounge, have a quiet few moments and talk to Jessie. 'It is so good to be home and for the war to be over.'

To which Jessie replies as she sits stroking Lucky, who has settled on her lap pointedly ignoring John 'yes it is, so much has happened with the war, family deaths and so many men in the area not coming home from the war. I am truly thankful that we can be together, do you know when they will release you?'

'My leave ends on the 28th Dec but they are being very cagey about our release date, we are not that busy and everyone wants to be home. I need to be home to help with the hotel and to help you, but they won't set a date. I will keep asking because I know how difficult it is here for you.'

'I am managing and we have a temporary manager in the hotel, so let's just enjoy the holiday and celebrate Xmas.'

He nods in reply looking thoughtful. 'Lucky seems to have deserted me now, he wasn't on the jetty and hasn't been to me at all, it's very strange.'

'I think he knows that you will be back shortly for good and is making sure of his place here. He has been very good company and you did save him so he owes you a lot.'

'Nellie is growing fast and so is young Jessie,' comments John.

'As soon as Jessie was born Nellie has looked after her, the two are inseparable and Nellie is very caring.'

'I see upon the mantelpiece a lovely brown and white porcelain dog ornament which looks fed up, that very unusual, where did you get it?' asks John.

'I was shopping with mother in the market, the children were with friends and she saw me staring at the dog on display. She told me that the dog and I had the same expression, which really surprised me, as I thought I was hiding my feelings well. She bought it and then gave it to me, now I look at it and remind myself to cheer up; I have grown to love it.'

'I love it too and am pleased that you have told me the story, we will treasure it. We have been a little distant with each other these last 4 years, which is not surprising, I can now admit to you that I was focussing all my efforts into doing my job as well as I could, hoping that would help me to survive.'

Jessie looks at him and smiles, 'I was frightened that you wouldn't come back to me and of course so many didn't. I also hid my worry because I did not want you to have that concern as well.'

A broad smile lights up John's face, as he rises and gestures for them to go upstairs, 'it's good to know all this now, nothing could have prepared us for this war, we survived and our marriage will be stronger than ever.'

Jessie rises and Lucky tries to hang on, but finally, he lets go and curls up in front of the dying fire, as the two climb the stairs to bed.

When John returns to Racer she is in dock with workmen hard at work repairing almost everything on board, his pleas to the Chief about a release date fall on deaf ears.

The other half of the crew are then off for their leave and by 11th Jan everybody is back on board.

On the 13th Jan, the Captain clears the lower deck, with every one ordered to report in their best uniform onto the jetty. Lining up on the jetty alongside the Racer, photographs are taken of the whole crew.

John turns to the Chief 'should we not have one of just the riggers as well he asks?'

'Good idea, riggers gather round, Sparks as well' and they include the ships mascot, Biddy.

Every night in the mess after dinner and yet another day of work maintaining their salvage equipment, talk turns to the only subject they are all really interested in.

'Are you ready to go home and get back to normal life, John?' Enquires his good friend Chas.

'I have been ready ever since this war finished in November, no-one seems to care about us and it's not as if we are doing any salvage work, just this dammed routine maintenance, day after day.' Replies John.

'Well, I am going to ask the Chief tomorrow, if we can have an interview with the Senior Naval Officer here in Aberdeen, I am ready to go home as well.' Is Chas's final announcement on the subject and sure enough the next day he carries out his promise to request a meeting.

What really surprises them all is that, 2 days later accompanied by the Skipper, Lt Harold Jones, all the riggers get their requested interview with the SNO.

'Sir, these riggers would like some idea of when they will be demobilised, it has been over 2 months since the war ended and there has been nothing heard,' begins Harold.

'Do any of you have anything to add to your Captain's opening comments?'

John steps forward, 'Sir, each of us has our own motives for wanting to go home, however, I will explain my own position. During this war, both my Parents have died. We run a hotel in Birkenhead and my wife has 5 children and a hotel to manage. We have all here worked so hard this last 2 years salvaging many ships, and now we are doing nothing but maintenance.'

Reaching into his pocket he brings out a sheet of paper, opens it out and hands it to the SNO.

'All ships in the navy have an honours board, last night I drew this one for RFA Racer which lists each of the vessels we have salvaged. We could do no more, and we were very successful. If we were still salvaging ships then I am sure we would feel different.' All of the riggers nod in agreement, Pony had seen John doing the drawing last night and wondered what was afoot.

The SNO studies the list of ships as the men wait for him. 'This list is very impressive and I can see that you have good reason to want to be demobilised, I will forward your case to the Admiralty immediately, but bear in mind that there are many people still in the same position as you.'

Back on board continuing with the maintenance they wait and hope, very impressed however with John's work which everyone wants to look at properly.

At the Salvage Section headquarters, Fred is in discussion with the 2nd Sea Lord trying to get a decision about the future of the Salvage Section and the demobilisation of the men.

'We now have almost no salvage work being carried out; many of the ships are sitting in harbour, and the crews naturally want to go home. I suggest that we gather them together in Southampton for disposal and demobilisation. I have selected RFA

Racer to work on the Laurentic gold recovery and will ask for volunteers to man her.'

Charles replies 'Excellent, and until the diving season starts the RFA Racer volunteer crew can look after the disposal of the remaining salvage ships and equipment.'

Fred feels somewhat happier as his boss departs; sorting out the demobilisation has been much more difficult than any salvage job.

A week later RFA Racer leaves Victoria dock and Aberdeen for the final time, heading for Southampton where all the Salvage Vessels are gathering.

USS Narragansett

On-board RFA Racer which is now in Southampton harbour, the day's work has finished and John sits down, to flip through the latest copy of The War Illustrated for Jan 1919 that he has bought.

As he turns the pages, he is staggered to see a whole page with pictures that he instantly recognises. 'Pony, Chas come and look at this' as he starts to read out loud the headline which says 'U-boat murderers meet the fate they merited' and then the storyline.

'That's UC-44' says Chas over his shoulder.

Pony asks 'what's the story then?'

'They are saying something about U44 and the sinking of the Belgian Prince, which took place 4 days before the submarine was trapped in a minefield. Apparently, after sinking the merchant ship, they mustered the ship's crew on the submarine casing, removed any means the crew had of floating and then dived. 3 men survived because they were wearing lifejackets under their coats but the rest of them drowned.'

'Unbelievable' says Chas and Pony looks aghast, as he remembers how they had honoured the dead crew of UC-44.

'There are a few things wrong with this story' says John, 'it says U44 which is a different submarine to UC-44, then it says the U-boat was trapped, but we know that she was sunk by her own mine. So it looks like propaganda to me, I intend to keep the page and look into it in the future.

Pony looks relieved and says 'that's many of us in those pictures and it has Lt. Davis as a Cdr., so he has been promoted.'

Chas pipes in with, 'I would not be surprised because most of those salvage officers were ok, compared with many others I have met.'

'I bet they don't have any trouble getting demobbed either, I just want to go home now the war is over' is John's final word as he rips the page out carefully, folds it and adds it to his growing pile of photographs and documents.

In the mess deck a few days later the Chief is giving them some news, 'it says here that RFA Racer is to be retained for future salvage work and they are looking for volunteers to man her, the existing crew will get priority, then the crews of the other salvage vessels. If you decide not to volunteer you will be demobbed in early March.' All their faces light up as they have at last got a date finalised.

'When do we have to let you know?' asks Pony.

'You can have the night to think it over and we will meet tomorrow morning', finishes the Chief.

The three friends gather together looking somewhat happier, 'I guess you're going home as I am John,' says Pony.

'I am, there is no choice for me really, what about you Chas' John replies.

'Staying is tempting but it's time for pastures new for me as well, although I will miss you both,' Chas finishes with as they head up top for more maintenance work, now they know that Racer will be continuing as a salvage ship the maintenance work has more point to it.

A few decide to volunteer for further service including riggers Furley, Kennedy, Redgrave, Heckett, Master rigger Dole and steward Weatherby but the majority decide to leave.

On the 1st Feb, there is a severe gale out in the English Channel, and one last job is unfolding, not very far from their very first salvage job, the SS Carl on the Isle of Wight.

The United States Transport troopship USS Narragansett is blown onto the rocks on Bembridge Point, at 0040 with 2200 troops on board. As the storm abates she has been driven high and dry, with fairly extensive damage to her hull, but disembarkation of her troops into Train Ferry No 2 is finally achieved.

John had noticed the large special gantry, at the end of the long jetty in the docks. Here whole trains are driven off and onto these specially designed ships, fitted with 4 sets of rails running the full length along the top deck. As far as he can find out there are more of these ships and there are other special jetties in both France and Britain. Apparently, these ships were very quickly loaded and unloaded which freed up many more merchant ships for more normal duties.

The Mariner is the first salvage ship to leave to help the Narragansett with Lt. Williams as Salvage Officer and they manage to install pumps in the stokehold, such that by the time the other ships arrive, she is able to raise steam herself. Now the ships engineers can get the engine room pumps started.

Racer still has most of her pumps ashore at the time, being maintained in local sheds, and it takes them 2 days of frantic work to put them back together, load them on board and then with Salvage Officer Lt. Jarvis on board they join the growing number of ships available to help.

Most of the other ships salvage ships still have men on leave so are unable to assist.

Eng.-Cdr. Vine is on board Narragansett, in overall command of the operation.

Other ships involved include RFA Reindeer, Salvage Vessel Corycia, SS Ellida, and even the US Salvage Vessel Favourite which arrives on 14th Feb because of course the ship is an American one[18].

The salvage riggers of Mariner and Racer work together, preparing purchases, cables and 3 anchors, which are laid off her stern. At high tide with Racer, Mariner and 2 tugs also pulling,

---

[18] Under guidance from The Royal Navy Salvage Section the American Navy quickly created its own salvage service. They were given all the information required as soon as they joined the war, much of it directly from Captain Young.

they start heaving on the purchases, but when the tow rope to one tug breaks, efforts are halted.

The next move is to lighten the ship as much as possible, which includes the jettisoning of ship's anchors, davits, fire-bars, rafts, paravanes, in fact, anything that is loose and easily disposed of.

Twice they have to go back to collect and lay even bigger anchors along with heavier duty purchases.

On Monday 17th February at 12.30, she slips off the rocks as the forces generated by the powerful purchases, and tows from Mariner, Racer, a tug Ellida and the Favourite finally pull her clear.

As she slips off the rocks, the wind then starts to take charge because the ship has flat sides acting like a large sail and the extra strain on Favourite's tow line causes it to snap, but the tug Ellida quickly changes position and saves the day.

The vessel is then berthed at Town Quay next to the collection of salvage ships, under the care of the Racer riggers who keep watches on her, whilst Divers examine her bottom and stop leaks. Eventually, they cement the tank tops where necessary such that she is fully watertight after which the vessel is then moored in deep water.

On 4th Mar. at 10.00am all the men to be demobilised, are sent to see the Admiralty Surgeon on board HMS Hermione for a medical examination which was necessary for everyone who was being discharged.

The next day, the 5th Mar most of the riggers walk over to the nearby Railway Station for their final journey home and board a train to Waterloo. In London they gather together for a short farewell, John is off to Euston for his train to Liverpool with a few others and his 2 friends are going to Kings Cross for their journey home to the other side of the country.

It has been a long War, the last two years have been very hard but rewarding, and this fine team is being broken up.

'Thank you both for your friendship and support,' is John's last words to Pony and Chas. They are all grown men but that does not stop them hugging each other, despite the stares of civilians on the platform.

John's journey home is tinged with sadness at leaving his friends, joy at going home and wonder at what the future holds for all of them. He knows he is fortunate, there is a job, loving wife and family waiting for him at home, and he has survived.

As he crosses the Mersey on the ferry, he can see Lucky sitting on the far harbour wall waiting to greet him first, obviously, the cat has now forgiven him. How he knows he is coming home is very strange, but he is grateful and happy to see him waiting because it means all is well at home.

It's going to take quite a while to get used to ordinary civilian life, not that he is abandoning the Navy.

Apparently, HMS Eagle has been renamed HMS Eaglet because the Admiralty want to use the name for another ship, but he doesn't mind because he plans to stay in the Royal Naval Reserve. Another name is just another ship to add to the list of ones he has proudly served on.

He is after all just an Able Seaman at heart and wherever life leads him, he will be proud of his time in the Royal Navy and all that they did.

On top of that, he has his many salvage pictures and documents which will allow him to relive his many adventures during this awful war, and show them to families and friends.

Secrecy

Ordering RFA Racer to abandon the salvage of the paddle minesweeper at Dunmore East was a surprise to me when I read about it, given that the Royal Navy's Salvage Sections number one priority was warships. These minesweepers were important and very effective, because of their shallow draft and this seemed suspicious to me, outside influences were at work.

Of course, they obeyed the order to salvage the U-boat UC-44 but also managed to recover the minesweeper as well.

As the salvage of UC-44 continued it was clear from the number of attempts to enter her, before bringing the wreck to the surface that they were looking for something inside. The listings of items recovered, only mention various documents, but now I believe that it was the special documents that they were looking for.

The final proof for me was found amongst the many documents recovered from the U-boat, the original UC-44 Funkspruchbuch or radio message coding book at Kew in our National Archives.

There is only one group of people in the Royal Navy who would want such an item, this was Room 40.

They salvage section even abandoned the salvage of another U-boat in Scotland. Then ordering UC-44 to be taken out to sea was odd, even though local companies had offered to scrap her. The materials she was made from were valuable and in very short supply.

May 1917 was the worst month for Allied shipping losses, and the introduction of the convoy system is seen by most as a turning point. Many believe that the Government of the day forced the Royal Navy to introduce Convoys.

My view is now different; Convoys escorts can only protect the ships in their charge, if they have some way of finding the U-boat and then attacking them, i.e. with sonar and weapons.

The best period in WW2's Battle of the Atlantic, was when Bletchley Park broke the Enigma code and directed the convoys away from this danger, those escort ships had radar, sonar, and effective weapons but taking the convoy away from danger was by far the best and most effective approach.

In WW1 the U-boat was almost impossible to find unless it was on the surface. Submarine detection equipment was in its infancy, being useless on a ship underway, and whilst the depth charge had been developed, it was only effective if dropped close to its target.

It is my view that the real success in WW1 was the routing of convoys away from the aggressor, this is what made direction finding the most significant contribution from Room 40.

The weakness of the German signal code system was the requirement for the unit identifier to be added at the start and end of the message; that is why direction finding worked.

Room 40 was also gathering intelligence about individual U-boats, using various sightings and other reports, so they had some idea about which of them were the most active.

A few U-boats apparently went out and just fired their weapons before returning. The German claims about tonnage sunk were exaggerated, but this is normal in a war.

They managed to read a few messages using code-breaking techniques, which were helped when German radio operators did not include random codes, along with some other mistakes.

Having the UC-44 codebook was the next real breakthrough, enabling all the messages to be read and this revealed a great deal.

That is why we were fully aware of the German plan "Der Tag", to lure our fleet into a minefield trap, which was laid by the UC class of submarines. Of course the intelligence service was worried that the German's would change their codes, fortunately, they believed they were unbreakable.

The codes were changed in the middle of 1918, but the tracking still continued uninterrupted, and Room 40 went back to code breaking.

Other UC-44 documents recovered included a list of the U-boat Commanding Officers, understanding your opponent is important.[19]

The delivery of the complete codebook to Room 40 from UC-44 did not actually make the code breakers redundant.

In fact, it gives them more work but of a different type. Now they can look at how the book is made, discover keys to its design, so that when the next code is issued they may be able to break it quicker.

It's a matter of getting inside the mind of the designer and the code breakers were very good at this. It must have been odd, for these people, to have in front of them, the very thing they have been struggling to defeat for so long.

Almost at the end of the war, a new codebook is finally recovered by the special diving team that was set up by the Salvage Section. Unfortunately, they had many failed efforts, it was much

---

[19] *The best use of intelligence material gathered was fundamental to the conduct of the war and the actions taken in WW1 were in many ways mirrored in WW2.*

Knowing a particular U-boat's position, many would be tempted to try and destroy it. Perhaps some would be destroyed if they tried this option, but this could lead to the U-boat command questioning the events, better just to know the danger points and keep convoys away from them.

What they may have done is send airships on patrol in the general area; this would have the effect of keeping the U-boat submerged which will really limit its ability to patrol.

harder than expected and by the time they managed it, it was too late. Look how difficult it was to get inside UC-44 before it was salvaged.

The German U-boats performed magnificently during the war, causing a great deal of damage, the working conditions on board these vessels were very grim. The German surface fleet, however, was never ready for the plan to lure the British Grand Fleet into their minefield trap. Although the mines were successfully laid by the UC class of U-boats, the German ship's crews mutinied at the end of the war and refused to sail. The mutiny was driven by many forces but mainly by the shortage of food and communist unrest, which in itself was driven by the way the German Officer class treated their men; it was this that stopped the plan in its tracks, which was just as well for them.

We knew what the plan was and simply filled the empty channels with our own mines and would have left them to sail into our trap.

For me, the final clues and proof about how important the intelligence work in WW1 was, is contained in the book Strange Intelligence, Memoirs of Naval Secret Service written by H C Ferraby and Hector C Bywater.

I believe Bywater was intimately associated with Room 40, so was in a position to know the facts. Much of what he says is guarded but I have yet to find any evidence that contradicts his many stories.

These are their quotes from the book:-

'To intelligence work, we owed in great measure the success of our anti-submarine campaign.'

'Not one of them could send a wireless message without letting us know exactly who was talking and whereabouts he lay.'

'German submarines now and again sank in water shallow enough to allow of salvage operations. In their case, the possibility of destroying the confidential books was small, as will be realised, and from the wrecked hulls, we now and again extracted useful papers. UC-44 was a case in point. So far as Naval Intelligence *work was concerned, the last three years of the war were almost exclusively concerned with the submarine campaign.'*

'And, to our astonishment, we learned gradually that the secret U-boat call signs did not alter. They remained the same month after month. Apparently, the highly-organised German system was such that it would not bear change.'

Of course, these statements fit in with all that I uncovered at The National Archives in Kew which is why the book has been written like this.

Our knowledge about the operations in Room 40 is limited, but until someone provides concrete evidence that contradicts my theories, I believe that Bywater's book may well be one more of fact than of fiction.

There are 2 other events that are worth considering, the first is the remarkable page from The War Illustrated, that was published in 1919 and John kept a copy of it. At first sight, the page just looks like propaganda and is using pictures of UC-44 simply to illustrate the Belgian Prince episode. This foul act was committed by U-44 which is a completely different class of U-boat but a similar name. Realising that Room 40 had the documents from UC-44 made me wonder if they had a hand in publishing this, in order to create confusion and misinform the Germans.

It is possible that stories were leaking out about UC-44, many people were aware of the salvage and maybe this was their way of diverting attention.

The Captain of the U-boat, Kurt Tebbenjohanns was also held as a prisoner of war and would have been released. On his return, the German Navy would certainly have debriefed him.

The other strange event I discovered was the manufacture of a U-boat model inscribed with UC-44, which was presented to the British inventor of the Depth Charge Herbert Taylor.

Inscribed on the port side is '*UC-44 salvaged off Dunmore Sept 30 17*', on the starboard side is written again UC-44 along with '*Cast from Starb^{d} Propeller Blade*'.

I am confident that UC-44 was not sunk using a depth charge.

Is this another Room 40 inspired confusion tactic?

In WW2 there are quite a few instances, where the Intelligence Services caused confusion or misled the enemy, perhaps they were doing this in WW1 as well.

Bletchley Park's heritage is without doubt Room 40, almost half of those who worked in Room 40 worked at Bletchley Park.

All of the documents recovered from UC-44 are lying in the vaults of The National Archives at Kew. Surely these should be on display to the public, especially as they are in such remarkable condition considering they are over 100 years old and have spent many weeks 90ft down on the seabed.

There are also artefacts held in The Imperial War Museum and the USA Navy College[20], these now have a far greater historical importance than would have been realised before.

---

[20] Although I have not been able to find documentation confirming that American salvage ships dived on UC-44, there are stories that they did and of course the items they hold came from this submarine somehow.

The RFA Salvage Section

At Commodore Sir Frederick Young's house, in the lounge, Fred and his son are deep in conversation. 'Dad, why don't you claim for all the salvage money you must be due, for all the ships that were salvaged in World War One; it would be an absolute fortune?'

Fred looks at his son and smiles, whilst he considers the question, in his normal unflustered manner, 'personally I have been well paid for the years of work that I did. I was awarded an OBE, then a CBE and now I am a Knight of the Realm plus an honorary Commodore in the Royal Navy. The country was at war, and the work we did, was more vital than you will ever know. My rewards mean a great deal to me and I am very content, it is a shame that my teams on their ships have not been recognised as well. Hopefully one day someone will write their story, the story of our salvage work and they will include the whole story because even I only know a small part of it and that is all I am prepared to say.'

His son is intrigued, but he knows that his dad will say no more, and he doesn't want to spoil their relationship.

RFA Racer was one of a number of vessels assembled by Captain Frederick Young in order to create the Royal Navy Salvage Section. Nowadays the Royal Fleet Auxiliary service is a very important part of the Royal Navy, performing many roles, including at times being in the thick of the fighting.

The model of getting suitably sized old RN Warships, modified for salvage and using skilled seaman volunteers from the

Royal Navy, worked extremely well. The story of RFA Racer could well have been the story of any of the other ships he assembled. They operated all around the UK and in the Mediterranean, where the German U-boats also did a great deal of damage.

The salvage riggers were mostly ex-Royal Navy regulars who joined the Royal Naval Reserve as ratings.

Many of the Ships Officers and Salvage Officers were also Royal Naval Reserve.

Both the officers and men were generally somewhat older than General Service ratings, and became extremely skilled at their work, bonding into very close-knit teams, working extremely hard.

During my 23 year career in the Royal Navy, I saw a great deal of the RFA's and know what important work they do.

I saw very little of the RNR, thinking of them mostly as part-timers supporting us. My view of them has changed whilst writing this book because I can now see what good work they can do, and how important both of these services are, especially in wartime.

The importance of all this salvage work; could be justified simply by the number of ships returned to the dockyards for repair. Building each new ship at that time took 2 years, however, a repaired ship would be back in service in just weeks or maybe a few months. The case of USS Armenia filled with grain and bags of flower adds a new dimension. She could have been salvaged a lot quicker, but the riggers spent 2 weeks working 20 hour days in the hold, removing this vital cargo to feed the population, because the cargo can be as important as the ship.

Lord Fisher had stated the following in 1903,

'in May we had 3 days food supply in the country,

in September there is 3 weeks supply,

so stop the supply for 3 weeks and we lose any war.'

Keeping Britain supplied was, therefore, the most important task carried out by our Merchant Fleet, and the men who operated them are also quite often forgotten, but should not be. Having enough ships was a crucial factor and the U-boats managed to sink 40% of our ships, it was a very close run thing.

I have written a great deal about UC-44 because as I delved deeper and deeper, into the mysteries of The National Archives at Kew, I discovered to my amazement, that the original documents recovered from this submarine are available.

Quite often I wonder if the men of RFA Racer knew just how important this particular job was, they probably had their suspicions, or why would John collect and keep such a set of documents.

We shall never know because everyone who was involved is no longer with us, but I have no doubt they were proud of all they did, each of the salvage reports heaps praise on them all.

Captain Young was eventually awarded the position of Honorary Commodore and was knighted by the King to become Sir Frederick Young. He well and truly earned this, remaining steadfast in the job for the whole war and quite a few years after. To find an assessment of his work, have a look at the book Wonders of Salvage which reveals how highly the Author thought of him.

Salvage work was very dangerous, because they operated close to land in stormy seas, with U-boats in the vicinity and the presence of mines, RFA Thrush was lost in a storm with 6 dead and other salvage ships were sunk in the Mediterranean.

Almost no individual medals were awarded for this vital work, but the same could be said for many who served in the trenches, so I am content simply to write the story for everyone to hopefully enjoy.

RFA Racer was the only Salvage Ship to remain in service after the war, because she was selected by Captain Young, to be used to recover the 42 tons of gold from HMS Laurentic in Lough Swilly. The salvage riggers could have stayed on, but most chose to go home, which was their right, they wanted to be with their families again.

Did Captain Young select RFA Racer because she had done such a good job for him, I think it is quite likely; it was his way of saying thank you to this fine ship.

John sketched out what I call an Honours Board for RFA Racer which shows the last ship as HMS Shirley so he probably did it once the war had ended, as there is no mention of USS Narragansett. His use of the drawing at the interview with SNO Aberdeen is fiction.

All warships have Honours Boards listing all the battles they took part in and this sketch is in that form, so perhaps he wanted to get a shipwright to make it up. He thought RFA Racer deserved it and he is probably right, each salvage job was a battle.

This led me to think about battles, there are 'The Battle of Britain' and 'The Battle of the Atlantic' in World War 2.

What sort of name could we use for all the work that went on in World War 1, trying to defeat those U-boats who almost succeeded?

My suggestion is that we could use 'The Battle of the British Isles', and honour all those who took part, the Merchant Navy, the Royal Naval Air Service, the civilian salvage firms, the Naval & Civilian Dockyards, and of course the Royal Navy, whose main contributor was the Salvage Section, flying the flag of the Royal Fleet Auxiliary, operated by civilians and many from the Royal Naval Reserve.

As a final comment, I refer the reader to Appendix C, which lists the clothing and more particularly the scale of rationing for the Salvage Parties. They were very well fed and in my view well looked after. This was because Captain Young knew how arduous the work was, and the hours required, so he made sure that they were looked after. This is the mark of a man who knew what he was doing, and what his men were being asked to do.

Epitaph

As I have researched and learned about the unheralded and magnificent efforts involved, both by the Intelligence Service and the Salvage Service, my pride has grown, as I understand their efforts for my country.

Winston Churchill's immortal words, about the performance of the RAF during the Battle of Britain, 'Never was so much owed by so many to so few' are remembered by everyone, justly so.

The battle against the U-boats in World War One is barely recognised today but was just as important to the survival of our island.

The 'Battle of the British Isles' as I have named it, was won mainly because of the efforts of Room 40 and the Royal Navy Salvage Section. The number of people involved in these 2 departments is less than 1000, far less than was involved in The Battle of Britain. Surely Churchill's words could just easily be applied to the efforts of these few people in WW1.

Appendix A. Salvage rating duties and RFA Racer conversion detail.

DUTIES

Salvage Foreman £15/month

Takes charge on the wreck of all salvage work to be done by riggers such as placing and connecting up pumps, discharge of cargo, moving weights, heaving ship off the beach, etc. being assisted as far as pumps are concerned, by Motor Engineers and relieve Salvage Boatswain when necessary.

Salvage Boatswain £13/month

Works all derricks lifting heavy weights, working wires, anchors, etc. and has issuing of all salvage and deck stores, giving storekeeper daily list of stores used, distinguishing between those used for salvage and ships.

Diver £16/month + Diving allowance 4/s per hour

Will be responsible for the care and maintenance and proper upkeep of the diving pumps and gear carried on board, and when diving will follow instructions given by Salvage Officer or Captain, reporting to them the progress of work and consulting them as to the methods to be employed below water. When not diving or overhauling their gear they will work with the riggers as required by Salvage Officer or Captain.

Must be able to use pneumatic tools, understand the methods employed to overcome leakages, use of hook bolts, etc. make templates and salvage experience should be shown.

Riggers £12/month

    Working under Salvage Foreman, have the same qualifications of the same nature.

Demobilized (retain 6p / day retainer) sign T124 Free victualling, 2 Blue Boiler Suits and free uniforms. Grog.

RFA RACER CONVERSION DETAILS.

General

    The vessel is to be reconstructed and as work proceeds, it is to be thoroughly surveyed and any defects made good. The wooden sides are to be made as flush as possible and all projections such as gun sponsons, davit sockets, etc. are to be removed. The poop and the after bulkhead of the forecastle are to be removed.

Watertight Bulkheads

    In order to provide space for the new machinery W T bulkheads at stations, 34 and 62 and longitudinal coal bunker bulkheads are to be removed and replaced by W T bulkheads with casings for the boiler room and engine room to be made from 8lb plating sufficiently stiffened.

    Hatches on the upper deck are required to be capable of being made watertight.

    Seatings are to be built as necessary for the new machinery. These should be as light as possible consistent with the necessary strength & rigidity.

Cable Lockers

    New cable lockers sufficient for holding 210 fathoms of 1 ¾" cable are to be built, a cable clench for securing the inboard end of each cable is to be fitted.

Ports

    Heavy U shaped iron castings, well rounded in way of chafe of ropes, etc. and having large outside flanges are to be fitted, two in way of the forecastle and three on each side of the ship in the bulwarks. Similar ports but rather smaller and lighter are to be fitted in the bulwark aft. Means for securely closing are to be provided. The sides of the ship immediately under these ports are to be specially reinforced. Freeing scuttles are to be provided as necessary, say 6 on each side.

Deck Machinery

The steam windlass, the winch, and two capstans, all Messrs Dunlop Bell's will be supplied by the Admiralty. The wood deck in way of these machines is to be lifted and ½" plate not less than 6" larger each way than the base plate is to be laid on the beams and securely riveted to them. The beams should be backed by angle. Teak about 4" thick is to be laid on the steel plates to form a bed.

Masts and Derricks

New steel lower masts about 55ft long tapering from 22" diameter at the foot to 17" diameter at the top and having telescopic topmasts are to be fitted. All rigging stays blocks, etc. is to be supplied and fitted. Scantlings of masts and rigging to be generally as per plans of Thrush.

A platform suitable for a 20" searchlight is to be built on the foremast; the searchlight will be supplied by the Admiralty. Pitch pine derricks are to be fitted and tested as follows:-

Fore derrick on the foremast	12 tons
After derrick on the foremast	16 tons
Fore derrick on the mainmast	12 tons
After derrick on the mainmast	16 tons

These are static dead load tests, the working loads being ½ of the above.

Plates indicating the working load are to be affixed to each derrick after they have been satisfactorily tested.

Heel fittings and eyes for blocks are also to be fitted in an athwartships plane so that any of the derricks can be used as side derricks if required.

Electric and oil mast head & towing lights are to be fitted to the foremast.

Three triangular sails and all rigging & fittings for working are to be supplied and fitted.

Accommodation ladders are <u>not</u> required.

Deck Plates

Eight strong eye plates about 18" long x 6" wide by 1" thick and having a large eye are to be supplied and fitted in approved positions on the upper deck and secured generally as described for bollards.

Boats & Davits

One 25ft motor boat, two 20ft diving boats and one 23ft lifeboat will be supplied by the Admiralty.

Davits and crutches are to be provided. The motorboat will be lifted out by the derrick.

Arrangements for Towing

A towing Hook of the general design of the one in Thrush is to be fitted to the main mast. Preventers between the Towing Band and The Engine Casing for reinforcing the mast against the strain of towing are to be fitted.

Two towing bows of suitable height to clear the steam capstan are to be fitted. They are to be built of 5" x 4" x ½" Tee bar with 2 ½" greenheart rubbing pieces.

Steering Arrangements

A combined hand & steam steering engine by Messrs John Hastie & Co. will be supplied by the Admiralty and is to be fitted up in the steering compartment. The existing mechanism for actuating the rudder is to be thoroughly overhauled and put into working order, the guide pulley for the 2 ½" F.S.W.R. to be reinforced if considered necessary on a survey. A spare wire is to be provided and tried in place.

A boat's compass is to be fitted on a pedestal or bracket in the after steering compartment and a 1 ½" voice pipe led to the steering position on the bridge. Brass steering wheel standard is to be supplied and fitted on the bridge and connected to the steering engine by tubular control rods, bevel wheels, universal joints, etc. Guards are to be fitted over these as usual in HM Ships.

Navigating Bridge & Chart Room

A navigating bridge and chart house are to be built. The bridge to be supported generally by 2" steel stanchions suitably attached to the main bulwark rail. The wings of the bridge are to be made portable. A teakwood windscreen with sliding windows is to be fitted. Canvas weather cloths are to be fitted. Two pattern 1385 semaphores are to be supplied and fitted, one on each side of the bridge.

A voice pipe is required between the upper bridge and the steering position on the lower bridge. A 1 ½" voice pipe is to be led from the bridge steering position to the engine room.

Engine room telegraphs are to be supplied & fitted.

An electric flashing lantern is to be fitted to the masthead.

A Kelvin sounding machine for taking soundings over the stern is to be provided and fitted.

Workshop

A workshop is to be built and fitted with a lathe, drilling machine, tool racks, bench, and vices.

Air Reservoirs

The fixed and portable air reservoirs will be supplied by the Admiralty. The former is to be placed above the boiler casing and a suitable stowage is to be supplied for the latter.

Marconi Radio

A house for Marconi W/T gear is to be built. Accommodation for the W/T operator is to be provided. The instruments will be supplied by the Admiralty and will be fitted up by the Marconi Co., the Dockyard to provide all necessary assistance.

Rating accommodation

Six in number double tier G.I. berths are to be supplied and fitted on No1 Mess Deck & 8 in number on No2 Mess Deck. Four double berth cabins are also to be built on No2 Mess Deck. (36)

A slow combustion stove is to be provided & fitted in the two mess decks.

The lower deck aft is to be reconstructed for the accommodation of the officers.

The cabin bulkheads are to be built generally of wood.

All cabins including those on No2 Mess Deck are to be provided with folding lavatories.

Heating stoves to Admiralty pattern are to be provided and fitted in the messes aft and in the Salvage Officers' day cabin.

Galley

A Galley is to be built with tiled floors & a 6ft Cooking Range fitted. A sink, all necessary shelves, locker, & coal bunker to be provided.

Magazine & Stores

Magazines, storerooms, etc. are to be refitted as necessary and made suitable for the purpose. Magazine flood valves should be adapted if possible to the new requirements and any not wanted are to be removed from the hull and made good.

Pumping Arrangements

The pumping arrangements of the ship are as far as possible to remain as they are. The new 50 ton Fire & Bilge Pump is to be provided with all necessary connections to enable them to pump the main W.T. compartments of the ship.

Fire Main

Three C.I. distribution valve chest for the wash deck and fire hoses are to be fitted on the upper deck, one on each side of the engine hatch about station 54 and one on the M.L. just forward of the workshop. Each chest to be fitted with two No.2 Nunan & Stove hose connections.

The valve chest is to be connected to the new fire & bilge pump.

The system is to be tested to 100 lbs for a working pressure of 50lbs.

A relief valve is to be fitted in the delivery from the pump.

Sanitary Arrangements

Four in number W.C's are to be fitted at the break of the forecastle. Two of the W.C's are to be appropriated for Officers. A 50 Gallon sanitary tank is to be placed above for flushing. A semi-rotary hand pump with sea suction is to be provided for filling this tank.

A locked draw off cock is to be fitted at the pump.

Washbasins enclosed by a canvas screen are to be fitted for the crew to use.

One W.C. and a Bathroom are to be built on the lower deck aft for the use of Officers. The former is to be of the usual destroyer below water pattern.

The bath is to be of the Shank's narrow rim, Yacht Pattern No 2349b, a semi-rotary hand pump being provided for emptying the bath.

Fresh Water Arrangements.

The existing freshwater tanks are to be removed and storage tanks having a capacity of about 10 tons are to be built into the ship. All necessary arrangements are to be made for filling these from the test tank and from water boats alongside.

A 150 gallon daily supply tank is to be fitted on the superstructure. A semi-rotary hand pump for filling from the main storage tank is to be provided and fitted. Connections with locked cocks are to be provided from this tank to a 50 gallon R.U. Tank to be fitted in forward mess and a 25-gallon tank conveniently accessible from the pantry aft to the seaman's washbasins, the Galley and Officers' Bathroom.

Reservoir Feed Tank
A tank having a capacity of 12 tons is to be fitted.
All necessary arrangements for filling from the distillers and deck are to be provided as well as connections to the feed pump and condenser.

Propeller
The design of the new manganese bronze propeller is to be submitted for approval as soon as possible. The propeller should be a 3 blade and have a diameter of 8ft 6ins and a pitch of 7ft 3ins, the extended blade area being 20 square feet.

Ventilation
It is desired if possible that the fan for Howden's forced draught be fitted so as to be capable of exhausting the Engine Room. Proposals showing the necessary trunking should be submitted for approval before putting the work in hand.
The ship is to be efficiently ventilated by natural usage. In addition, fans are to be fitted as follows:-
7 ½" supply for No. 1 Mess Deck.
7 ½" supply for No. 2 Mess Deck.
7 ½" supply for Officers' living spaces aft.
The storerooms are to be ventilated by exhaust pipes led to the upper deck & fitted with mushroom tops. In addition, the three 7 ½" fans above are to be fitted with hose connections so that ventilation hoses can be led down to any storerooms if required.
The main W.T. Bulkheads are not to be pierced by ventilation trunks.

Lamp Room

A lamp room with all necessary shelves and fittings is to be provided.

Line Throwing Gun

Line throwing guns will be supplied by the Admiralty.
A tank about 3ft x 3ft x 3ft fitted similarly to a pistol tank for storing explosives is to be fitted in an approved position below the W.L.

Fenders

Special cane fenders etc. will be supplied by the Admiralty

Painting

The ship is to be painted throughout as usual for vessels in H.M. Service. The hull to be black and topsides grey.

Appendix B. Salvage Riggers

Figure 2.Salvage Riggers – RFA Racer in Aberdeen Jan 1919.

Back left to right - Salvage Rigger Henry McDonald, Salvage Rigger Henry Furley, Salvage Rigger W (Lofty) Harris, Salvage Rigger Thomas E Robinson, Salvage Rigger James W Jones, Salvage Rigger B McAteer

Middle Row left to right - Salvage Rigger Herbert Redgrave, Salvage Rigger Thomas (Pony) Moore, Salvage Foreman William Dole, Salvage Bosun Fred Collins, Salvage Rigger John (Jack) Foulkes

Front Row left to right - Salvage Rigger E Coone, Salvage Rigger Chas G Abrams, Biddy (Ships Mascot)

RFA Racer Salvage Team December 1916 to 1919

Riggers History
Salvage Foreman Thomas Pearce (Liverpool) Left 16/10/1917
Replaced by **Salvage Foreman William Morris (Liverpool)** joined 1/9/1917 to 18/1/1918
Replaced by **Salvage Foreman William (Billy) Dole (Dartmouth)** joined 15/1/1918 to end

Salvage Bosun John Meek (Liverpool) left
Replaced by Salvage Bosun Fred Collins (Liverpool) (Ex. "RFA Thrush") (ex. "ONYX" submariner) joined 22/5/1917 to end

Henry (Mac) McDonald (Peel, Isle of Man) Whole period

Henry Furley (Liverpool) Whole period

Thomas E **Robertson (Liverpool)** Whole period

James W Jones (Portsmouth) Whole period

Herbert Redgrave (Brighton) 138994 All (Q10 9 Aug 16 to 25 Nov 16 Supr.)(Joined RN 23 Oct 1889 left to RFR 13 Jun 1901)DOB 23rd Oct 1871

Thomas (Pony) Moore (Sunderland) SS336 All ("HMS Centurion" 26 Mar 16 to 25 Nov 16 Supr.)(Joined RN 1904 left to RFR 1909) DOB17 Sept 1885

John (Jack) Robert Foulkes (Liverpool) 196192 All ("HMS Centurion" Supr.) DOB 2nd Sept 1882

E Coone (Southampton) Whole period

Ernest Symons (Newlyn Cornwall) Whole period

Wilfred Kennedy (Southampton)(Born Ardwick Lancs) 196722 All (HMS Suffolk VG Supr.) (Joined RN 25 Mar 1900 left to RFR 24 Mar 1912) DOB 25th March 1882

John Tremble (Mayport) left 18/8/1917
    Chas G (Ikie) Abrams (Middlesbrough) Whole period, Stoker until 25/8/1917

George Reasey (Belfast) left 11/3/1918
    W Youldren (Brixham, Devon) joined 13/3/1918 to end Hospital 5/12/1918 to 23/1/1919

William Hall (Liverpool) left 31/3/1918

William Lofty Harris (Dover) joined 29/4/1918 to end.

Thomas Charles (Chas) Coale (Ilford) 211115 left 10/5/1918 (HMS Aurora VG Supr.) (Joined RN 18 Jan 1903 to RFR 22 Mar 1910) DOB 18 Jan 1885
    Bernard McAteer (Surbiton) 180795 joined 14/5/1918 to end. (Wildfire, Hilary, Victorious 2 Sat) (joined RN 16 Jun 1896 to RFR 14 Jun 1908) DOB 16 June 1878

Signalmen
V White 9/11/1917 to 28/3/1918

William M Hall joined 1/4/1918 to end.

Divers
J Keam Whole period.

J Tomkins 19/4/1917 to 20/8/1917
    John Forsyth 3/2/1918 to end.

M J Smith 7/5/1917 to 21/6/1918

Frank Pegrome Eaglestone (West Ham Essex) 220100 UC-44 salvage only DOB 7 Nov 1886

Appendix C. Admiralty Form D Clothing and Service Standard Rations Ratings.

Men

(5) The crews, of both Mercantile and Naval ratings, are victualled on what is known in the Service as the 'General Mess System,' and the Accountant Officer is to provide a sufficient and suitable dietary.

(6) The cost of the meals provided should approximate, over a period, to 1s. a head daily; and having regard to the fact that the bulk of supplies are obtained from Government sources and charged for at cost prices, it should be practicable under ordinary conditions to keep near this figure. Latterly, however, the prices of goods purchased from the shore to supplement the Government stores have advanced, and it has been found necessary in many ships to exceed the 1s. in order to maintain a sufficient scale of messing. It is expected, however, that even under these abnormal conditions the daily cost will not exceed 1s. 3d. If Accounting Officers find that they are unable to keep even to this enhanced figure they should report the fact to the Director of Victualling, enclosing a copy of a typical weekly menu and explaining where the excessive cost mostly occurs.

(Note,-Extra issues authorised by the Commanding Officer under Art. 1690, clauses 2, 3, 4 and 5, King's Regulations, will be in addition to the rate per head allowed for the General Mess, and such issues are to be accounted for separately.)

(7) The Accounting Officer will find it convenient to draw up a weekly menu for guidance, and for the purpose of estimating beforehand the cost of the proposed scheme of messing. The Service Standard Ration (see Table A) may well be taken as a nucleus to work up from; its cost at the current issuing prices (copy attached) is about 7*d*., so that even by working up to 1*s*. a day there is a margin of 5*d*. to expend in providing something extra for breakfast and supper and puddings for dinner.

(8) The Navy spirit ration (1/8 pint daily) is to be issued in addition to the general messing to all ratings, as in H.M. ships, and grog money at the authorised scale is to be credited to men who do not receive the ration in kind.

TABLE A. (See paragraph 7.)
SERVICE DAILY STANDARD RATION.

1 lb	Bread
½ lb	fresh meat
1 lb	fresh vegetables
4 oz	Sugar
½ oz	Tea
½ oz	Chocolate
¾ oz	condensed milk
1 oz	jam, marmalade or pickles
4 oz	Preserved meat on one day of the week in a harbour or on two days at sea
	Mustard, pepper, vinegar and salt as required

Substitute for sift bread when the latter is not available:-

½ lb	biscuit or
1 lb	Flour

Substitute for 1 lb. fresh vegetables for the issue with fresh meat when the former are not available:-

Salt Pork Day:

½ lb	salt pork
¼ lb	split peas

Celery seed, ½ oz. to every 8 lbs. of split peas put into the coppers. ½ lb. potatoes, or 2 oz. Haricot beans or 2 oz. Marrowfat

On Alternate *Preserved Meat Day:-*

6 oz.   preserved meat

8 oz   Flour

         ¾ oz. suet or 4 oz. rice

         2 oz. raisins or 2 oz. jam

         ½ lb. potatoes, or 2 oz. haricot beans or 2 oz. marrowfat peas.

In addition, a spirit ration of 1/8 pint daily is issued.

Table B

UNIFORM FOR MERCANTILE RATINGS IN ARMED AUXILIARIES.

Petty Officers and Men

Each man will be supplied with uniform as follows, viz.:-

Men not dressed as Seamen (viz., Donkey men, Artisans, &c.).	*Men dressed as Seamen* (viz., Greasers, Firemen, Trimmers, &c.)
1 serge jacket, single breasted.	1 serge jumper.
1 serge waistcoat.	
1 pair serge trousers.	1 pair serge trousers.
Working suit	Working suit
1 duck jacket, single breasted.	1 duck jumper.
1 pair duck trousers.	1 pair duck trousers.
2 check shirts.	2 flannel vests
6 collars	2 jean collars.
1 necktie.	1 black silk handkerchief.
1 peak cap.	1 cap and ribbon
2 cap covers.	2 cap covers.

The men, however, are to be allowed when on board to wear clothes of their own. Officers' stewards and cooks will be given a gratuity of £1, 10s to provide themselves with a suit of uniform such as they usually wear.

1900.-Rationing of Salvage Parties.

Salvage Parties consist of men belonging to some or all of the three classes,

i.e.: (a) Salvage Ratings (signed on T.124 agreement and entitled ordinarily to Naval Rations); (b) Dockyard Labourers and Mechanics; and (c) hired Mechanics who are employees of Private Firms.

2. As these different classes are employed together on salvage work, and in order to avoid any discontent arising from being on different scales of rationing, the Admiralty have arranged with the Ministry of Food that all men belonging to Admiralty Salvage Parties shall be authorised to obtain food on the scale approved for seamen serving on weekly articles, and it is to be noted that this concession on the part of the Ministry of Food has been granted in view of the very arduous nature of salvage work, and the fact that the men thus employed work in all weathers and at all times of the day and night.

Appendix D. Notes written by John on the back of the photographs.

Figure 7	UC44 German Sub Mine Layer brought out of 14 fathoms of water. Containing 9 live Mines & 2 torpedoes and 30 Bodies.
Figure 8	Live Mines being lifted out of the Mine chamber of the German Submarine Minelayer UC-44 you will notice the chamber underneath the grating. Alongside her is the lighter that we lifted her we used 8. 10' wires to lift her she was 4½ miles of the Hook lighthouse Entrance to Waterford River.
Figure 10	SS Antwerpen torpedoed and beached in Mounts Bay Penzance. Broke in halves during the salvage
Figure 11	Another view of SS Antwerpen with Racer alongside her.
Figure 13	Side view of Admiral Cochrane as she was run in at Dartmouth and beached right in the stairway of the harbour.
Figure 14	S/S Admiral Cochrane torpedoed off Berry Head 3.20 pm Jan 22nd, 1918. Sank at the entrance to Dartmouth Harbour at 6.30 pm the same day. Re-floated and re-grounded in Dartmouth Harbour Jan 29th, 1918 J Foulkes
Figure 15	One of the holes of Torpedo on the Admiral Cochrane.

Appendix E. References, The National Archives.

File Reference	Record Description
ADM 53/13974	13 August 1898 - 07 October 1899 HMS Hood.
ADM 53/16041-3	HMS Theseus ships log. 26/12/1898 to 28/5/1902
ADM 53/16041	Admiralty, and Ministry of Defence, Navy Department: Ships' Logs. THESEUS.
ADM 53/16042	Admiralty, and Ministry of Defence, Navy Department: Ships' Logs. THESEUS.
ADM 53/16043	Admiralty, and Ministry of Defence, Navy Department: Ships' Logs. THESEUS.
COPY 1/449/349	Photograph of the Russian ironclad coast defence ship, "Khrabry", aground in the harbour of the Piraeus on 11 February 1901, boats of HMS Theseus assisting
HW 3/3	Clarke's history of Sigint in Room 40,
HW 3/6	Room 40 Pen portraits
HW 3/5	Setting up Room 40
HW 3/1	Room 40 Naval Section
HW 3/8	Frank Clarke Room 40
ADM 137/4155	U-boat history sheets compiled by Lt. Cdr. Tiarks in chartroom of Room 40
ADM 53/37449	Admiralty, and Ministry of Defence,

	Navy Department: Ships' Logs. CENTURION.
ADM 53/37450	Admiralty, and Ministry of Defence, Navy Department: Ships' Logs. CENTURION
ADM 53/37451	Admiralty, and Ministry of Defence, Navy Department: Ships' Logs. CENTURION.
ADM 116/1423	Salvage Record No. 1 AWO 2002 Salvage Ratings
MT 23/514/4	Correspondence and Papers. Particulars of ratings for salvage vessels.
ADM 116/1510A	Salvage Record No. 24 RFA Racer conversion.
MT 23/541/28	Slow progress on the conversion of certain salvage vessels.
ADM 116/1506	Salvage Record No. 5. SS Carl, Lt Kay initial report.
ADM 116/1587	Salvage Record No 7. SS Carl.
ADM 116/1587	Salvage Record No. 7 TB 24.
ADM 116/1503	Cases. Salvage - Case No. 2. Lifting Barges.
MT 23/543/11	Admiralty, Transport Department: Correspondence and Papers. Hopper barges required as lifting craft for salvage. Approval to requisitioning of four barges.
ADM 116/1589	Salvage Record No. 10 SS Quantock Q5.
ADM 116/1588	Salvage Record No. 8. HMS Q19.
ADM 116/1425	Salvage Record No. 9 HMS C16.
ADM 137/3897	German submarines UC 16-UC 44:

interrogation of survivors, translations of German officer's diary, and letters ...

ADM 116/1632	Salvage Record No. 20 UC-44 & HMS Haldon.
ADM 116/1592	Salvage Record No 13. List of Photographic Equipment.
ADM137/4239	German documents concerning wireless. UC-44.
ADM137/4240	German papers concerning North Sea outposts UC-44.
ADM137/4241	Mineseekers and auxiliary mine seekers: tactical organisation: North Sea Fleet UC-44.
ADM137/4242	War orders of the day for German High Seas Armed Forces UC-44.
ADM137/4244	Translation of log books UC-44.
ADM137/4245	W/T log UC-44.
ADM137/4248	W/T codebook UC-44.
ADM137/4249	W/T codebook: amendments UC-44.
ADM137/4251	German code word/call sign list UC-44.
ADM137/4253	Miscellaneous papers UC-44.
ADM137/4255	1st Flotilla orders UC-44.
ADM137/4256	Miscellaneous documents UC-44.
ADM137/4259	Clear texts of messages received UC-44.
ADM137/4261	Submarine orders UC-44.
ADM137/4262	W/T log of enciphered messages UC-44.
ADM137/4810	Messages to and from UC-44 relating to the war against commence.
ADM137/4811	UC-44: translation of W/T log book Mar 1 - May 30
ADM 137-3871	Specifications, administration, personnel, tactics, and salvage of German submarines.
MT 25/21	Ministry of Shipping, 1917 - 1921: Correspondence and Papers. Ministry of Shipping, 1917 - 1921: correspondence

	and papers. Submersible pumps
Series No4 Feb 1917 Submersible & J-L Motors Ltd. Southall.	Instructions for Care and Management of Submersible Generating and Pumping Plant. Admiralty Motor Alternator Type. (in MT 25/21)
ADM 116/1595	Salvage Record No. 16 SS Antwerpen.
ADM 116/1598	Salvage Record No. 27 SS Antwerpen.
ADM 116/1641	Salvage Record No. 36 SS Antwerpen.
ADM 116/1637	Salvage Record No. 31 USS Armenia
ADM 116/1639	Salvage Record No. 34 SS Comrie Castle.
ADM 116/1643	Salvage Record No. 39 SS Admiral Cochrane.
ADM 116/1639	Salvage Record No. 34 SS India.
ADM 116/1643	Salvage Record No. 39 SS Celtic
ADM 116/1596	Salvage Record No 17. HMS Magic & HMS Shirley
ADM 116/1639	Salvage Record No. 34 Esperanza de Laringa.
ADM 116/1858	Salvage Record No. 38 SS Oriana
ADM 116/1631	Salvage Record No. 19 Standard Patch
ADM 116/1595	Salvage Record No. 16 Standard Patch
MT 23/514/4	Particulars of ratings for salvage vessels. Pay & Uniform.
MT 23/515/5	H.M. Salvage Vessels. Uniforms for crews.
ADM 116/1425	Salvage Record No. 9

	RFA Thrush stranding.
ADM 116/1853	Salvage Record No. 23
	Demobilization.
ADM 116/2010	Salvage Record No. 44
	USS Narragansett
ADM 53/57031	RFA Racer Ships Log, November 1918.
ADM 53/57032	RFA Racer Ships Log, December 1918.
ADM 53/57033	RFA Racer Ships Log, January 1919.
ADM 53/57034	RFA Racer Ships Log, February 1919.
ADM 53/57035	RFA Racer Ships Log, March 1919.
ADM 116/1639	Salvage Record No. 34
	Rationing of Salvage Parties.
ADM 116/1853	Salvage Record No. 23
	List of Salvage Officers plus Salvage
	Ship Officers and crew.
ADM 116/1742	Salvage Record No. 28
	Salvage Fleet 1917 & Policy.
MT 23/515/5	H.M. Salvage Vessels. Uniforms for
	crews.

Appendix F. Other References

Able Seamen The Lower Deck of the Royal Navy 1850-1939	By Brian Lavery	ISBN: 9781844861408
Manual of seamanship for boys' training ships of the Royal Navy.	By Fox, Lieutenant Cecil H, RN	ISBN 10: 1894572785
British Vessels Lost at Sea 1914-18	HMSO	ISBN: 9781852601348
Mr. W. R. Macdonald	British Patent No. 19384/1908	an a.c. motor whose stator winding was rubber-covered cable.
The Wonders of Salvage	By David Masters	John Lane The Bodley Head Ltd.
The War Illustrated	25th January 1919 Page 398	U boat Murderers Meet the Fate they Merited.

Strange Intelligence memoirs of Naval Secret Service ISBN978-1849548847	By Hector C Bywater and HC Ferraby	First published Constable & Co Ltd 1931, then Biteback Publishing 2015
London Gazette supplement	dated 7 Jun 1918	(Medals Issued)
MUN 239	88mm Shell, cartridge & ready-use case from UC44	Imperial War Museum
MUN240	Incendiary Device from UC44	Imperial War Museum
MUN241	Fabric charge bag for 88mm Shell from UC44	Imperial War Museum

Appendix G. Service Records

Name		Service Number	TNA Reference
Frederick William Young	Salvage Section OIC	CW53257	ADM 240_49_641
William Dole	Salvage Foreman	1071034	BT 395_1_25527
Herbert Redgrave	Salvage Rigger	P138944	ADM 188_192_138944
Bernard McAteer	Salvage Rigger	C180795	ADM 188_300_180795
Wilfred Kennedy	Salvage Rigger	D196722	ADM 188_340_196722
John Robert Foulkes	Salvage Rigger	C196912	ADM 188_340_196912
Thomas Charles Coale	Salvage Rigger	P211115	ADM 188_369_211115

Thomas Moore	Salvage Rigger	SS336	ADM 188_1094_336
Thomas Moore	Salvage Rigger		BT 351_1_99689
Ernest Symons	Salvage Rigger	C1532	BT 377_7_33776
William Morris	Salvage Rigger	C1804	BT 377_7_34048
John Tremble	Salvage Rigger	C3095	BT 377_7_35334
William Hall	Salvage Rigger	D1745	BT 377_7_41738
Ernest Symons	Salvage Rigger	D2477	BT 377_7_42465
Frank Pegrome Eaglestone	Diver	C220100	ADM 188_387_220100

Photograph Index[21]

---

[21] The quality of the photographs is the best available. The originals are very small and have been well thumbed over the years. Extensive digital work has improved them to the present standard which is the best that could be done.

Cover Photograph

Front Cover   John on HMS Centurion c1916

Figure 1 HMS Centurion

Figure 2 RFA Racer riggers 1919. See Appendix B for names.

Figure 3 RFA Racer after refit

Figure 4 SS Carl Freshwater Bay

Figure 5 Salvage Scene on Postcard (RFA Thrush)

Figure 6 RFA Racer Radio Room

264

Figure 7 UC-44 in Dunmore East

Figure 8 UC-44 Mine being removed after salvage

Figure 9 Submersible Pumps being maintained after use

Figure 10 SS Antwerpen awash

Figure 11 SS Antwerpen with RFA Racer alongside

Figure 12 USS Armenia Salvage Repairs

Figure 13 SS Admiral Cochrane in Dartmouth Harbour

Figure 14 SS Admiral Cochrane in Dartmouth Harbour

Figure 15 SS Admiral Cochrane Torpedo Hole

Figure 16 SS Admiral Cochrane Pumps in the hold

Figure 17 SS Comrie Castle

Figure 18 SS Comrie Castle with steam pumps in the hold

Figure 19 SS Anchoria

Figure 20 Submersible Pumps in the hold of SS Anchoria

Figure 21 SS Celtic torpedo hole

Figure 22 SS Celtic being towed away after salvage

Figure 23 SS Esperanza de Larringa

Figure 24 Convoy, SS Manora aground

Figure 25 Convoy, H M S Mystic port wing escort

Figure 26 Convoy, SS Oriana Port Side

Figure 27 Convoy, SS Oriana Starboard Side

Figure 28 Convoy, SS Oriana & HMS Mystic

Figure 29 HMS Magic

Figure 30 HMS Shirley repairs

Figure 31 HMS Shirley being towed in

Figure 32 HMS Shirley close up of pumps

Figure 33 HM Tug Oceana

Figure 34 RFA Racer dressed for Armistice in Aberdeen

Figure 35 USS Narragansett close up of bows aground

Figure 36 USS Narragansett with RFA Racer alongside

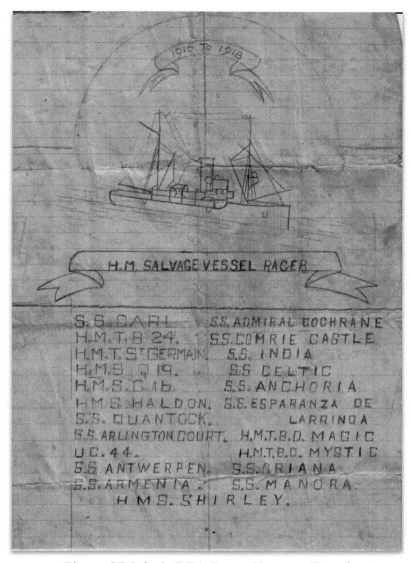

Figure 37 John's RFA Racer Honours Board

Figure 38 War Illustrated UC-44.

The Author

Anthony Babb served for 23 years in the Royal Navy as a Weapons System engineer and was awarded the British Empire Medal in the 1988 New Year's Honours list for services to the Royal Navy.

Since retiring he has lectured on cruise ships many times, and the pictures in this book formed a significant part of his very first lecture, which was presented on the P & O ship Oriana in 2012.

Many of the fictional incidents in the book are based upon his own naval experiences.